The Ethics of Practice with Minors

Books Also Available from Lyceum Books, Inc.

Advisory Editors: Thomas M. Meenaghan, *New York University*
Ira C. Colby, *University of Houston*

STRAIGHT TALK ABOUT PROFESSIONAL ETHICS,
by Kim Strom-Gottfried

SECONDARY TRAUMATIC STRESS AND THE CHILD WELFARE PROFESSIONAL,
by Josephine G. Pryce, Kimberly K. Shackelford, and David H. Pryce

THE DYNAMICS OF FAMILY POLICY,
by Cynthia J. Rocha and Alice K. Johnson Butterfield

SOCIAL WORK WITH VOLUNTEERS,
by Michael E. Sherr, foreword by John G. McNutt

EMPOWERING VULNERABLE POPULATIONS: COGNITIVE-BEHAVIORAL INTERVENTIONS,
by Mary Keegan Eamon

SOCIAL WORK PRACTICE WITH FAMILIES: A RESILIENCY-BASED APPROACH,
by Mary Patricia Van Hook

SOCIAL WORK IN A SUSTAINABLE WORLD,
by Nancy L. Mary

SCHOOL SOCIAL WORK: PRACTICE, POLICY, AND RESEARCH, 6E,
Robert Constable, Carol Rippey Massat, Shirley McDonald, and John P. Flynn

The Ethics of Practice with Minors
High Stakes, Hard Choices

Kim Strom-Gottfried
University of North Carolina, Chapel Hill

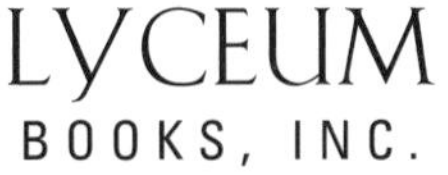

Chicago, Illinois

Published by

Lyceum Books, Inc.
5758 S. Blackstone Ave.
Chicago, Illinois 60637
773+643-1903 (Fax)
773+643-1902 (Phone)
lyceum@lyceumbooks.com
http://www.lyceumbooks.com

ISBN 978-1-933478-12-8

12 11 10 09 08 1 2 3 4 5

Library of Congress Cataloging-in-Publication Data

Strom-Gottfried, Kim.
The ethics of practice with minors : high stakes, hard choices / Kim Strom-Gottfried.
p. cm.
ISBN 978-1-933478-12-8
1. Social service—Moral and ethical aspects. 2. Social ethics. 3. Social work with children. I. Title.
HV10.5.S77 2008
174'.93627—dc22

2007041353

To Mom and Dad, my aunts and uncles, and the surrogate parents in Camden, Maine
Your influences endure.

Contents

About the Author

Kim Strom-Gottfried, PhD, LISW, is the Smith P. Theimann Distinguished Professor of Ethics and Professional Practice at the School of Social Work at the University of North Carolina at Chapel Hill. Professor Strom-Gottfried teaches in the areas of direct practice, communities and organizations, and human resource management. Her practice experience in the nonprofit and public sectors focuses on suicide prevention, intervention, and bereavement. Professor Strom-Gottfried's scholarly interests involve ethics, moral courage, and social work education, and she is active in training, consultation, and research on ethics and social work practice. She has written numerous articles, monographs, and chapters on the ethics of practice. Professor Strom-Gottried is also the author of *Straight Talk About Professional Ethics* and coauthor of *Direct Social Work Practice* and *Teaching Social Work Values and Ethics: A Curriculum Resource.*

PREFACE

Is it ethical to withhold information about a child's diagnosis from him because the parents insist that he not be told?

What are the ethical considerations in medicating youngsters for ADHD?

How much weight should be given to a minor's wishes in foster placement, child custody, or health care decisions?

When are diagnoses, family difficulties, test results, and prognoses constructive pieces of information for minors, and when do they create distress and even life-limiting prophecies?

Is it fair to withhold information on controversial topics such as contraception, sexually transmitted diseases, homosexuality, and abortion from teenagers because organizational or social policies require that social workers do so?

Social work practice with children and adolescents takes place at the complex intersection of legal, ethical, clinical, and developmental considerations. How can professionals interpret and apply the concepts of self-determination, confidentiality, and informed consent with a client whose rights and choices are constrained by his or her age and maturity, and legal and parental prerogatives?

This book provides the tools professionals need to bridge those tensions to deliver effective, ethical services. It offers a useful, easy-to-remember framework for considering ethical dilemmas that will help readers develop critical thinking skills in arriving at ethically sound decisions. It is written in a direct and conversational manner intended to make ethics accessible to students and experienced practitioners alike. It applies practical guidance and sound resources to an array of clients, settings, and issues. It goes beyond presenting problems to guide the reader through the considerations that must be made to resolve complex right-vs.-right dilemmas.

How is it organized? The book begins with a discussion of what ethics means and what it means to be ethical. This section lays an important foundation for all that follows and contains useful case material as well. The second chapter offers a framework for examining ethical dilemmas and weighing the options for addressing them, and it gives examples, drawn from one of the questions above, that apply that framework. Two subsequent chapters provide critical information about the developmental considerations in serving minors of different ages and capacities, and the prevailing norms and paradigms found in various child-serving systems. Both chapters focus on what these features mean for ethical decision making and for protecting the interests of minor clients amid sometimes hostile, confusing, or conflicting organizational imperatives.

Each of the remaining chapters focuses on a particular category of ethical dilemmas, weighing competing goods such as the needs of individuals versus those of the community, short-term versus long-term considerations, and value conflicts such as justice versus mercy or truth versus loyalty. In each of these chapters, a consistent format is used: two cases are presented to reflect the particular type of dilemma on which the chapter focuses, and each is reviewed using the ethics framework introduced in chapter 2. Sometimes this analysis will result in one clear conclusion, and sometimes the analysis will simply reveal the pros and cons of several options, none of which may seem ideal. The book does not and cannot provide a conclusive answer to every ethical problem. Rather, it equips the reader with the tools and considerations for deliberately and effectively responding to ethical dilemmas.

Readers may find the cases and characters in the book familiar. Each case is a composite of a commonly occurring dilemma, sometimes one that has been created from an actual dilemma, or in some instances one that is just made up. Only the cases in the first and last chapters are real, though I hope you find them all authentic, compelling, and useful. In addition to sending your feedback, please send me your dilemmas so that others can benefit in the future from novel, life-like examples.

Many people deserve credit for the inspiration and creation of this work. Thanks to Martin Hall, Joette Woody, and Tonya VanDeinse for their research and critical thinking, and the hot afternoons spent putting it all together. Thanks to Dr. Andrew Gottfried for his assistance in understanding medical conditions. Thanks, too, to Shelley Cohen Konrad, David Hussey, Tina Souder, and Joanne Caye; each has clinical acumen, sound judgment, and a firm moral compass and was kind enough to share them all in this work. I'm grateful to my students, workshop participants, and colleagues for generously sharing their ideas and struggles. I appreciate the enduring support of my friends and colleagues, and especially my sweet husband, for cheering this book across the finish line.

Chapter 1

UNDERSTANDING ETHICS

On January 2, 2002, the last day of his school's winter break, twelve-year-old J. Daniel Scruggs hanged himself with a necktie in the bedroom closet of the small apartment he shared with his mother and nineteen-year-old sister. Six days earlier, the Department of Children and Families had dismissed allegations of neglect against Daniel's mother due to a lack of evidence.

Daniel was small for his age, weighing only sixty-three pounds. He was different from his classmates in other ways, too. He liked wearing a jacket and tie to class; sometimes, in response to a teacher's question, he would stand up and act out the answer. He loved Harry Potter and magic shows. Although he had an IQ of 139, his school performance was much less impressive, and he was placed in special education classes for an undefined learning disability. However, the school dropped him from special education classes in the sixth grade without conducting the required testing to determine if he could rejoin a mainstream classroom.

Daniel was bullied a great deal in school. Other children reported that he was pushed, hit, kicked, and choked and had his belongings stolen on a regular basis. Daniel's home conditions were appalling and unsafe. He stopped showering and brushing his teeth, and in an apparent strategy to get sent home from school early, he would routinely urinate and defecate in his pants. Teachers reportedly covered their noses around him and appeared relieved when he was absent from class. The guidance counselor tried to work with him on hygiene but made no referrals in that regard. The school nurse stated that she was embarrassed to talk with him about his hygiene and, further, that doing so was not her responsibility. In the sixth grade, Daniel was absent or tardy over one-third of the school year. Of the seventy-eight school days before the winter break in his seventh-grade year, Daniel was absent forty-four days and tardy twenty-nine days, which means that he only spent five full days in school.

Daniel's mother, Judith, worked approximately seventy hours per week as a teacher's aide at Daniel's middle school and also as a part-time employee at a large national discount store. According to his obituary notice, Daniel had two married sisters, a married brother, and another sister, all living in the same state. Judith Scruggs claimed to have suffered physical abuse from Daniel's father, whose whereabouts were unknown. Daniel had reportedly been very close to his grandparents, who had died within months of each other less than two years before Daniel's suicide.

One year after Daniel's death, the Connecticut Office of the Child Advocate released a report of all the instances in which agencies and adults failed him. It recommended sweeping changes to the school system, the Department of Children and Families, and the juvenile justice system. On October 6, 2003, Judith Scruggs was convicted of felony risk of injury to a minor, which carried a possible ten-year prison sentence. Her attorney vowed to appeal, and her supporters contended that she was twice victimized: by unresponsive social and educational services and by the justice system. In 2004 she received an eighteen-month suspended sentence with five years of probation, mandatory counseling, and one hundred hours of community service. In addition, she was required to take a parenting class should she ever become responsible for or have occasion to supervise a child under the age of sixteen; in 2006 the conviction was overturned (Heyman, 2003; Makwana, 2003a, 2003b; Office of the Child Advocate, 2003).

Thankfully, few cases in the health and human service systems end as tragically as that of Daniel Scruggs. However, every day social workers and their colleagues in other helping professions strive to meet crushing human needs in an often fragmented and frustrating social service environment. While few cases generate the level of public attention that the Scruggs case warranted, there are cases every day in schools; hospitals; and child protective, residential, and other kinds of settings where a delicate balancing act takes place between the constraints of policies and resources and the needs of clients. In addition to providing services that are clinically sound and responsive to clients' needs, social workers must also be attuned to the ethical dimensions their cases present. They must apply principles such as confidentiality, informed consent, and self-determination with clients whose rights and choices are constrained by age and maturity, and legal and parental prerogatives. This book examines how social workers can ethically bridge those tensions to deliver effective, ethical services.

ETHICS AND ETHICAL DILEMMAS

Our journey begins with a discussion of what we mean by ethics and ethical dilemmas. At its most basic level, ethics is the study of doing what is right or good and the bases by which we determine the "right" course of action. As we shall see in chapter 2, ethical practices in social work are shaped by a number of factors, including personal and professional values, organizational and social policies, laws, and the ethical standards found in codes of conduct and codes of ethics. Through our personal upbringing and professional socialization, we develop the capacity to distinguish right from wrong in our practice as social workers. Through virtue ethics (character) and principle ethics (our professional codes), we choose to do the right thing when faced with right-or-wrong choices such as taking a client's money, divulging a client's secrets to our friends, or reporting to our agency that we provided services we really did not. Yet having a clear compass for distinguishing right from wrong doesn't spare us from ethical dilemmas. Ethical dilemmas commonly arise under five circumstances:

1. When the application or boundary of an ethical standard is unclear
2. When standards conflict with institutional demands
3. When there are conflicting loyalties
4. When a professional finds it difficult to adhere to an ethical standard
5. When good solutions seem unattainable

In each of these scenarios, the social worker must decide between two goods, or two compelling "right" choices. In the first case, the worker's dilemma may concern carrying out a given standard. For example, what are the limits of confidentiality when a client is engaging in dangerous behavior, albeit behavior that falls short of the standard of creating "serious, foreseeable, and imminent risk to themselves or others" (NASW, 1999, 1.02)? It is good to comply with the Code and it is good to support one's clients. Where should the worker draw the line on each?

This dilemma of how to apply standards is compounded in practice with minor clients, because the intent of the standard, even if it is clear, may conflict with other laws or policies granting parents rights. "Social workers respect and promote the right of clients to self-determination and assist clients in their efforts to identify and clarify their goals" (NASW, 1999, 1.02), but how does a clinician reconcile a youth's rights with those of his parents, who may have referred him for treatment with an entirely different goal in mind? Is informed consent relevant for clients who have no legal right to give consent? What are the boundaries of confidentiality for a youth whose parents are paying for her treatment and are worried for her well-being? How should a social worker uphold his or her responsibility to the client and the commitment not to abandon the client when the child's parents abruptly remove him from treatment? It's easy to see how dilemmas can arise when the clarity of standards is applied to the vagaries of practice!

At other times, the dilemma may arise when an organization's policies or practices conflict with professional standards. For example, a juvenile detention facility may store records in an area where all staff can have access to them, with the rationale that services are provided by a team and all members of the team need to keep abreast of cases. This is an admirable goal in that it is meant to facilitate continuity of care in a facility with twenty-four-hour interdisciplinary responsibility for high-risk youths. However, the social worker in the facility may be uncomfortable with that policy, in light of NASW (1999) standards about protecting information received from clients and guarding "the confidentiality of clients' written and electronic records and other sensitive information. Social workers should take reasonable steps to ensure that clients' records are stored in a secure location and that clients' records are not available to others who are not authorized to have access" (1.07l). It is possible that the agency's authorization of a large number of employees to have access to records upholds the letter rather than the spirit of the standard. The type of information divulged to the social worker may be particularly sensitive and thus worthy of greater protection than the organization would afford it. Do the nurses on the night shift need to know that a youth is questioning his sexual orientation or that another's mother is a crack addict? If the social worker seeks clients' informed consent about this information-sharing arrangement, will that impair their trust and willingness to share their concerns?

A third type of dilemma arises when the worker has conflicting loyalties. Sometimes, as in the case above, that may mean loyalty to one's employer versus one's professional code or responsibilities. It is good to be loyal to both, but some situations render them mutually incompatible. At other times, these dilemmas may speak to conflicting responsibilities or conflicting loyalties to different parties in a case. If a teen in treatment discloses troubling behavior, such as drunk driving or a planned liaison with someone he or she met on the Internet, the social worker must choose between principles of confidentiality and safety and between loyalty to the client and loyalty to the parents or guardians.

The fourth category of dilemmas involves those that arise within the worker. A good deal of professional preparation involves personal development, as practitioners examine their motivations, vulnerabilities, and values and the ways that these may facilitate or impede effective practice. While important, that work does not preclude difficulties when a worker's values collide with an ethical standard. Cases frequently arise where the law requires that a report of child endangerment be filed but the clinician's experience indicates that the report will lead to little change, except greater risk and distress for the child. In other cases, such as those involving risk of harm, professional standards may urge confidentiality but the worker's values or apprehensions may favor openness. Even when it is clearly right to follow the law or put one's responsibilities to clients before one's own needs, is it always right to do so? How can the worker tell the difference?

We've talked so far about situations involving competing good or rights, as opposed to right-vs.-wrong dilemmas. But sometimes the dilemma seems to arise because there are no good solutions, and the decision seems to be one in which a choice between competing bad choices must be made. In fact, the word "dilemma" describes decisions that must be made between two unsatisfactory alternatives (Loewenberg, Dolgoff, & Harrington, 2000). A child must be removed from an abusive situation (protecting his safety) yet he pleads to be allowed to stay (upholding his self-determination). A young man is distraught about keeping his sexual orientation a secret yet knows that if he tells his family, he will be forced to leave home. A school social worker arranges for a young girl to get a winter coat, but her family makes her return it, refusing what they see as charity. Divorcing parents each insist on having custody of their children, and the children only want their parents to remain together. In each situation the dilemma emerges from the apparent absence of a desirable solution.

Understanding and categorizing dilemmas is an essential first step in beginning to solve them. Identifying the nature of the conflict allows the worker to move from discomfort and confusion to action. The categorization helps to isolate the elements of the dilemma so that options for resolution can be developed. The organization of dilemmas into the five types described above is one method for describing ethical problems. The next model offers a framework where the dilemmas come about as a result of the tension between competing principles.

Kidder (1995) suggests another paradigm for classifying ethical dilemmas. His, too, represents different types of right-vs.-right conflicts. While Kidder's research shows that all dilemmas fall into one of these four frameworks, he notes that some fall into multiple frameworks, which represent different types of tensions. The later chapters of this book are organized around these four polarities: justice versus mercy, short term versus long term, individual versus community, and truth versus loyalty.

In justice-vs.-mercy dilemmas the worker is caught between acting to uphold laws, policies, principles, or agreements in a fair and just manner and acting with forgiveness and compassion. This is exemplified by the troubled teenager who makes the track team and appears to be thriving in school as a result. When he is caught shoplifting, the coach and his counselor meet to tell him he will be dropped from the team for his clear violation of team and school rules. He begs for their forgiveness, making a case for how much progress he has made, and assuring them that he has learned his lesson and it won't happen again. He says regretfully, "I just didn't see any other way to get those running shoes."

The coach and counselor must weigh two goods: upholding an explicit policy without making special exceptions based on the context of the situation or the individual involved, and showing leniency and sympathy due to the circumstances and individual involved. Each choice offers promises and pitfalls. In acting with justice, they validate the importance of following this and other school rules, and they ensure fairness for other students who may have been held to the policy's consequences in the past regardless of how compelling their case might have been. Upholding the policy may help the youth understand the seriousness of his actions and learn from the consequences.

In showing mercy, the counselor and coach may teach the youth a lesson about the consequences of his behavior, but the nature of the lesson is unclear. Will he swear off shoplifting after this close call, or will the lasting message be that he can avoid consequences by making a compelling argument? Making an exception in his case may keep him involved in pro-social activities and encourage his success in school, while holding a hard line may result in a discouraging turning point and the loss of his recent gains. When is a second chance an opportunity, and when is it an unfair exception? It is good to be fair and it is good to act with mercy, and it is difficult to do both at the same time.

As the name suggests, short-term vs. long-term dilemmas balance choices that may be advantageous in the short run with the resulting long-term effects. The case of the shoplifting teen could be construed as a short-term vs. long-term dilemma in that the options can be examined in light of the immediate and eventual consequences they will have on the youth and other stakeholders. As another example, consider the advertising some child welfare agencies use to secure adoptive homes for hard-to-place children. Children available for placement are pictured and profiled in newspaper columns, brochures, and public service segments on the television news, with the hope of attracting interested families. Is this ethical? Do the ends justify the means? What are the short-term effects on the children involved, and are these outweighed by the prospect of the child being placed permanently with a loving, stable family? Is it right for other principles such as the right to privacy and dignity to be sacrificed for a greater good down the road?

The third category of dilemma weighs the tensions between the interests of the individual vs. the community or between individuals. Imagine a teen who learns that he is HIV positive and refuses to tell his parents because the diagnosis will raise suspicions regarding how he acquired the disease. While the clinic social worker might understand his apprehensions, he or she may also feel that the parents have a right to know that their son has a grave condition. The dilemma exists between two goods: the benefits the teen might reap in keeping his diagnosis a secret, and the benefits for his family, who may feel it is their right and responsibility to monitor his health care.

Truth-vs.-loyalty dilemmas are essentially dilemmas of promise keeping. The case of the HIV-positive teenager can also be viewed through this framework. The social worker, having made a commitment to keep the client's information confidential, must do so (acting with loyalty or fidelity) even though he or she might feel that honesty requires him or her to tell the truth to concerned others or to persuade the teen to do so. As we can see from this dilemma, the principles of truth and loyalty are not simply personal values. Rather, they spring from the social worker's professional duties and responsibilities. The worker is true to the promises made to the client not simply because he or she is a trustworthy person but because the professional role demands it.

Privacy is accorded a high priority in clinical practice because it is the basis on which clients feel safe to share their histories and their deepest troubles and aspirations. Minors are typically accorded confidentiality on matters involving sexually transmitted diseases on the presumption that it encourages them to seek help and thus stem the transmission of diseases. The right to an expectation of privacy (and the limits of it) is articulated explicitly through informed consent procedures at the outset of the treatment relationship. Hence, the client expects the clinician's loyalty to this principle and to the contract. However, there are many situations in which truth telling is also a responsibility of practice, such as when a child is being abused or when a person is placing him- or herself or another in danger. Social workers who serve minors often have a responsibility to tell the truth to parents, in their capacity as the child client's legal guardians and concerned stakeholders, and this responsibility may conflict with the expressed and implied loyalty to the child. Can the professional be both loyal and honest? How can those principles be reconciled when they are in conflict? This is the crux of the truth-vs.-loyalty dilemma.

Like the five-type categorization of dilemmas, Kidder's framework gives us the tools and language to dissect and discuss ethical problems. Both schemas address competing-goods or rights-vs.-right dilemmas, as there should be no struggle when one is choosing right from wrong.

Each framework views dilemmas as clashes between principles, standards, values, or roles. In this way, ethical quandaries are distinct from clinical quandaries. There are an infinite number of problems that may arise in clinical practice: a child is ineligible for a promising program, a therapeutic group appears to be of no benefit to some members, a treatment team is in conflict over the most efficacious intervention, a supervisor is unhelpful, a parent is resistant to family therapy, funding is cut for an after-school program. There is no doubt that these are vexing problems for the professionals involved. They clearly lead to dilemmas, but they are not evidently ethical dilemmas. As a result they are not amenable to ethical analysis and decision making. The classifications described above and the decision-making framework introduced in the next chapter are built on different premises and principles. As we look back to the case of J. Daniel Scruggs, there may have been an array of clinical problems in the case, but there no doubt were ethical dilemmas as well. In the next section, we use the two classification systems to analyze some of them.

ETHICS IN ACTION

As bystanders reviewing the case of Daniel Scruggs, how might examining the problems in the case through the lens of ethics help us better understand them? Let's select three issues for review: Judith's care of her son, the school's response to Daniel's bullying and hygiene, and the Department of Children and Families' decision not to substantiate neglect charges.

Judith

In reports on the case, Daniel's mother was criticized for keeping a filthy home, for not ensuring that Daniel attended school, and for being noncompliant with the school's recommendations. A clean home and active, responsive parenting are both good things to provide. Judith Scruggs's case might simply be viewed as a right-vs.-wrong decision where she failed to do what was morally and legally correct. On the other hand, if you were working as Judith's advocate or as the family's social worker, what other insights might emerge as you consider the ethical dilemmas in this case? Perhaps her failure to keep a clean home and ensure Daniel's attendance stemmed from her own history of deprivation or a depression that made it difficult to do more than the basics of daily life: work and sleep. It is right to expect parents to care for their kids, but it is also right to sympathize with and assist people who lack the knowledge or ability to do what we ask of them. In this framework, hers is a justice-vs.-mercy paradigm where the laws and societal standards would hold her accountable for her son's care, but a belief that she was doing the best she could against terrific odds might engender mercy.

We might also wonder what effect Judith's work schedule had on her ability to keep up with her housework and her son. Was she caught between competing responsibilities to her employers and to her son? Is a society that requires parents to work seventy hours a week in order to make a living wage ethical? Perhaps she was trying to reconcile two incompatible imperatives: maintaining a clean home and making enough money to provide the home in the first place. In that case, hers is an example of a short-term vs. long-term dilemma where excessive work hours led to short-term benefits but at long-term costs. As such, it may have also reflected a bad-vs.-bad dilemma, where no acceptable options were apparent. In the absence of a caring social network, it is not surprising that good options were hard to come by.

The School

The investigation into Daniel's death held the system responsible for not addressing Daniel's bullying and for the failure of key staff, including the nurse and guidance counselor, to respond to his needs. What are the ethical elements in this finding? Competence would be a concern if the workers failed to understand their jobs or did not possess the diagnostic or therapeutic tools necessary to understand Daniel's hygiene and behavioral problems. While it is wrong for people to practice without the competence to do their jobs, perhaps these staff members were focusing on problems that were more common in the school, leading to a right-vs.-right, individual-vs.-community, competing-loyalties dilemma where the needs of some students were weighed against the needs of others. In a similar vein, we might imagine the school board and administrators facing a competing-responsibilities paradigm as they sought to make effective use of scarce funds. One can understand how the school's need to choose between required services such as special education and important but not required services such as social work or bullying prevention is also an ethical dilemma.

The workers may also have been stymied by Judith's unresponsiveness. They might have embraced their professional responsibilities in the case but faced dilemmas about how to carry them out without the consent of the student's mother. Perhaps confidentiality (an ethical issue) or fractures in the service delivery system (a clinical issue) meant that the service providers in the case lacked the capacity to share their perspectives with each other and thus act on full case information. If so, this would constitute a truth-vs.-loyalty dilemma.

Department of Children and Families

The Department of Children and Families' decision not to keep the Scruggs case open by substantiating educational or physical neglect is troubling, as it might have provided an avenue to bring services to the family and would have reinforced the importance of Daniel's school attendance. Surely the workers in the case understood their mandate from the state and the importance of securing child safety. Why would they fail to substantiate a case as clear as this? Perhaps the workers had a competing imperative, to limit their caseloads or to conserve resources for the most critical cases (individual versus community, ethics versus institutional demands). Perhaps they assessed that a youth of Daniel's age was capable of taking care of his hygiene and getting himself to school and therefore constituted a low priority for their intervention or protection (competing loyalties or responsibilities). Perhaps they assessed that his poor attendance was caused by the bullying he was experiencing and thus a remedy was out of their jurisdiction (a bad-vs.-bad scenario).

The available records on Daniel Scruggs's case don't reveal the inner thoughts of the employees of the Department of Children and Families or school personnel. As a result, we can't speculate about whether personal values were in conflict with ethical standards or even if the workers ever perceived the ethical dimensions of this case. Yet from the extensive examination the case received due to its tragic conclusion, we can consider the perspectives of various actors in the case to uncover and identify ethical dilemmas that might have been addressed.

SUMMARY

This chapter introduced you to the purposes of the book and the ethical and clinical dimensions of practice with children, using the Scruggs case as a guide. We covered examples of right-vs.-right dilemmas in practice with minors and Kidder's classification system in order to help you hone your skills in identifying and understanding ethical dilemmas. Now that we have developed some efficacy in identifying dilemmas, what do we do about them? The next chapter will offer a guide for ethical decision making.

Chapter 2

Ethical and Clinical Decision Making

When asked what process they use for resolving dilemmas, professionals often respond, "I trust my gut." Sometimes gut-level decisions are the result of an internalized, almost automatic ethical decision-making strategy honed over years of use until it develops into a reflexive response to addressing dilemmas (Gladwell, 2005). In other cases, though, intuition is a fly-by-the-seat-of-your-pants enterprise, where decisions are independent, inconsistent, ungrounded, and unexamined (Gambrill, 1997). This is a hazardous approach, as it raises questions about the quality of the decisions that result and the efficacy of the social worker who reacts without forethought or consultation.

Another subset of practitioners relies on a codified decision-making schema, reporting, "I resolve ethical decisions by finding out what's legal," "I decide whom I'd rather be sued by," or "I do what the Code says." In contrast to gut responses, these decision-making processes have the advantage of being grounded in *something* (laws, liability, ethics codes), but they too have disadvantages. The first is the imperfect correspondence between what is legal and what is ethical. There are many activities that are legal (suspending a teen from school for fighting) that are not ethical (suspending a teen of color for fighting while sparing a white teen the same consequence). There are also activities that are illegal that are not unethical (exceeding the speed limit when driving to the hospital with an ill family member or acts of civil disobedience, such as sit-ins or protests). Using the law alone as a guide leaves a lot of decisional territory uncovered, as there are many areas in which the law is of no assistance.

Practicing from a liability-averse perspective yields a different set of problems. While clinicians are wise to engage in sound practice, making case decisions based on the fear of a lawsuit or ethics charge is unrealistic (anyone can complain about anything at any time: there are no risk-free decisions). This strategy is also likely to disadvantage those who are already powerless and most in need of the social worker's help. Risk-driven decisions, by definition, put the professional's needs before the client's.

Ethics codes, while an important resource in decision making, are useful but insufficient. Like laws, codes only address a limited array of issues: those dilemmas and circumstances of special concern to the profession's activities. Even in areas addressed by codes, the user will find that elements of a particular code may be in conflict with others—in upholding one standard, the worker may be running afoul of another. For example, in order to protect others from harm, a clinician may need to compromise a client's privacy or impinge on his or her autonomy. As we saw in the previous chapter, while autonomy, privacy, and safety are all important concepts, sometimes they cannot be reconciled.

A further limitation of code-based decision making is that even when codes address an issue, they make use of relative or qualifying language that can stymie the practitioner looking for answers. For example, the NASW (1999) Code states that social workers should set "clear appropriate and culturally sensitive boundaries" (1.06c) with clients and should break client confidences only for "compelling professional reasons" (1.07c). While the responsibility to set boundaries and maintain confidences is clear, the times and mechanisms for doing so are open to interpretation, as various practitioners may disagree on the meaning of terms like "clear," "appropriate," "compelling," and "professional." Codes of ethics are not legal documents. They do not strive to address every possible permutation of a case. Rather, they provide guidance that must be applied contextually based on the facts of the case at hand. Because codes are inherently ambiguous, they rely on the thoughtful, principled application by users in order to have the intended effect.

Finally, we note an additional concern about the limits of ethics codes that is particularly salient for this volume. Codes are not typically written with minor clients in mind. In social work that means that many of the standards in a code cannot be applied without qualifications to minors. For example, the NASW (1999) Code of Ethics stipulates that social workers should provide clients with "reasonable access" to their records (1.08a). If a minor client makes a request to review his or her case file, what role do the child's parents have in such a request? Must they be consulted? What actions should the worker take if the parents disallow such access but the NASW Code encourages it? What effect would refusing the child's request have on the therapeutic relationship? These and other questions must be addressed by workers in applying a code's provisions to minor clients.

What options exist if instinctual decision making is flawed and rule-based strategies aren't adequate? We advocate the conscious use of a decision-making model to ensure ethically and clinically sound decisions that takes into account the array of options, guidelines, and consequences that may come to bear in any given case. What's our rationale for the model? Ethical decision making is a complex skill and, as such, requires practice before it becomes second nature. It is a high-stakes process wherein bad decisions can have negative consequences for the client and for the practitioner. Decision making is further complicated by the endless variations in cases and concepts, so that while workers can build on past decisions, each dilemma requires fresh examination. Adopting and incorporating a decision-making framework helps to ensure that bases have been covered and that the resulting decision is made with full awareness of the risks and benefits.

While dozens of decision-making models exist, researchers are hard pressed to find clinicians who use them (D'Aprix, 2005). Typically, workers complain that such models are both cumbersome and unhelpful. Let's examine each of these criticisms in turn.

Some models are in fact complex and much too long, which makes them hard to remember and employ. Sometimes, though, the perception of complexity may simply be an artifact of the learning curve. Decision-making models appear awkward and unwieldy at first, just as a snowboard does to the first-time snowboarder and yarn and needles do to the first-time knitter. The learning curve may also make models time consuming to employ at first, a disincentive for the busy practitioner. Yet we'd argue that increased facility with the model ultimately leads to increased efficiency. We also note that bad decisions cost time, money, and psychic energy, which makes them inefficient in the long run. Further, when elements of the decision-making process are routine, they are less awkward to employ. For example, supervisors can institute regular slots of time to talk about ethical dilemmas with their supervisees, clinicians can use time spent traveling and other downtime to reflect on cases, and documentation can be incorporated in existing recording processes. While employing decision-making models may not be easy, especially at first, they may not be as unwieldy as they first appear.

The complaint that models are unhelpful also has legitimacy. No model will point to a particular decision as the right one for any given circumstance. In part, this is because there may be no one right decision. The beauty of a model is that it forces the user to uncover and consider a number of options, tossing out those that are inappropriate or unwise and examining the array of viable choices based on sound clinical, ethical, and legal criteria. Rather than being disappointed in the model for failing to suggest a single perfect answer, we must be grateful that it generated several answers and provided us with a basis on which to choose the one we will pursue. This last point is an important one. Should our decision be called into question by a client, a colleague, or a court, the use of a decision-making model provides our choice with legitimacy. Question: "Why did you tell my mom I was sneaking out of the house to get high?" Answer: "Because I agreed to let her know when your safety is in jeopardy, and I felt this was too risky to keep to myself."

This volume presents a model designed to encourage critical thinking about ethical dilemmas, accompanied by an easy-to-remember mnemonic device to prompt a thorough response to dilemmas. After it is introduced in this chapter, the model is then employed throughout the book in examining cases. If it does not resonate with you, please examine instead any of the array of models available from Congress (1999), Corey, Corey, and Callahan (2003), Loewenburg, Dolgoff, and Harrington (2000), Reamer (2006), and others. Whichever framework you choose, the goal is for you to find a schema you can remember, practice, and eventually use with ease. In doing so you can become part of the growing band of professionals whose gut-based decisions are head based as well!

THE MULTIPLE-PERSPECTIVES MODEL

Though ethical decision-making frameworks vary in their level of detail and elaboration, they entail similar steps: understanding the dilemma, generating options, seeking the wisdom of others, and recording and assessing the resulting actions. The framework presented here distills these elements into a five-part process that is as easy to remember as the ABCs.

A—Assess options
B—Be mindful of process
C—Consult
D—Document
E—Evaluate

Before we examine and apply the elements of the model, let's look at some features of this critical thinking framework. The first is its organization. While the last step of evaluation might only take place once the decision has been made, the first four parts of the framework are not intended to be done in any particular order. They may be done simultaneously or in varying sequences. For example, the social worker may document concerns and questions prior to consulting with a supervisor, then the two together can evaluate options and consider implementation of the decision. Or a worker may independently weigh the choices and then consult a colleague about the outcome or process. Or the worker might seek the input of others in generating options and document that advice before individually deciding what to do. The key is to ensure that all the steps are taken, regardless of the order in which they are done.

The second element to discuss is one's timing in employing the model. While it is intended to be used *before* one acts on an ethical dilemma, in practice, practitioners may be called on to act first and evaluate later. For example, consider a case in which a child surprises the worker with the gift of a paperweight she has made or a teenage client says, "I have something important to tell you but you have to promise not to tell anyone else." In these instances the worker must respond in the moment, hopefully guided by sound experience and practice wisdom. Yet the fact that the moment for decision making has passed does not mean that there is no need for critical thinking. In fact, examining our decisions after the fact is an essential step in building a foundation for future decisions. That is, thinking critically about the choice and opening it up for examination and consultation can reveal options we overlooked but might employ as alternatives in the future. In this retrospective analysis, the worker asks him- or herself, "What other things might I have done? What are the pros and cons of those compared to what I did do? Are there risks in the choice I made that I hadn't considered? If so, how can I be alert to them in making future decisions?"

A-B-C may seem like an infantile schema for an activity as important as ethical analysis. Our goal is to make the model memorable and useful without in any way trivializing the difficulty and importance of the process it represents. As each of the elements is examined in the following sections, feel free to choose whatever terms and phrases you find acceptable and helpful for internalizing the decision-making process.

Assess Options

A key element of decision making in any field involves the generation of an array of ideas and their examination through various perspectives. The critical examination of ethical dilemmas involves the same process. Workers, alone or in concert with colleagues, should look at the problem from various viewpoints and formulate as many responses to the dilemma as possible. While generating alternatives, workers may simultaneously begin evaluating the merits of each. How do we decide what is ethical? How do we distinguish the actions that are unwise from those that are sound? A variety of variables must be taken into account in sorting good choices from bad. In order to help you remember them, we offer yet another rubric. We refer to these critical elements by the mnemonic ELVIS, as in:

E—Ethical theories and principles
L—Laws and policies
V—Values
I—Information
S—Standards

Each of these variables offers a particular form of guidance for decision making. Taken individually or together, they may lead decision makers to different places. That is, a legal analysis may favor one option, but an examination of the implications of that choice may render it undesirable. Don't despair. The value of these screens is in their complexity. Think of the popular Web site that provides maps and directions. It offers the user the choice of getting to his or her destination most quickly, via the most scenic route, through metropolitan areas, or around them. Different routes have different merits and drawbacks, and so it is with our ethical options. ELVIS provides us with different methods for assessing which is "best."

Ethical theories and principles. In the long tradition of moral philosophy, many theories of ethics and ethical behavior have emerged and evolved (Rachels, 2003). Two theories in particular have endured and constitute the most prominent points of reference for ethical decision making. The first, utilitarianism, concerns itself with the consequences or effects of a decision. Most often associated with the work of Jeremy Bentham and John Stuart Mill, this ends-based perspective posits that the risks and benefits of a decision are what matter and should be given the most weight as we evaluate its goodness (Bandman & Bandman, 2002; Kidder, 1995). This premise is typically captured in the question, "Which option creates the greatest good for the greatest number?" Though this aphorism doesn't do justice to the complexity and permutations of the theory, its emphasis on the consequences of a decision distinguishes it from philosophical traditions that are more absolutist in nature.

Deontological or rule-based ethical theories stand in contrast to utilitarianism. The theories in this area are concerned with duty, obligations, and universal moral principles. This perspective emphasizes that some actions are inherently right or wrong regardless of the context or the outcomes they might generate. Most commonly associated with the work of Immanuel Kant, deontology posits that decision makers should follow the categorical imperative to "act only according to that maxim that should become universal law" (O'Donohue & Ferguson, 2003, p. 6). Phrased another way, Kant would have the decision maker ask, "Is this how I would want everybody to behave?" and on that basis determine the permissibility of an action.

The advantages and disadvantages of utilitarianism and deontology have been thoroughly examined (Darr, 1997; Rachels, 2003; Reamer, 2006). Critics note that the benefits, goods, or "pleasures" in ends-based approaches may be different for different stakeholders, and thus hard to evaluate and open to broad interpretation. The common standard requiring decisions "in the best interest of the child" demonstrates these frailties (Braver, Ellman, & Fabricius, 2003). Is it in the child's best interest to be placed with a parent who has significant financial means or another who has abundant time to spend with the child? Is the greater good found in living in a loving home or a clean and safe home? It is clearly best to have both, but when the choice must be made between the two, what then constitutes "best"? A further concern with the perspective of "the greatest good for the greatest number" lies in its capacity to powerfully disadvantage the minority while maximizing benefits for the majority of citizens. The staff and residents of a runaway shelter may benefit from knowing a resident has AIDS. However, the focus on the greatest number may result in significant harms to the individual who is marginalized or stigmatized following revelations regarding his health status.

Critics of deontological perspectives argue that obligations or duties are not hierarchical and thus may exist in conflict with one another. Further, from a pragmatic perspective, they argue that consequences can never be totally eliminated from decision making (Bandman & Bandman, 2002) and thus pure deontology is more an intellectual exercise than it is useful in real life.

While each of these landmark perspectives has flaws and fissures, these do not render them meaningless for our assessment of options. Once we are familiar with these and other ethical theories, they can be employed to help us understand our preference for one action or another (Do we tend to be ends based or rule based?) and to generate a broader array of choices (We know what a consequentialist would suggest we do, but what would a deontologist say?). As we examine dilemmas in this text, we will refer to these theories and the solutions they suggest.

Beyond the two contrasting ethical theories, six ethical principles are commonly utilized in evaluating desirable acts in the health and human services: autonomy, beneficence, nonmaleficence, fidelity, justice, and veracity (Beauchamp & Childress, 1994; Corey et al., 2003). The principle of autonomy refers to the individual's right to make his or her own life decisions without undue or unwarranted interference. Beneficence refers to the importance of doing good by enhancing another's well-being. Its corollary, nonmaleficence, refers to the duty to prevent or reduce harm. Fidelity is the principle of behaving in a trustworthy manner and keeping one's promise or word. Related to fidelity is the principle of veracity, or the commitment to truthfulness. Justice is the premise that individuals in similar circumstances will be treated equitably, thus resulting in the equal distribution of risks and benefits. The principle of justice should also be construed in its broadest sense, meaning nondiscrimination and the fair distribution of scarce resources.

These principles can be used to generate alternatives (What actions would meet the principle of beneficence? That is, what would promote the client's interests? What decision would be just?). The principles can also be used to evaluate choices (Is this action truthful? Which of my choices results in the least harm for the stakeholders involved?). In addition to giving us tools to assess our choices, these principles, which transcend the helping professions, provide us with a common language to employ in discussing dilemmas with others.

Laws and policies. While ethical theories and principles provide one set of lenses through which to view ethical dilemmas, our choices are also governed by a continuum of laws and policies. Laws or statutes are developed at the federal, state, and local levels, while case law is shaped by court decisions rather than the actions of a legislative body. Regulations and administrative codes are typically issued by agencies with financial or other rule-making authority over an area and are intended to interpret, specify, or codify legislation. For example, the federal No Child Left Behind Act establishes an enhanced role for the federal government in public education and puts forth stipulations intended to improve students' competencies and hold schools accountable for performance goals. Beyond the legislation, however, government agencies such as the U.S. Department of Education and its state equivalents promulgate administrative regulations to define terms, clarify processes, and set performance standards.

While laws, statutes, and regulations cover geographic jurisdictions, policies are typically formulated at the organizational level. For example, agencies in the same geographic area may have different policies regarding the treatment of minors without parental consent. The differences may be attributed to the agency's mission, philosophy, funding source, or statutory responsibilities. For example, the policies of a school that accepts funding from sources that advocate abstinence-only sex education will prevent a social worker from discussing contraception or abortion, even with a student who asks for that information. In a district with a different philosophy and funding stream, the social worker will have more latitude for that discussion. And, as chapter 4 reveals, the nature of the youth's problem may also dictate policy regarding his or her treatment. For example, services for substance abuse or sexually transmitted diseases may be afforded greater confidentiality than services for depression or anorexia (Kuther, 2003).

As competent practitioners, all helping professionals should be familiar with the laws and policies that commonly affect practice. These include confidentiality, mandatory reporting, the duty to warn others, record keeping, licensure and certification, and parental rights (Corey et al., 2003). When faced with dilemmas, social workers must be able to identify the laws and policies that may impinge on their decisions. Sources of information about relevant laws and regulations include texts such as Madden's *Legal Issues in Social Work, Counseling, and Mental Health* (1998) and Saltzman and Furman's "Law and Using the Law" (1999), the *U.S. Code* for federal statutes, and the *Code of Federal Regulations* for administrative law (Dickson, 1998). State social work licensure and certification board Web sites may have links to relevant administrative codes for the profession. The U.S. Library of Congress operates several Web sites that offer information on federal, state, and international law, including the U.S. Law Library of Congress (www.loc.gov/law) and the Global Legal Information Network (www.glin.gov). Other general legal Internet sites such as Nolo (www.nolo.com), Westlaw (www.westlaw.com), and the

Legal Information Institute (www.law.cornell.edu) may be of assistance as well.

These resources, while helpful for locating laws and policies, may not be sufficient to help the worker interpret the particular statute or provision's meaning for the case at hand. To this end, we recommend coursework or continuing education programs on social work and the law, or on the laws relative to particular practice areas. In addition, consultation (addressed below) and experience in a particular subfield will help workers build expertise in this area.

Values. Values refer to our beliefs about how things should be, about what is preferable or right. Our personal values regarding money, recreation, time with family members, and the like, affect the choices we make in how we conduct our lives. Professional values refer to the ideological underpinnings of particular occupations. In social work, these values reflect the historical tradition of the profession and the beliefs that are shared by those who choose to practice as social workers. The NASW (1999) Code of Ethics articulates six core values: service, social justice, emphasizing the dignity and worth of the person, the importance of human relationships, integrity, and competence.

Service refers to the value placed on assistance to the other over self-interest. It also indicates a commitment to address larger social conditions as well as individual problems. The value that the profession places on social justice reflects its commitment to critical social issues such as poverty and marginalization and the expectation that social workers will endeavor to address the causes and results of various forms of injustice. By emphasizing the dignity and worth of each individual, social workers demonstrate their dedication to treating all people with respect and working to create social conditions that offer all people the opportunity to function at their highest capacity. This provision also reflects the belief that social workers must act responsibly in addressing both the needs of the individual and those of society. The value placed on human relationships reflects the belief that human interactions are the medium for creating change, and that social workers have the responsibility to assist in strengthening the relationships between all types of social systems. The value of integrity is similar to the ethical principles of veracity and fidelity described earlier. The profession expects that its practitioners will strive to understand the mission and ethics of the profession and will uphold them in practice with clients. Competence refers to the belief that social workers must be equipped with the knowledge, skills, and values needed for practice, and that they will be responsible for developing ongoing competence as the knowledge base of the profession evolves and changes.

When it comes to ethical decision making, two particular implications of values stand out. The first is the importance of self-awareness, which means that practitioners must be alert to their personal values and the ways that these preferences shape their view of the decisions they must make. When these values are incongruent with other elements of decision making, such as the profession's values, the client's interests, agency policies, or ethical standards, the worker should seek out consultation and assistance. While the professional may be uncomfortable acting in conflict with his or her personal beliefs, it is also improper to put those values ahead of one's professional commitments. Consultation may be helpful in finding and negotiating other alternatives.

A second consideration in using values for ethical decision making is the clarity with which we can translate those values into action. For example, we may embrace the social work value of competence but be hard pressed to explain what that means in practice. Competence is good, but what does that mean for the novice social work student seeing a new client or the clinician who is trying a new intervention for the first time? Further, we may understand and live up to a value but find that doing so is part of our ethical dilemma. For example, imagine the rural practitioner who has no experience in practice with children but is asked to lead a support group for children with cancer. When the value of competence collides with the value of service to others, where can the clinician turn?

In the realm of professional values, at least, we are assisted in our quest to apply values to ethical dilemmas by our codes of ethics, which translate the values of the field into ethical standards that help guide practice. Because, as we shall see, the standards themselves have limitations, workers must think critically about these ideals and the ways that they inform ethical matters.

Information. This step asks us what facts and other information come to bear on the dilemma. This can refer to clinical knowledge, research findings, or details about the case at hand. For example, would knowledge of Daniel Scruggs's bullying or home conditions have led workers to handle his case differently in holding him accountable for his truancy? Would information on precedents for case continuation have helped concerned people advocate for the Department of Children and Families to keep his case open? Would knowing that he had relatives nearby have helped authorities craft a back-up plan in light of the decision to close his case? What were Daniel's wishes and preferences regarding his custody and care, his classroom placement at school, or his treatment by his teachers and counselors?

As demonstrated in the Scruggs case, information can be an elusive element in decision making. In most cases, particularly those involving children, knowledge is situated with different individuals associated with various aspects of the case, and it is hard to bring it all together in a timely fashion. In other cases, there is no time to do research, as urgency demands that decisions be made and actions taken with incomplete or unsatisfactory information. At other times the pursuit of information can stymie decision making when, due to "analysis paralysis," the worker delays inexorably, waiting for the one last piece of information that never comes or is never enough.

The opinions of those most directly affected by a decision are desirable pieces of information for decision making. Sometimes it is possible to ask the client directly about his or her wishes. In other cases, one must use the individual's previous statements (living wills, for example) as evidence of his or her wishes. At other times, parents, guardians, or family members may serve as proxies for the client in declaring his or her preferences. This is often the case for child clients, whose decision-making rights are limited by the client's competence, developmental stage, and cognitive capacity.

Developmental considerations are central to ethical decision making with minors. Going beyond mere chronological age, evaluations of a youth's cognitive functioning, judgment, and maturity determine the extent to which he or she is capable of making a reasoned decision; anticipating the import of various choices; and generating acceptable options. These and other elements of competence affect the degree to which a minor might be included in decision making and the degree to which his or her decisions should hold sway. Because determinations of competence are so crucial to ethical decision making, chapter 3 is dedicated to the elements of such judgments.

While minors may have limited rights in decision making, this does not mean they have limited rights to express their wishes and opinions. We advocate inclusion of the voices of child clients, even while recognizing that children's wishes may be skewed by divided loyalties, lack of life experience, despair, or poor judgment. It will ultimately be up to the decision makers to decide how much weight to give the child's opinions, but seeking his or her views does not mean that those views will be given precedence over other factors.

Another way to consider the client's perspective in a case is to consult the literature by and for consumers, which provides insights about those directly affected by social and health care services. These views can be obtained from consumer Web sites and discussion groups (for example, www.nami.org, www.kidshealth.org, www.spanusa.org, www.diabetes.org), and from novels, memoirs, self-help guides, and other resources created by people who have faced similar decisions (Christ, Siegel, & Christ, 2002). Clearly, care must be taken in using such materials—one person's decision to forego chemotherapy may not be right for others faced with the same choice. However, familiarity with these experiences and perspectives may reveal implications and options not previously considered.

To fulfill the information step in assessing options, decision makers should ask themselves what clinical and case-specific information is relevant to their choices, what other data they might seek to better understand their choices, what written or human resources they can draw upon to learn more, and how they can seek input in a way that upholds privacy principles.

Standards. When evaluating options, social workers should pay special attention to two types of standards that govern ethical decision making: ethical standards and practice standards. Ethical standards are derived from the profession's values and principles, as well as from laws and policies. In social work, ethical standards are found in codes of ethics put forth by professional organizations such as the National

Association of Social Workers or the Clinical Social Work Federation. Codes are also generated by licensing or regulatory boards that are empowered to regulate the practice of social work. In this text, we will refer to the standards in the NASW Code of Ethics, a broadly applied and widely utilized document for ethical guidance.

The NASW Code of Ethics contains 155 standards organized by different areas of professional responsibility, including the social worker's responsibilities to clients, to colleagues, to practice settings, and to society at large. Thus, in addressing a concept such as nondiscrimination, the code applies it in different ways, depending on the arena in which the decision must be made. Social workers must treat clients in a nondiscriminatory fashion, but they must also treat colleagues fairly and without prejudice and work to eliminate discriminatory practices within society as a whole. The NASW Code contains both aspirational and enforceable standards: those that are more general and reflect the ideals of the profession and those that the clinician is expected to uphold under the possible penalty of professional or legal sanctions.

Beyond the NASW Code of Ethics, individual practitioners may look to other codes or documents for guidance on ethical standards, such as those affiliated with their particular practice setting, their licensure, or other credentials. Often these are more specific or narrowly focused than the larger professional codes (concerned only with the protection of clients, for example, as opposed to collegial relationships and other areas of conduct). At times the provisions of some codes may be at odds with the NASW Code, and the provisions within a particular code at odds with each other. While these discrepancies can be disturbing for the practitioner who wants clear and undisputed guidance, they are a hallmark of the ambiguous and contextual nature of ethical decision making.

Beyond reviewing ethical standards, workers must be familiar with professional or practice standards in order to adequately address ethical dilemmas. Practice standards may be codified, such as those from the National Association for the Education of Young Children that articulate expectations for professional preparation or quality programs, or those from the National Association of Social Workers that offer guidance on practice in child welfare settings, clinical practice, health care, and end-of-life care, to name a few. Many associations that support and regulate work with minors have published standards that can shed light on vexing practice questions.

In addition to written standards, social workers may look to the best practices that have evolved in a particular practice environment or with a particular population. Workers can learn the norms of practice that will help in generating and weighing choices from research articles, case presentations, and continuing education. Whatever avenue you use to learn about ethical and practice standards, we recommend that you do so in anticipation of ethical dilemmas, rather than in response to them. The competent and evolving professional should continually build his or her knowledge base in this area, making adjustments in practice accordingly, so that ethical mishaps can be avoided and dilemmas addressed adroitly.

As you can see, it is not easy to generate and evaluate options in response to ethical dilemmas. We hope that the mnemonic device with which we provide you will help you do so more systematically, uncovering the ethical theories, laws, values, implications, and standards associated with various choices. Alas, assessing options is only the first in our five-step alphabetical decision-making process.

Be Mindful of Process

At its heart, this step requires the worker to go beyond considering *what* actions he or she might take to consider *how* he or she will enact them. If the clinician decides that she must divulge private information about a teen client, what steps will she take with the teen and with other stakeholders to mitigate damage from the decision and to maximize positive outcomes? If a worker must decline a gift from a child client, how should he do so in a way that is sensitive and understandable to the youngster? As much as anything, this element of decision making is about the application of clinical knowledge and skill. It is not just about deciding what is right but about doing it. It is about strategy deployed with professional skills. Let's look at an example.

Gary is a social worker at the local mental health center. Yesterday, as he and his wife were leaving the house for a dinner date, his wife introduced him to the new babysitter she hired—a young woman named Maya whom she had met in her role as a soccer coach. Unbeknownst to Gary's wife, Maya had recently been in Gary's eating disorders treatment group. Maya looked awkwardly at Gary and did not indicate that she knew him when they were introduced.

Gary quickly concluded that it would be inappropriate to employ Maya as a babysitter, as that would constitute a dual relationship. He was also aware that he could not divulge Maya's status as a client to his wife, as that would violate Maya's privacy. He asked to speak with Maya privately for a moment and said, "I apologize for the confusion here. As you can see, my wife and I don't talk about our work relationships at home, so she is unaware that you were my client. As your therapist, though, I can't also be your employer. She and I will need to make other plans for this evening, and we'll pay you for the time you would have spent had you done the babysitting. I'll talk with my wife and let her know you won't be able to work for us, but I won't divulge why or anything about the nature of the services you received at the center."

Gary was attentive to Maya's reaction to this news. She shrugged and said, "Okay. But I can tell her, can't I, that you were my counselor? I don't want to talk about the group, but I don't want her to think it was for something dangerous or bad that would get me kicked off the team." Gary replied, "The choice to tell her or not is entirely up to you. Just know that even if you do, that's not something I will talk about with her."

Gary went in the house and said to his wife, "We'll need to make other plans for tonight, as I've asked Maya not to babysit for us after all." When his wife pressed him for a reason, he simply replied, "I can't talk about it further. Please trust me and let's leave it at that."

As you read this case, you may have thought, "I'd have handled it differently" or "I wouldn't have worded things that way." Indeed, practitioners may arrive at different conclusions and develop different strategies for carrying out their choices, depending on their clientele, the setting, and their own experiences, theoretical orientation, and personal style. There are, no doubt, other acceptable ways to address the challenges this case offers regarding confidentiality and dual relationships. In keeping with this step in the decision-making process, being mindful of process, Gary had to be careful not to carry out his decision in a way that would have been disturbing, invalidating, or anxiety provoking for Maya. His decision to handle it the way he did was attentive not only to the ethical prescriptions at play but also to the clinical dimensions of the case. In speaking directly and honestly with Maya, Gary demonstrated respect, concern for her well-being, and a belief that she would understand the rationale for his action. Was his the best choice under the circumstances? Is there anything further he should do, such as speak with her parents? Is there a way to avoid such incidents in the future? Consultation, even after the fact, will help Gary to explore and refine his actions in the case.

Consult

If the descriptions of steps A and B seem complex to you, it should be clear why consultation is a necessary part of decision making. Even the most gifted clinicians struggle in generating a comprehensive set of solutions and weighing their merits. The professionals most closely involved in a decision may be hesistant in taking necessary action and require encouragement to rise to the ethical and practical demands of a case. We all need an extra set of ears to hear us as we talk through our ethical dilemmas, extra eyes to see opportunities, and extra minds to think through them. Consultation, which can be a first step in ethical decision making or the final step before a decision is made and acted on, provides just such a vehicle.

Who can social workers turn to for consultation on ethical decision making? The first response is the clinician's immediate supervisor, who has responsibility for ensuring that the worker's practices are in keeping with the agency's goals and objectives. Several factors, however, can hamper the use of supervisory support and consultation. Workload factors diminish the amount of time supervisors have for supervisees and supervisory sessions for reflection and professional development. Features of the relationship such as trust and professional respect play a role in consultation: when either is lacking, the supervisee may be reluctant to share challenges or may be skeptical of the quality of the advice given. Even when mutual respect exists, the evaluative aspect of supervision may inhibit the worker from sharing ethical dilemmas for fear that it will reflect poorly on his or her performance or out of discomfort about how prior decisions in the case will be construed. A final reason that workers may not use supervision for ethical discussions is to preserve their autonomy. Will supervisory consultation tie the worker's hands, limiting his or her options rather than opening up an array of options for discussion? In fact, it might. In representing the agency's interests, the supervisor may advocate or even mandate a course of action that the worker finds unhelpful or even unethical. The possibility that this or any of the other possibilities mentioned above will occur is not a reason to avoid seeking ethical guidance in supervision. If supervision is bad, ill informed, or unavailable, the ethical course of action is to attempt to improve the supervision, not avoid it. Should a worker's decision come under scrutiny, the failure to seek supervision raises red flags about the worker's judgment and commitment to good practice. The explanation that supervision was in some way deficient won't hold much water.

Agency-assigned supervisors aren't the only resource for consultation on ethical decision making. Workers can formally contract for supervision to enhance their practice and establish credentials for licensure. They can also create alliances such as peer consultation groups when supervision is not available or adequate for their needs. In these, consultation is enhanced by the ongoing relationships in which advice is given. The trust and knowledge that develop over time in a supervisory or group relationship facilitate the sharing of dilemmas and enhance the quality of the feedback. Consultants may be freer than supervisors to offer frank assessments because the information is given in the context of an ongoing, trusting relationship. Their advice may also be more useful as a result of the consultant's knowledge of the decision maker that has developed over time. In addition to facilitating the provision of consultation, the relationship may also make the feedback easier to take.

When consultants are outside the auspices of the employing agency, the clinician should be mindful of provisions in the NASW (1999) Code that recommend, "Social workers should not disclose identifying information when discussing clients with consultants unless the client has consented to disclosure of confidential information or there is a compelling need for such disclosure" (1.07q), "Social workers should keep themselves informed about colleagues' areas of expertise and competencies. Social workers should seek consultation only from colleagues who have demonstrated knowledge, expertise, and competence related to the subject of the consultation" (2.05b), and "When consulting with colleagues about clients, social workers should disclose the least amount of information necessary to achieve the purposes of the consultation" (2.05c). Consultation groups may also develop their own written agreements detailing the expectations of group members and stipulations regarding confidentiality, fees, participation, and termination. These contracts add legitimacy to the consultation process, demonstrating that these are not casual personal conversations but substantive discussions designed to provide support and improve professional practice.

Other group venues may also be appropriate for ethics consultations, including staff or team meetings or even workshops on ethics. While participants must be careful to protect patients' privacy in such venues, group consultations can help workers uncover various interpretations and applications of practice concepts. Earlier in this chapter we discussed the use of relative language in ethics codes and how terms such as "appropriate," "feasible," and "reasonable" might be open to interpretation. Even on an ad hoc or one-time basis, group consultation provides us with benchmarks by which to assess our interpretation of such terms. What would our mentors consider appropriate boundaries with clients? Under what conditions would they deem it feasible to notify a client in advance that his or her privacy must be breached? What constitutes providing a client reasonable access to records? Discussion about various interpretations of these terms opens up options and offers a compass by which individual workers can gauge their own appraisals.

Beyond general assistance in decision making, consultation can involve seeking out expertise on the specifics of a case. A lawyer may help us to understand case precedents around parental rights, a minister may help us understand a family's faith and their reluctance to approve needed mental health services, a physician may help us understand the biological factors impinging on a child's behavior, and so on. Ideally, an agency would offer just the kind of interdisciplinary resources needed to provide ready consultation. Having built-in resources facilitates communication about cases. Such communication takes place in the context of existing relationships, so that advice is founded on a common understanding of the organization's mission and the clients' needs. When consultants are not available in-house, though, social workers must seek out and build a network that they can turn to when faced with questions outside their scope of practice.

While social workers should look to supervisors, peers, and experts to broaden their perspective and knowledge regarding ethical dilemmas, they should not turn to family members and friends for assistance. Even though our social networks are familiar to us and easy to access, they are not typically equipped to offer advice from the professional framework that ethical decisions demand. Those who care about us are likely to put our concerns before the client's interests. And even those friends and family members who are professionals themselves and subscribe to the values, laws, and standards of social work are still not entitled to the private information of the clients we serve.

Consultation is an important element of ethical decision making, but the resources we use should be carefully selected and consistently used.

Document

The fourth element of the critical thinking model is documentation. Unfortunately, in the press of other responsibilities and the need for action, record keeping can be pushed aside. Clinicians may also be wary of recording their options and choices, lest the paperwork be used against them in the future. Despite these constraints and reservations, documentation is essential. The clinician should detail what factors he or she considered in making the decision, the resources and individuals consulted, the decision itself, and the basis for the decision. Information about the effects of the decision and any efforts that were made to address untoward outcomes should also be included.

Documents related to ethical decisions may be kept in different places, including the client's case records, the therapist's clinical notes or personal journal, and the supervisory record. Should the case be litigated in some way, these records may be discoverable, meaning that they could be subpoenaed as evidence in the case. However, this should serve as an impetus for documentation rather than a disincentive. The clinician's account of his or her actions, however meritorious, has little meaning without supporting evidence recorded at the time the decision was made. Risk management experts agree that thorough and well-constructed records substantiate rather than undermine good decisions (Houston-Vega, Nuehring, & Daguio, 1997).

Beyond providing security amid the specter of liability, documentation in ethics cases helps the worker develop decision-making capacity, as the effort to record and reflect on decisions provides a foundation for enhanced decisions in the future. And, like many tasks, documentation is less onerous when done incrementally. Rather than waiting for the case's conclusion, the worker should record consultations and decisions as they occur, capturing them in a timely manner to create a comprehensive record.

Evaluate

As the worker implements the decision, he or she must be alert to the effects of the decision. Did it go forth as planned? Did the expected results materialize? If not, what was different? Were there problematic outcomes for the client or others involved? Were there ways those outcomes could have been avoided? What steps can the worker take now to diminish negative effects? If the decision was successful, should the worker implement it in future cases? The evaluation phase is essential for the worker who aspires to internalize an ethical decision-making schema, as it provides a feedback and refinement mechanism and thus the foundation for future decisions.

In the context of ethical decision making, evaluation may be an individual process where the worker engages in personal self-reflection. It may also be incorporated into supervision and consultation processes, in which other professionals are involved both in examining the effects of the decision and participating in a process of self-correction as their input and advice are examined and refined. Depending on the circumstances, too, the worker might seek the client's input, soliciting feedback on the outcome and process of decision making and juxtaposing it with the worker's impressions.

The key in evaluation is to close the decision-making loop so that the process is improved based on the results achieved, so that poor results are ameliorated, and so that the worker learns not just what works but why it works and under what conditions it may (or may not) work in the future.

WHAT YOU DON'T KNOW WON'T HURT YOU

How does this multiple-perspectives model work in practice? The following case integrates the elements of the framework and applies it to a situation involving a minor client.

Leticia is twelve years old. She was admitted yesterday to the burn unit of a local hospital following a tragic house fire in which her stepfather perished. She is currently under heavy sedation as the medical team addresses her injuries, and Leticia's mother, grandmother, and uncles have told the nursing and social work staff that they do not want her to know about her stepfather's fate until she is ready to return home. The team has concerns about this request. The nurses and social workers are concerned that this is an unfeasible plan, and that at some point, Leticia will seek that information from the hospital staff or learn the devastating news from a well-meaning visitor who may be ill equipped to deal with her response. The family's answer to these concerns is that Leticia will be told that her stepfather is fine, which the family believes is an honest answer, as they believe that he is now in heaven with his Lord and Savior.

Leticia's treatment team can foresee a dilemma arising in the future as they manage the tension between her guardians' wishes and her requests to know the whereabouts of her stepfather. Following the decision-making model (figure 1), the team must begin by developing and examining their choices.

FIGURE 1 The Ethical Decision-Making Model

Assess options

- Ethical theories and principles
- Laws and policies
- Values
- Information
- Standards

Be mindful of process
Consult
Document
Evaluate

Assess Options

Four options are immediately evident in Leticia's case. While other possibilities may emerge in the decision-making process, we will start by examining the first four.

1. Adhere to Leticia's mother's wishes and say that her stepfather is fine
2. Comply with Leticia's mother's wishes that they not tell Leticia of her stepfather's death but refer her to her family when she raises questions about him
3. Assess the situation over time and work to try to change the family's mind
4. Answer Leticia's questions honestly, despite her family's wishes

How do these choices measure up when we look at each through the ELVIS framework?

Ethics. Let's look first at the consequences of each choice, using a utilitarian perspective. While Leticia's family may honestly believe that her stepfather, in death, is "fine," would Leticia have the same belief, or would telling her he is fine be construed as a lie? If the latter is the case, what are the implications of lying to this patient? It may undermine her trust in the team at the very time she most needs to depend on their expertise, thus breaching the principle of fidelity. It would certainly violate the ethical principle of veracity and potentially those of beneficence and nonmaleficence too if Leticia's health and well-being are compromised when the lie is revealed. An additional effect of this decision is that it may not put an end to her questions but rather lead to more, each with its own challenges and sequelae. One could expect her to ask, "If he is fine, when is he coming to see me?" or "Why doesn't he visit me?" which then may lead to more prevarication and relational damage and, potentially, distress and distrust for the client. The team's choice to honor her mother's autonomy could have problematic consequences for Leticia.

Refusing to address questions about the stepfather also honors Leticia's mother's rights as a decision maker but does not require the team to actively participate in what they perceive to be dishonesty.

Saying, "You'll need to discuss that with your family," may not satisfy Leticia, but it upholds the principle of veracity. While option 2 will probably result in less harm, it may still raise concerns about fidelity, leading Leticia to wonder what secret her team is keeping and whether there are other parts of her care about which they are not being forthright. And this response may not be in Leticia's best interest if in fact the team believes she should know about her stepfather. In other words, if Leticia ultimately feels betrayed by her family, have her needs been adequately served by the team's choice to simply defer to them?

What are the consequences of option 3, of stepping back to see if it is possible to eventually change the family's position? This offers the advantage of allowing more time for a relationship to develop between the family and the team, and for the team to better understand their motivations and perhaps find ways to persuade the family to reconsider. On the other hand, the family may not capitulate, and if the team puts all its eggs in this basket, it will have missed the opportunity to pursue other options. In addition, the family may feel badgered by the team about what they consider to be a firm decision, and continued discussion could alienate them, which would not benefit Leticia and could impede needed collaboration for her recovery. On the other hand, if successful, this choice would honor the family's autonomy, is aboveboard (meeting the standards of fidelity and veracity), and could avert further anguish for Leticia and her family (beneficence).

The question one must ask in examining option 3 is "How likely is the family to change their minds?" Our answers to this come from our information or assumptions about the basis for their decision. Is it is a matter of firm faith or belief in the family that children are not entitled to certain information? If so, how amenable are those core values to the team's opinions and appeals? Is the family's position a function of their own trauma and grief? If they received needed care, could they think more openly about Leticia's needs? Are they trying to protect Leticia from heartache? Would information on the negative effects of withholding such information and the advantages of informing her in an intense treatment environment change their opinions? The team's calculations about the family's motivations can help them evaluate the benefits of this option.

What about option 4, overriding the family's request? To tell Leticia against her family's explicit instructions would violate their autonomy and legal and moral authority. It would likely lead to a rift between the family and the team, which might ultimately work against Leticia's improvement and interests. While truthful, the team's actions may not engender trust with Leticia and might cause her distress as those she relies on for care, her family and the hospital, are pitted against each other. This decision would undermine the family's trust in the hospital staff, and perhaps their comfort in complying with other treatment recommendations. The team's subversion could also result in legal or disciplinary action by the family, a detrimental consequence affecting not only the team but the hospital as a whole. That legal liability could cause potential damages well beyond this individual case, thus violating the principle of nonmaleficence.

Having viewed the case through a utilitarian lens, what path would we choose if we were to subject it to the categorical imperative? Should professionals ever be untruthful or withhold information from their clients, if asked to do so? Should professionals overrule a parent or guardian because his or her position differs from what they think is best? Would we want either to become a universal law? Our answer to these questions may depend on whose perspective we adopt in the case. From a patient's perspective, we might determine that it is never right for a clinician to withhold or distort information in answering our questions. Doing so undermines the fiduciary relationship in which patients place trust in doctors and others to act on their behalf. On the other hand, if we put ourselves in the parent's shoes, is it right for professionals, whose provision of care is time limited, to overrule our decisions, when we as parents are legally and morally charged with caring for and acting on behalf of our children? Yet even if we accept that the law supports the right of Leticia's mother to demand silence from the treatment team, can the professionals in the case live, ethically and clinically, with that rule?

Laws and Policies. As described above, the law in this case favors Leticia's legal guardian. It is highly unlikely that the team can construe her mother's decision as resulting in sufficient harm to warrant taking away her parental rights. The team should consult the hospital's legal department, but it is certain that they will support the parent's prerogatives in this case. The legal team may not rule on *how* the team must comply with her, only that they *must*. That is, the law and policy may not distinguish between options 1, 2, and 3, but they would rule out option 4.

Hospital policies may address conflicts between parents and health care providers regarding the treatment of a minor patient; however, whether Leticia's knowledge of her stepfather's condition should be considered a component of her treatment is unclear. Further, hospital policy will likely suggest a process for decision making or recommend a series of action steps rather than provide a clear resolution (i.e., by outlining the appropriate actions and communication chain for the medical team involved in addressing the dilemma, or encouraging the health care providers involved to seek consultation from the hospital ethics committee).

Values. How do the options we generated stand up in the arena of values? We can't explore the values of the individuals in a hypothetical case, but we can surmise that values play a part in the family's insistence that Leticia not be told. Values are also at play on the hospital team's side. Regardless of what they value—their patient, their scientific knowledge, their livelihoods, their reputations, or their power—these personal values will significantly influence the appeal of the various options.

We note that the professional values of service, integrity, and competence would encourage the team to act honestly on their knowledge and beliefs, neither defying the family nor carelessly capitulating. Embracing the value of social justice might lead the team to follow the mother's directive in deference to her cultural background or religious beliefs, or in support of her relatively powerless position in the medical establishment. Other values seem to speak to all the options. For example, in upholding Leticia's dignity and worth, is the team discrediting her mother's (and vice versa)? In acting on the importance of human relationships, will the team damage one relationship (with the mother or daughter) in fostering the other?

As suspected, values alert us to different merits in different options, and they highlight what values might be forsaken in the selection of some options over others. They also require us to adopt the perspectives of various actors in the case. While the treatment team may construe Leticia to be their client, their decision must acknowledge the positions of other stakeholders too.

Information. What additional information might be useful in weighing the options? Data on Leticia's biopsychosocial functioning prior to the fire, her relationship with her stepfather, and the prognosis for her healing will provide guidance about what kind of impact news about her stepfather will have, and when such information might be shared. In addition, it will help to know facts about the fire itself and whether Leticia might feel any culpability for her stepfather's death. The team will want to know the family's plan for telling Leticia the news if they insist that it cannot be done while she is in the hospital. Perhaps the team can assist the family, prepare them, or arrange resources so that anticipated problems are mitigated.

Clearly, it would help to know what Leticia wants, but since her unawareness is at the crux of the case, it may not be possible to find out her preferences. However, two other options might help in discerning her wishes. We might construe her requests for information about her stepfather as demonstrating her interest in knowing his fate, regardless of whether the news is good or bad. We might also consult the literature to determine what youths like Leticia tend to desire in regard to their treatment. Online resources, books, and articles would suggest that Leticia should receive the information in forthright, sensitive, and age-appropriate terms; such resources provide assistance in both the process and aftermath of such disclosures (Christ et al., 2002; Dougy Center, n.d.; Weir, 2003).

Learning more about the family's history, particularly regarding other losses, and how grief and death are commonly handled will enhance the team's understanding of the family's perspective. Where is Leticia's father? What are his rights regarding decisions that must be made about her care? Who is Leticia close to within the family? Who in the family might be amenable to the team's position and willing to bridge the gap between the perspectives of the family and the team?

Regardless of which option they choose, the team should act on the best available knowledge about the issues in Leticia's case, such as the effects of traumatic experiences, disenfranchised or delayed grief, and the impact of distressing information on recovery from significant burns. If such clinical information is compelling, it may variously redouble the team's efforts to come to agreement with the family, support their decision to subvert the family's wishes, or convince them that they cannot be party to the decision, whereas weak or equivocal empirical support would support them in choosing option 1 and acceding to the mother's wishes.

Finally, it will be useful to know how the treatment team came to know of the stepfather's death. If the information was provided by a family member within the context of a confidential relationship, another layer of protection may be afforded the information. On the other hand, if the information was public (in the local papers) and generally known, sharing it, while problematic given the family's wishes, would not be a violation of someone's privacy.

Standards. Several standards in the NASW Code of Ethics speak to the options generated in this case. In describing social workers' commitment to clients, it states, "Social workers' primary responsibility is to promote the well-being of clients. In general, clients' interests are primary. However, social workers' responsibility to the larger society or specific legal obligations may on limited occasions supersede the loyalty owed clients, and clients should be so advised" (NASW, 1999, 1.01). This suggests that the treatment team (or at least the social workers on the team) should give precedence to Leticia's mother's legal rights, but that they should also inform the patient that they are deferring to her mother's wishes regarding her interests. This standard seems to affirm option 2.

The candor demanded in ethical standard 1.01 is also reflected in provisions on informed consent and on potential conflicts of interest: "Social workers should use clear and understandable language to inform clients of the purpose of the services, risks related to the services, limits to services because of the requirements of a third-party payer, relevant costs, reasonable alternatives, clients' right to refuse or withdraw consent, and the time frame covered by the consent"

(NASW, 1999, 1.03a) and "When social workers provide services to two or more people who have a relationship with each other (for example, couples, family members), social workers should clarify with all parties which individuals will be considered clients and the nature of social workers' professional obligations to the various individuals who are receiving services" (NASW, 1999, 1.06d). These standards appear to affirm option 3, encouraging the treatment team to be frank with Leticia's family about their perspective on the case, their obligations to Leticia, and the risks and benefits of withholding information about her stepfather's death.

The last set of ethical standards with bearing on the case addresses professionals' responsibilities when working with clients of different cultures. The NASW (1999) Code states, "Social workers should have a knowledge base of their clients' cultures and be able to demonstrate competence in the provision of services that are sensitive to clients' cultures and to differences among people and cultural groups" (1.05b) and "Social workers should obtain education about and seek to understand the nature of social diversity and oppression with respect to race, ethnicity, national origin, color, sex, sexual orientation, age, marital status, political belief, religion, and mental or physical disability" (1.05c). These provisions, too, would seem to favor option 3. To the extent that Leticia's family's wishes are culturally or religiously derived, it is vital that team members endeavor to understand them.

The practice standards in health care would seem to encourage the hospital staff and family to find common ground in their shared concern with helping Leticia experience a full recovery. The staff should explain that while they value the family's position, they are under an ethical mandate to involve minors in their own treatment to the highest degree possible. Such a mandate would preclude deliberately misleading a minor patient.

Beyond the principles in the case, keeping the secret is unfeasible. The hospital could not absolutely prevent Leticia from learning the truth. A phone call from a classmate or a get-well card from a cousin could undermine disciplined attempts by staff to keep the secret. And what of Leticia's intuition? If she is informed that her stepfather is fine, then what will be the response to her requests to visit or phone him? Ultimately, such an elaborate lie would likely be deemed both undesirable and untenable. Instead, practice standards suggest assisting the family to develop a plan for disclosure. Davis and Shah (1997) note that such a process might involve regular dialogue between staff and family; decision making in the case should be perceived as a process, not a single occurrence. Although every attempt should be made to prevent the development of an adversarial relationship, practice standards might call for mediation by the hospital's ethics board to resolve the impasse.

Be Mindful of Process

Whichever option the team selects, they must consider how they will carry out the decision. How can the team mitigate the negative effects and enhance the likelihood that the decision will have the desired outcome? For example, if the team decides it will refer Leticia's queries back to the family, how will they make sure everyone is onboard with the plan? What precisely will they say? What tone will be used? There is a difference between saying brusquely or uncomfortably, "You'll have to ask your mother" and saying warmly, "Your mom has told us that she prefers to talk with you about that, so you'll need to ask her when she visits." There is no guarantee that tone, wording, and preparation will preserve Leticia's trust in the team, given their evasion of her question, but if it might, a carefully considered strategy is essential. The team should inform Leticia's mother of their strategy so that she understands in advance how the team plans to balance her wishes with Leticia's inquiries.

Let's look at the process issues if the team decides to pursue option 3. Will the effort to understand the family's position come from a genuine desire for understanding or an attempt to get close to the family with the hope of changing their minds? What strategies are likely to lead to improved give-and-take, and which may be perceived as an abuse of professional power? Who on the team will take leadership in learning more about the family and forging a relationship with them? How will this new knowledge be shared with other team members? Within each option there are embedded questions of process.

As the team hones in on a decision, it must think carefully about how the decision will be executed most effectively.

Consult

The team as a whole and its individual members will likely seek consultation. For example, the team may talk to the hospital's legal department, ethics committee, quality assurance and patients' rights representatives, or other administrative personnel. Various professionals on the team may seek supervision on the case. Some may do research on aspects of the case such as culturally derived beliefs, grief reactions, and developmental issues. Team members may discuss issues embedded in the case (but not the case itself) with representatives of their professional association, licensure board, or malpractice carrier to evaluate professional standards and the liability issues related to the various options.

Document

Each member of the treatment team is responsible for documenting his or her actions or decisions on the case. Some of this may be part of the hospital's record-keeping protocol, and some may be idiosyncratic to the worker involved. For example, the results of the team's consultation with the legal department might go in the client's record, but a social worker's findings about developmental considerations might go in the individual worker's journal.

Evaluate

Let's play out the decision in this case. After trying option 3, the team continued to find itself at a stalemate with Leticia's family. Their consultation with the legal department and the hospital administration led them to rule out option 4 on liability grounds. They ruled out option 1 on the basis of ethical principles and standards. They decided to follow option 2 and consistently referred Leticia's questions about her stepfather to her mother, who responded that he was fine. After initially pushing her relatives for more information, Leticia seemed to accept this response. If she was unsettled by it or distrustful of it, it had no apparent negative consequences for her recovery.

The team heard later from the home health worker that Leticia learned of her stepfather's death the day she returned home. She was reported to be extremely distraught and inconsolable, despite the ministrations of her extended family, who had gathered around when she was given the news. It is unclear to what extent her reaction was a result of her surprise at the news versus the death itself. While the team didn't witness her reaction firsthand, the information they received reinforced their concerns and affirmed their attempts to resolve the matter forthrightly while she was hospitalized.

In evaluation, the members determined they had done everything in their power to create a better outcome, and that only a change in parents' rights would have altered the course of the case. That change, they determined, was well beyond their capacity and, even if it had occurred, would have caused more long-term problems for Leticia despite the resolution of the short-term problem of disclosure about her stepfather's death. Ideally, the team would have liked to follow up with Leticia's mother to revisit the case and get her perspective on how the entire situation might have been better addressed. However, the team had no continued contact with her, which effectively closed off an avenue that might have generated better feedback and improved practices in the future.

SUMMARY

Ethical dilemmas are troubling and high-stakes aspects of practice in the helping professions. To arrive at decisions that are ethically and clinically sound, social workers must examine the case from multiple viewpoints. This form of decision making is a complex skill, developed through practice and application. This chapter introduces readers to an ABCDE framework for building critical thinking skills. The model involves assessing options, being aware of process and strategy, seeking consultation, and documenting and evaluating decisions. Within the process of assessing options, it offers an outline (ELVIS) to assist users in exploring all facets of a decision: the ethical theories and principles, the legal and policy implications, the role of values, relevant case and clinical information, and the guidance provided by ethical and practice standards. Applying the model to an ethical dilemma reveals the various elements of the decision to be made and its overall utility in solving ethical problems.

In subsequent chapters, we use the competing-values framework from chapter 1 to categorize dilemmas, and the multiple-perspectives model to address the dilemmas that can arise in practice with minors. First, however, it is important to understand the developmental parameters we must take into account in practice with minors and the characteristics of the agencies that serve them. The next two chapters address these issues and provide an important foundation for the informational and policy elements we will need to consider when unpacking future dilemmas.

Chapter 3

Understanding Minor Clients

David Hussey, PhD

The issue of competence rests at the core of all discussions about ethics and minors. What are minors able to understand? Are they capable of rendering judgments? These questions of competence are inextricably linked to minors' developmental capacities and the factors that influence those capacities. This chapter explores markers of competence across the developmental spectrum and highlights relevant concepts for ethical decision making.

HISTORICAL AND LEGAL PERSPECTIVES ON MINORS' RIGHTS

In ancient and medieval times, sanitary conditions were poor, disease ran rampant, life expectancies were much shorter than they are today, and childhood was brief and harsh. Commencing at a young age, children often worked alongside their parents in the fields. Childhood was not regarded as a separate phase of life; children were looked upon as miniature adults. Gradually, during the Renaissance and Enlightenment, the special qualities of childhood began to be recognized and depicted in paintings and literature. Famous seventeenth- and eighteenth-century philosophers such as John Locke and Jean-Jacques Rousseau emphasized the need to protect children from the evils of society and guide their development. In spite of this novel way of thinking, children were regarded as the property of their parents, particularly their fathers, rather than individuals in their own right. As such, children's rights were strongly predicated on the nature of their value in relation to property and the corresponding rights of legal property holders. In the colonial period, a father could hire out his children for wages or apprentice a child to another family without the mother's consent. Indeed, fathers were responsible for moral, educational, and vocational rearing, and the state only stepped in in cases of parental death, financial hardship, incompetence, or illegitimacy.

Although parental sovereignty dominated, children's status as property evolved over time into a "partial-person" status. In the mid- to late 1800s, the idea of children's rights as distinct from those of adults took root in recognition of the need for laws regulating child labor and requiring a certain amount of schooling for children working in factories. It wasn't until the twentieth century, however, that civic-minded "child savers" successfully advocated legal reforms needed to protect children that required compulsory school attendance and established separate juvenile courts.

By the mid-1960s, during the civil and women's rights movements, children were finally considered individuals in their own right and protected by the Bill of Rights. Prior to the Supreme Court decision *In re Gault* (1967), juvenile courts were deemed to be acting in the best interests of children under the doctrine of *parens patriae*, or the "state as parent," performing parental functions for those deemed legally incompetent. A related concept, *in loco parentis,* originally derived from British common law, is Latin for "in the place of a parent" and refers to the legal responsibility of a person or entity, such as the state, to take on certain parental functions or responsibilities. This was presumably done in the best interests of the child but was historically carried out in a fashion that violated fundamental civil liberties.

Gerald Gault was a fifteen-year-old probationer who had been arrested for making an obscene telephone call and remanded to a state facility until the age of twenty-one. An adult convicted of the same offense would have been given a maximum punishment of a $50 fine and two months in jail. There were no records of the hearing, no transcripts, and no specific charges (except that Gault was delinquent), and fundamental facts regarding the case were in dispute. After unsuccessful attempts to appeal at the state level, the U.S. Supreme Court ruled that basic due process rights (e.g., notice, hearing, opportunity to be heard and represented, rights against self-incrimination) should have been afforded to Gault. The case decision, later expanded by several subsequent court rulings, extended the Fourteenth Amendment protections of the Bill of Rights to minors, recognizing that fundamental rights such as substantive due process, or fair treatment in criminal legal matters, are not for adults alone.

Today minors as well as adults are protected by the Constitution and possess constitutional rights; however, the state has somewhat broader authority to both protect children and regulate their behavior. In most circumstances, parents of children under the age of eighteen are still empowered to make legal decisions for them. Parents and guardians have broad decision-making authority for their children. The "best interest of the child" standard that first emerged in the late 1800s provides a guiding conceptual foundation for many types of cases. It establishes that in cases involving custody, adoption, and delinquency, the child's welfare should be given priority when courts are forced to decide between the interests of the child and competing adult interests. Thus it is generally assumed that parents know best regarding the interests of their child, and judicial proof is usually required in order to rule that parental decision making is detrimental to the child's welfare.

One of the practical difficulties with the best interests standard is that it is broad and subject to a wide degree of interpretation. Goldstein, Freud, and Solnit's critical works *Beyond the Best Interests of the Child* (1973) and *Before the Best Interests of the Child* (1979) helped to shape much of the child welfare debate regarding the best interests of the child in the 1970s and 1980s. Goldstein and his colleagues emphasized how psychoanalytic notions such as the importance of "continuity of relationships" and the primacy of the child's perceptions of his or her "psychological parent" need to be considered in balancing the rights of biological parents with the best interests of children who have experienced serious maltreatment. In effect, they argued that in some instances the best interests of the child may be best served by the "least detrimental alternative" for safeguarding his or her growth and development (Goldstein, Solnit, Goldstein, & Freud, 1996).

Other interpretations of best interests depend on whether we're referring to what a child would choose for him- or herself or a more objective interpretation of what may be best for a child. This issue often arises in medical care, where the limited benefits of multiple and painful diagnostic procedures have to be carefully weighed against the pain and suffering that a youth faces, particularly if these procedures are done on a nonvoluntary basis. Interpretations of the best interests standard may also vary depending on whether we're referring to a child in a specific situation or to children in general. For instance, in child welfare policy, the standard usually does not require a child's parents to provide more than an adequate threshold of care. However, in a disputed custody case involving two special-needs adoption placement options, the standard may be far different, requiring more than merely adequate care. A careful and thorough estimation of the caretakers' abilities and resources in light of the health and psychosocial needs of a particular child would be required to determine which of two completely adequate potential adoptive families may be better able to meet the best interests of a particular special-needs youth. While the best interest standard is an intuitively appealing norm that is used in ethical decision making, it is not as straightforward in practice as it might appear.

STATUTORY PERSPECTIVES ON DECISION MAKING

While most states consider adolescents to have limited decision-making ability, there are circumstances where adolescents can give consent for services without parental approval. In these situations, a minor's right to privacy or consent for treatment may even be protected by law, based on his or her situation or status and/or on the type of services being sought.

Situational or status considerations are extended to minors who are seeking emergency services, particularly when parental consent is impractical, and legally emancipated minors, who are viewed by the court as adults. In the case of emergency services, the treatment must be needed immediately in order for the child to avoid death or disability. If clinicians determine the situation to be an emergency, they usually opt to err on the side of caution and intervene to prevent harm without delaying care to obtain consent. An emancipated minor, on the other hand, is a youth who has approached the court to become legally separated from his or her parents or legal guardians. Once emancipated, these youths, regardless of age, are entitled to consent to or refuse treatment and make decisions as if they were adults. Typically, emancipated minors are expected to be self-supporting and relinquish the right to parental support, though state statutes establish the criteria for emancipation, and thus there is wide variation among jurisdictions. Legal emancipation is rare due to the difficult and cumbersome legal process required to establish independence.

A more common situation that social workers may encounter involves the "mature minor" exception, which refers to a youth who has not legally reached adulthood, as defined by law, but may be treated as an adult for certain purposes. In the United States, the mature minor exception was created as a result of *Smith v. Seibly* (1967), a court case that allowed health care providers to treat a youth as an adult based on assessment and documentation of the youth's maturity. In treatment situations, the doctrine requires youths to demonstrate an understanding of the relative risks and benefits of the proposed treatment. The doctrine was developed to prevent the usual requirement for parental consent from becoming a barrier to treatment in situations where youths may be reluctant to inform their parents. It is also used in situations in which treatment refusal by the parent or child may not be in the best interest of the child. Health care professionals typically ask a series of questions to determine if the minor is mature enough to consent to treatment and then document the criteria supporting their decision. This assessment takes into consideration age, living arrangement, intelligence, maturity, economic independence, conduct, and marital status. The nature, intensity, or permanence of the service requested is also taken into consideration. For instance, a mature minor may be able to fully understand the implications of receiving an oral contraceptive prescription, but less capable of consenting to sterilization or abortion. Treatment decisions made using the mature minor exception require careful documentation of the circumstances and criteria used to support the determination that the minor was mature enough to render consent.

Aside from situational or status considerations in which minors may be able to give consent, there are also statutorily protected areas governing informed consent that pertain to the type of care being sought. For example, minors in most states can give their own consent when seeking treatment for drug or alcohol abuse, mental illness, and sexually transmitted diseases; pregnancy-related care; and contraception. Often there are age requirements (e.g., thirteen years of age or older) associated with specific types of treatment consent, and these vary considerably from state to state. In situations where minors request confidential services, providers may explore the reasons why they are reluctant to include parents or guardians in their decision making. This usually involves understanding the minor's concerns or fears regarding parental participation in decision making, and correcting any misconceptions that may underlie those concerns.

DEVELOPMENTAL PERSPECTIVES

Minors are not simply small adults, and there are significant physical, emotional, and cognitive differences that influence their independent functioning. Our understanding of child development and the related capacity for decision making is shaped by various theories.

One way to understand child development is to consider the different stages that children pass through before they reach adulthood. In the early 1900s Sigmund Freud (1923-1973) and other adherents of psychoanalytic theory focused on the importance of early childhood experiences related to critical and invariant stages of human development. Freud and other stage theorists portrayed childhood growth as a sequence of age-related periods, each with its own defining characteristics and challenges.

At least five stages have been identified by developmental theorists: infancy (birth to age two), early childhood (ages three to five), middle childhood (six to eight), pre-adolescence (nine to eleven), and adolescence (twelve to eighteen). In infancy, a child is completely dependent on a caregiver. Behavior begins with simple reflexes to ensure food intake and progresses to an expanded repertoire of motor skills that includes smiling, crawling, and walking. During this period children are most vulnerable to injury or death arising from deficits in caretakers' capacities. Infants require the greatest amount of attention and protection due to their dependency and vulnerability.

In early childhood, play becomes very important, as children are both mobile and vocal, and therefore able to initiate interactions with other children and adults. Cognitively, children begin to develop symbolic reasoning, whereby they are able to consider things that are not present and develop a basic understanding of right and wrong. In middle childhood, children learn rapidly, attend school, and begin acquiring a great many skills. During this stage children become more cognizant of the opinions of others, particularly their peers, as they begin to experience the effects of peer pressure. Intellectually, their increased ability to remember, pay attention, and speak allows them to express their ideas, although typically in a concrete black-or-white fashion. During pre-adolescence, children begin to develop a more specific sense of self and find it important to gain social acceptance and recognition for their achievements. Close friends are almost always of the same sex, and youths at this stage generally develop hobbies and interests. Intellectually, they are able to understand concepts without direct hands-on experience. In adolescence, a major task is the creation of a stable identity and becoming a competent and productive adult. Dramatic physical, emotional, and intellectual changes occur that lead to both increased opportunities for engaging in risky behaviors (e.g., reckless driving, substance abuse, and sexual promiscuity) and emerging cognitive capacities to plan and think in a reflective, hypothetical cause-and-effect manner.

Erik Erikson (1963), perhaps the most widely studied of the stage theorists, identified eight psychosocial stages of development, which he characterized as crucial struggles between individual psychological growth and interacting societal supports and pressures. Each stage is marked by a crisis for which successful resolution revolves around an important event, such as struggles between trust and mistrust, autonomy and shame and doubt, initiative and guilt, industry and inferiority, and identity and role diffusion. Erikson believed that the most important experiences during adolescence, the last childhood stage, involve peer relationships. Peer relationships provide the vehicle for adolescents to experiment and discover a deeper and truer sense of self. For Erikson, the ever-changing developmental landscape requires that practitioners assess emerging physical and psychological capacities from the perspective of "maturation," or movement through life stages, which involves adapting and responding to new psychological and social challenges.

In contrast to Erikson, cognitive theorists focus on the way children think and construct knowledge (Piaget, 1970). Cognitive development refers to the evolution of the thinking and organizing systems of the brain. These systems include language, reasoning, problem solving, and memory. Cognitive differences in capacity development are particularly important when we consider the ways children reason, understand, and solve problems. Piaget identified four primary cognitive structures, or patterns of physical or mental action that govern intelligence. Thus, children progress from an understanding based on intuition and immediate sensory experiences (sensorimotor, birth to age two, and preoperational, ages three to seven) to an understanding based on objective, logical mental processes (concrete-operational, ages eight to eleven) and ultimately to formal-operational stage thinking (ages twelve to fifteen). During this stage, the form of thinking, not just the content, is important. Consequently, the adolescent learns to think in an abstract manner and recognize underlying connections and relationships in such a way as to respond to hypothetical problems or generate solutions to situations that may never actually occur (Dilut, 1972). Some theorists speculate that this type of cognitive maturity is related to the thoughts associated with adolescent depression and suicide (Zahn-Waxler, Kochanska, Krupnick, & McKnew, 1990). The ability to feel such emotions as guilt and hopelessness may be predicated on an ability to imagine and long for a world that ought to be better, yet some succumb to despair and conclude that life is hopeless.

While the ability to engage in more sophisticated and adult-like abstract and hypothetical thinking is a significant developmental advancement, recent research regarding adolescent brain development has found that although teens may look and sound like physically mature adults this does not mean that they are able to think and act in that fashion. Studies suggest that the human brain might not reach full maturity until the mid-twenties (Sowell, Thompson, Holmes, Jernigan, & Toga, 1999; Sowell, Thompson, Tessner, & Toga, 2001). The dramatic physical and psychological changes occurring during adolescence are thus not fully accompanied by corresponding maturation in adolescent brain development, particularly in the frontal cortex and in executive functioning governing cause-and-effect thinking. For instance, the amygdala, which is the center of impulsive and emotional reactions, matures earlier than the frontal cortex, which is responsible for executive decision making and is the last area of the brain to mature. In short, the adolescent brain may not be able to fully anticipate the outcomes of hormone-driven decisions (Strauch, 2003).

Cognitive differences are particularly important when we consider the way adolescents are able to reason and solve problems. One of the paradoxes of adolescence is that although indicators of health (strength, stamina), ability (speed, reaction time), and resilience (immune responses) are extremely high during this period, so is adolescent mortality. In fact, adolescent mortality increases dramatically between childhood and late adolescence; these mortalities are primarily caused by problems adolescents have controlling behavior and emotions. For example, suicide mortality rates for fifteen- to nineteen-year-olds are more than six times those for ten- to fourteen-year-olds, while mortality rates from homicide are nine times higher for older teens than for ten- to fourteen-year-olds (Centers for Disease Control and Prevention, 2006).

In contrast to theorists who believe that children universally pass through invariant stages or processes during the course of development, sociocultural and social learning theorists prefer to emphasize the importance that parents, teachers, peers, and others have on child growth and skill acquisition through an ongoing series of social and culturally based learning experiences. A major theme is that social interaction plays a pivotal role in the development of child and adolescent cognition. Child development is influenced by continuous and reciprocal interactions between cognitive, behavioral, cultural, and environmental influences rather than a series of more linear universal stages.

Regardless of one's theory base, important developmental considerations must be factored into ethical decision making by or on behalf of children. The use of developmental theory situates the child in a developmental context that encompasses an array of interacting physical, environmental, cognitive, cultural, and emotional capacities that influence actions and decisions. For example, beyond normative developmental considerations, the presence of disorders characterized by abnormalities in cognition, emotion, mood, or behavior further complicates ethical decision making. Estimates suggest that approximately 20 percent of children have mental disorders or at least mild functional impairment. Anxiety, mood, and disruptive behavior disorders are the most common (U.S. Department of Health and Human Services, 1999) and may be associated with cognitive or information-processing deficits. For instance, information-processing research has identified differences in how disruptive and aggressive children encode and process information. These youths, specifically those who have been repeatedly exposed to violence, may develop deficits in information-processing skills that can lead to such things as misattributions or "false judgments," which occur when they infer threat or danger from false cues of hostile intent on the part of peers or playmates (Huesman, Eron, Leftkowitz, & Walder, 1984; Lochman & Dodge, 1994). These children lack basic and necessary social problem-solving capacities and tend to be hypervigilant, expecting the worst and responding aggressively to perceived hostility from peers and authority figures. Clearly, developmental considerations must be assessed along with other factors, such as the cognitive-developmental deficits resulting from exposure to violence, in order to determine a minor's decision-making capacity.

DEVELOPMENT AND DECISION MAKING

Anyone who works with minor clients must confront the challenge of making decisions on their behalf. When workers understand the interplay between child development and the ethical decision-making assumptions and models that they use as a guide, they are able to address these challenges more effectively.

Several core assumptions already introduced in this volume are worth restating here. First, models can help workers systematically sort through options when dilemmas emerge. Second, minors' rights and abilities to make well-informed decisions are at the center of most ethical dilemmas that arise in social work practice. Children are generally perceived as dependent and vulnerable, and therefore in need of protection. It is generally assumed that certain proxies, particularly parents, can decide on behalf of children, who are not able to make independent life decisions due to age, vulnerability, dependency, or lack of capacity. At times, these factors can interact in complex ways, creating murky ethical situations.

The notion of child vulnerability is related to children's evolving capacities or, more precisely put, their unevolved capacities from which protective rights derive. In introducing the concept of "evolving capacities," the United Nations Convention on the Rights of the Child noted that parents or caretakers providing direction or guidance must take into account the capacity of a child to exercise rights on his or her own behalf (Office on the Higher Commission on Human Rights, 1990). In practice, one accords children rights commensurate with their evolving capacities, based on age and maturity, to understand and participate in any procedures or decisions concerning them. Likewise, one affords children protection based upon their un-evolved capacities, or their inability to exercise rights on their own behalf. It is necessary, therefore, to understand the elements of informed decision making and their relationship to these various capacities. Each critical aspect of informed decision making must be assessed in relation to the individual child's competence to participate in his or her own protection and his or her ability to make reasoned choices in decisions affecting his or her life.

Five key elements are required in fully informed decision making: information, understanding, competency, voluntariness, and decision-making ability (i.e., reasoning). By briefly examining these five key elements, we can see that minors, regardless of age, usually do not meet a reasonable threshold for independent informed decision making.

Information

This refers to the communication of essential information, including data that might reasonably be expected to influence a person's decision or willingness to participate in decision making. Information refers to both the quality (e.g., developmentally appropriate) and quantity (e.g., too much, too little) of communication. The use of simple, plain, informal language gives the child the best chance of understanding the information presented. In communicating information to children, it is a good idea to use common or everyday words, avoid long sentences, use active voice rather than passive voice, and avoid unnecessarily technical language (Green, Duncan, Barnes, & Oberklaid, 2003). Children should be granted access to records and allowed to participate in treatment and planning discussions, and any risks or dangers associated with procedures or therapy should be disclosed.

While the quality and content of communications are important, another aspect of information exchange involves timing. In some instances, social workers may delay discussing a painful medical procedure, a court date, or a conflicted custody visitation due to the realization that advanced notice just makes a particular child more anxious. In other instances, children may benefit from being told in advance about these events and what to expect. The social worker's knowledge of the individual child's concerns and capacities is essential in this type of decision making.

Understanding

Obviously, the volume, nature, and complexity of information provided to clients must take into account the child's capacity for understanding. Understanding is the ability to comprehend the information presented. In minors, understanding is linked to developmental capacity and an appropriate level of comprehension. Younger children (i.e., pre-adolescents) might not have the capacity for abstraction that comes with formal-operational thinking; however, they may be able to understand information presented in a way that corresponds to their developmental levels. We can expect younger children to be knowledgeable about the concrete issues related to their decision, while adolescents may be able to understand the more abstract factors that frame decision-making contexts or processes. For example, a nine-year-old may know that his mother needs to stop using drugs and enter a drug treatment program before the judge will agree to reunification. A sixteen-year-old may realize that his mother must first abandon her dependent relationship with her violent, drug-dealing boyfriend before she will be able to pursue drug treatment and recovery. In fact, children over the age of fourteen are generally thought to be able to reason as well as competent adults (Koocher & DeMaso, 1990), although they often lack the life experiences necessary to inform their discernment process. In effect, an adolescent may be able to explain and describe how the future may be different as a result of a decision that he or she makes now; however, the adolescent's ability to truly appreciate what it would be like and how it would actually feel under a variety of circumstances is limited by a lack of life experience. This is not surprising, as even adults are poorly equipped to accurately predict their feelings and responses to future situations that are radically different from the present.

Competence

Competency is the capacity to act on one's own behalf and involves the capacity to understand, plus the ability to weigh potential outcomes, and also the foresight to anticipate future consequences of a decision. Full competency is a prerequisite for both informed consent and autonomous decision making.There are many aspects of child development that act to inhibit or enhance competency and the ability to give consent. A minor's competency is a function of age, cognitive abilities, and life experiences. Competency evolves in large part in response to the experiences that an individual has had and the world he or she grows up in. Life experiences can relate to social, cultural, political, and economic conditions or the child's familiarity with the circumstances or events related to the decision. For example, an adolescent with a chronic medical condition who has experienced numerous painful treatment procedures is probably in a better position to assess the pain, discomfort, and rehabilitation requirements of a new treatment procedure than a healthy adolescent who has had few, if any, life experiences related to hospitalization, surgery, and recovery. Child competency is not only circumscribed by age, but also by social, emotional, cultural, and environmental influences. These influences often frame the range of decision-making autonomy that youths are given.Too little autonomy can limit a youngster's ability to develop and practice independent decision making.Too much autonomy can overwhelm youngsters and place them in situations that they are not equipped to handle. Foster care youths in transitional or independent living situations epitomize this struggle.While these individuals may range in age from fifteen to twenty-two years old, their level of competency can vary considerably based on a range of environmental factors and life experiences. An assessment of their competency to function independently and to successfully manage their lives involves much more than just knowing their chronologic age. Informed and caring adults who are familiar with the child's unique social and developmental experiences and capacities serve an essential role in supporting minors in developing competency and exercising autonomy to the greatest degree possible.

Voluntariness

Voluntariness is the freedom to choose a course of action, such as the decision to participate or refuse participation in therapy or a research study. It implies freedom from coercion, duress, or undue influence. Several conditions can affect voluntariness, including discrimination and power imbalances between social institutions, parents, and youths. Minors, even more than adults, are subject to the influences of their social context and conditions. Youths who internalize negative attitudes held within their community may lower their own expectations regarding their capacity to make important life choices. Children who experience discrimination and social exclusion have less opportunity to acquire the cognitive, social, emotional, and physical competencies that others derive from more validating social contexts. Factors such as social class, economic dependence, gender, ethnicity, and disability can have an effect on these important capacity-building opportunities. The cumulative result of such limiting or marginalizing life experiences is likely to be a skewed reflection of a child's true potential. Youths who are given opportunities to participate in decisions affecting their lives and are supported in doing so generally develop greater decision-making capabilities, as well as a sense of independence and autonomy, which in turn enhances the quality of their participation.

Power imbalances can also affect a child's voluntariness in decision making. A classic example is when children are caught in custody or visitation conflicts between divorcing parents. Children may be highly emotionally conflicted and therefore should not be placed in a position of having to choose one parent over the other. It is incumbent upon practitioners to recognize the dilemmas that children may face and help them to negotiate the nonvoluntary aspects of their circumstances. Even though children may not be completely free to make a choice, they may be able to select from an array of reasonable options. Often there is significant psychological benefit in having one's fears acknowledged and validated, and being given the option of choosing from a menu of reasonable alternatives.

Reasoning

Decision-making ability refers to the capacity to render a reasoned choice and to express it clearly (Lidz, Meisel, Zerubavel, Carter, Sestak, & Roth, 1984). Decision making encompasses the totality of communication, understanding, competency, and voluntariness that enable a child to make a free and informed choice.

In practice, tension exists between minors' rights and liberties and the realities of their dependence and vulnerability. Those who work with minors have an obligation to negotiate both sides of this tension, respecting children's rights and liberties while protecting them from harm. A useful ethical principle that can guide and inform practitioner decision making is an appreciation of client autonomy. Social workers have an ethical duty to promote the autonomy of their clients by involving them as much as possible in their decision-making process. In work with minors, a full appreciation of the principle of client autonomy is strongly connected with an accurate understanding of a child's abilities, particularly the status of his or her evolving capacities. Rather than simply protecting children from adverse circumstances or seeing them as helpless and vulnerable, professionals should engage children as much as possible as active agents in their decision making and protection. They do not have to be fully autonomous and independent decision makers in order to be treated with respect as autonomous individuals. Even very young children have views on matters affecting them. The key is to develop strategies to help them articulate these views. Given support, encouragement, and the proper developmental focus, children can acquire the skills necessary to participate appropriately and meaningfully in informed decision making.

TYPES OF INFORMED DECISION MAKING

Sometimes in documenting child decision making we distinguish between consent, assent, and permission. This commonly occurs in health care decision making and when minors participate in research studies. In most instances minors are not considered competent to give legally binding informed consent. Consent assumes that there is a process in which a fully informed individual or client can participate in making decisions. As we have seen, legally informed consent is predicated on the client's autonomous legal status and the five elements of informed decision making. Consent also requires the client, having already been determined to be a competent and voluntary agent, to participate in a documented discussion of the nature of the decision or procedure (e.g. intervention, research study); other reasonable alternatives or options; and the risks, benefits, and uncertainties involved. There must also be documentation of the client's understanding of the decision or procedure, as well as documentation of his or her decision or acceptance of the procedure.

As opposed to consent, assent means affirmative agreement for those who lack decision-making capacity. Children as young as five years old are thought to be capable of giving assent (Meaux & Bell, 2001). Therefore children's assent is typically sought for participation in treatment or research. Assent is usually paired with parental or guardian permission because parents and guardians are still considered responsible for protecting their children from unjustified risks. Permission is something that is granted by another person or entity who has recognized responsibility for another. Once parental permission is obtained, then child assent can be sought. Identical information does not have to be given to parents and children, as the information given to the minor should correspond to his or her developmental and maturity level. Usually this means that the information is simplified, more pictures and diagrams are used, and relevant comparisons are provided to improve the child's understanding. It is important to keep in mind and clearly document in client records these distinctions between consent, permission, and assent. In some social work practice settings, particularly those that sponsor research, all three forms of decision-making agreement may be utilized.

SUMMARY

Practitioners need a strong developmental focus to be able to assess the capacities of minors and their ability to participate in decisions regarding their welfare. It is best to work *with* minor clients, not just *for* them. Participation in decision making can enhance the evolving capacities of children, as it offers them opportunities to acquire negotiation and communication skills and to develop trust and confidence. In addition, children learn to respect the rights of others when their own rights are carefully considered and affirmed. Partnerships with adults are beneficial to minors and allow them to draw on adult support and experience to aid in their personal development and participate meaningfully in decisions that affect their lives.

Service providers should be aware of the different types of informed decision making (consent, permission, and assent) and the situational and status considerations that affect minors' rights to make independent decisions, such as emancipation and the mature minor exception. Developmental, situational, and status considerations must be taken into account as professionals endeavor to seek solutions to ethical dilemmas involving minor clients.

Chapter 4

UNDERSTANDING THE SYSTEMS THAT SERVE CHILDREN

David Hussey, PhD

The major child-serving systems—child welfare, juvenile justice, mental health, education, substance abuse, and health—all embrace distinct philosophic orientations, policy mandates, values, and interventions. These variables influence the ways that ethical dilemmas are approached and resolved in those settings. The decision-making framework used in this book encourages multiple grounded perspectives for resolving dilemmas and therefore requires consideration of the unique characteristics of the settings in which decisions are made.

This chapter highlights some of the dominant historical policy and practice dimensions of three major child-serving systems in order to illuminate contextual features that create ethical dilemmas and inform decision making. While evidence suggests that workers are most comfortable when their decisions satisfy both client wishes and organizational mandates, it can be challenging to achieve such a balance in any system (Walden, Wolock, & Demone, 1990).

MENTAL HEALTH

At least three dominant practice paradigms operate within the child mental health field and frame the context for ethical decision making: systems of care, managed care, and evidence-based practices. The philosophic and organizing principles of each of these paradigms clearly influence the emergence of dilemmas, particularly those involving boundary and role challenges. They also create ethical tensions for mental health practitioners in ensuring that clients receive effective evidence-based treatments in any given service delivery model.

Systems-of-Care History and Philosophy

In 1992, the federal government's Center for Mental Health Services adopted the system-of-care model as a way to organize, coordinate, and deliver mental health services and supports for children, adolescents, and their families by giving grants to states to develop such systems. The 121 grantees in the program's history range from neighborhoods to entire states, each of which has been charged with developing a broad array of community-based, culturally competent, family-driven, and strength-based services to improve outcomes for children with serious emotional disturbance and their families. They do this by integrating public and private child- and family-serving agencies into a comprehensive system of care.

Systems of care are guided by a core set of principles. They are intended to be child centered and family focused, meaning that the needs of the child and family dictate the types of services provided. The focus of services as well as management and decision-making responsibility should rest at the community level. The system of care should be culturally competent: agencies, programs, and services must be responsive to the cultural, racial, and ethnic makeup of the populations they serve.

Systems of care are widely thought of as a central feature of any modern children's mental health system. The federal government and most practitioners in the children's mental health field have adopted or support this approach for serving children with serious emotional disturbances (many of whom receive some services from multiple agencies). Increasingly, organizations outside the mental health system, including substance abuse treatment centers and the child welfare, juvenile justice, and education systems, are incorporating the systems-of-care model.

Managed Care History and Philosophy

Managed care is a health care arrangement that attempts to deliver high-quality cost-effective services by monitoring and managing the use of care as well as the costs. Health maintenance organizations (HMOs) are one type of managed care organization (MCO). While HMO development was fostered in the 1970s, the 1990s saw accelerated growth, during which time the vast majority of private insurance companies adopted some form of managed care and incorporation into Medicare and Medicaid plans as well.

The primary intent of managed care is to reduce health care costs. MCOs frequently contract with a group or panel of health care providers, who are expected to deliver services in accordance with the guidelines set by the MCO. MCOs can specify which caregivers an insured individual or family can use and may also limit the number of visits and kinds of services that are covered by insurance. Care is allocated through a series of gatekeeper policies that require individuals to get referrals for specialized treatment. Often there are also financial incentives for providers to limit services and thus contain costs. Providers also agree to treatment and referral guidelines and are held accountable if their services are deemed unnecessary by utilization review procedures. It appears that mental health and substance abuse services incur greater restrictions and heightened scrutiny under MCOs. As a result, advocates for mental health and substance abuse service consumers argue that parity, or equality of coverage, is necessary for these disorders so that they are treated in a manner similar to other health problems.

At the heart of many ethical debates in managed mental health care is the perceived trade-off between the goals of cost containment and those of quality care. This tension can result in conflicts for practitioners, who in a sense operate as double agents in acting on behalf of both the client and the MCO in the proper allocation of limited resources. Such role confusion creates issues of divided loyalty as workers strive to help clients while endeavoring to meet cost-containment targets and brief treatment standards. What should workers do when clients are denied necessary treatment in order to save money or boost profits? Dilemmas are also embedded in questions of allocation. For example, should finite resources be prioritized for prevention or for those with acute long-term problems?

Evidence-Based Practice

Mandates to provide effective treatment are driving transformational changes in both public and private mental health practice. Over the past ten years, increasing efforts have been made to encourage the adoption of best practice interventions within the field of children's mental health. Evidence-based practice refers to the use of the body of scientific knowledge regarding the effectiveness and efficacy in improving client outcomes of different service interventions in the provision of services and recommendation of interventions to clients. Methodologically sound practices are typically divided into different categories (i.e., research-validated evidence-based practices and promising practices), in recognition of the strength of evidence regarding the intervention's effectiveness.

Research shows that few mental health programs provide evidence-based services to the majority of their clients (Drake, Goldman, Leff, Lehman, Dixon, Mueser, et al., 2001). While evidence-based interventions have worked well in research settings, these strategies often do not have the same positive results when transferred to practice settings. This gap between efficacy (results obtained in more ideal laboratory and research settings) and effectiveness (results obtained in routine and real-world practice settings) is a sobering reminder of the challenges practitioners face in their everyday work as they adapt interventions to meet client needs based on available resources, agency mission, funding streams, client subgroup differences, client capabilities, and the worker's own competence. While funding initiatives have focused resources on improving the process of translating science-based practice into community-based services, almost all the attention has been unidirectional. Recent shifts in thinking have highlighted the complex multidirectional nature of practice improvement, endeavoring to improve both the "science to service" and the "service to science" pathways. Until these improvements materialize, the ethical and clinical dilemmas will continue to abound. What constitutes adequately effective practice? How can professionals obtain proper informed consent from clients in light of the equivocal nature of the evidence supporting the interventions they are recommending? How do professionals meet the standard of competence in new and emerging interventions? How can the long-term negative effects of medications and other mental health interventions be predicted and reconciled with short-term needs?

Ethical Dimensions

It is understandable that the different variables that influence mental health services in systems of care, managed care, and evidence-based paradigms give rise to ethical dilemmas. For example, do evidence-based practices or managed care processes take away from truly individualized service planning and leave clients with little autonomy or choice at the expense of expediency or paternalistic beneficence? How effective (minimally effective to optimally effective) should the services that clients receive be, and how should these be allocated based on cost and need? How do services in any mental health framework account for application barriers, organizational constraints, and the lack of needed resources? How can provisions for confidentiality, resource allocation, accountability, and competence be ensured, given the variety of disparate providers in the systems-of-care model?

Transparency, integrity, and competence are necessary to improve the quality of mental health services. Money saved from the discontinuation of ineffective, excessive, or harmful services could be spent on those that have been critically tested and are properly allocated. While most professionals agree on the importance of effective mental health practice, there remains considerable room for debate about which practices are most effective with which clients under different circumstances.

CHILD WELFARE

Child protective service workers make hundreds of thousands of complex decisions each day. These decisions are influenced by workers' personal characteristics as well as the unique features of the child welfare setting (Smith & Donovan, 2003), including environmental constraints such as heavy caseloads and resource and time limitations. CPS settings are rife with ethical and value dilemmas as workers attempt to reconcile the needs for safety, permanency, and well-being. Child welfare values range along a continuum from first supporting families to intervening around child protection, planning for permanency, achieving psychological permanency, and finally enhancing the child's well-being. Decisions are usually based on general principles that do not enable practitioners to predict an individual's behavior. For example, risk assessment measures do not enable staff to calculate with certainty whether a particular parent will continue to abuse a child. Decision making in CPS often involves choosing between competing values such as whether to protect children from abuse or to support the rights of parents and preserve families. Sometimes the right choice, even when clear, is not easy. For example, while children should be protected from harm, CPS workers may not be empowered to require a standard of parenting beyond the lowest threshold necessary to protect a child's welfare.

Clearly, personal values, agency practices, and policy mandates can collide in the attempt to balance the three cornerstone priorities of child welfare: child safety, permanency, and well-being. This intersection results in complex ethical dilemmas, such as the tensions between a minimal standard of adequate parenting and a higher standard of good care; between the needs and interests of children, including their right to protection (safety), and their parents' needs, interests, and religious and cultural values; and between defining permanency as a legal and a psychological construct. By contrasting two major influences guiding contemporary child welfare practice, we can see how ethical decision making regarding safety, permanency, and child well-being may be influenced by legal mandates and organizational practices and values.

Adoption and Safe Families Act

A key piece of legislation organizing child welfare practice is the Adoption and Safe Families Act (1997), or ASFA, which amended Title IV-E of the Social Security Act. ASFA was initiated to increase accountability in the child welfare system due to the long delays that children experienced in obtaining permanent placements. The focus on reunifying children and their families had led to some placement decisions that were not in the best interests of children and did not promote child safety. ASFA prioritized the issue of safety by adding language on the "safety of the child" to every step of the case plan. Then, in order to move children into permanent homes in a timely manner, states were given stricter placement and reunification guidelines. Thus, legal time frames are set for permanency decision making; first reasonable efforts to achieve reunification are made, and if these are not successful, then efforts are made to place the child in an alternative permanent (usually adoptive) home. In support of this goal, ASFA requires states to initiate court proceedings to free a child for adoption once that child has been waiting in foster care for at least fifteen of the previous twenty-two months. Apart from cases presenting exceptional circumstances, ASFA promotes the creation of a secure legal status for children who cannot return home.

Family to Family

The Family to Family (F2F) initiative was created to foster public policies, human service reforms, and community supports to more effectively meet the needs of vulnerable children and their families. F2F was designed to help communities redesign and reconstruct their foster care systems in order to do a better job of screening children being considered for removal from home; to determine what services might be provided to safely preserve families and/or meet children's needs; to bring children in congregate or institutional care back to their neighborhoods; to involve foster families as team members in family reunification efforts; to provide a neighborhood resource for children and families and invest in communities from which the foster care population comes; and to provide children with permanent families in a timely manner (Annie E. Casey Foundation, 2002).

Workers can achieve child safety by supporting and strengthening families (preservation and rehabilitation), or by legally protecting children from continued abuse by placing them in stable and permanent alternative settings. For ASFA, legal permanency by way of adoption is the central priority when reunification cannot be safely accomplished. For F2F and other community-based child welfare models, a child's right to be with his or her own family or kin is a central priority, and is sometimes given greater priority than legal permanency mandates of ASFA. F2F values "psychological permanency" and acknowledges the importance of attachment and the feeling of belonging that a child can have in a permanent caretaking relationship with a relative or even a foster parent. This emphasis on psychological permanency can mean that the past or current relationship that the child has with a relative or other caretaker is weighed more heavily than a future legal relationship with a new adoptive parent. Placement with a permanent legal guardian with whom the child has an attachment is acceptable if the child cannot return to his or her birth family. In addition, F2F places a higher priority on maintaining the continuity of cultural, racial, and community ties than do the ASFA mandates.

Under both the F2F and ASFA guidelines, workers must manage the ethical tensions that arise from the pressures to obtain timely permanent placements for children. In concurrent planning, one strategy for meeting this goal, potential adoptive parents become foster parents for children not yet legally free for adoption. Concurrent planning reduces the number of placement disruptions that a child has to experience, which is beneficial due to the significant correlation between such disruptions and an array of negative outcomes, including more time spent in temporary placements and higher levels of psychiatric symptoms (Hussey & Guo, 2005). With concurrent planning, if efforts to rehabilitate the family are not successful, the child doesn't go through another move from the foster home to an adoptive family, which facilitates a smooth and timely transition. While concurrent planning can have many benefits, workers may find that they have contradictory roles to both rehabilitate the natural family and prepare for a permanent outplacement through adoption. Potential adoptive parents can develop strong emotional ties to the child that make rehabilitation of the natural family a secondary priority; concurrent planning can also create loyalty conflicts for all involved, especially the child. Workers need strong case planning and supervision structures to negotiate the ethics of role and responsibility conflicts.

Ethical Dimensions

Child welfare decision making is an uncertain and complex endeavor. Workers who possess an understanding of the philosophic and practice contexts of CPS and other child welfare organizations are better prepared to find solutions to the problems that arise from questions such as, how do we ensure a child's safety and right to protection while trying preserve and rehabilitate families? Are families referred to CPS held to fair and appropriate standards for parenting? How do organizational and legislative mandates interface with child welfare practice values and philosophies? Is it ethical to exclude safe and loving foster or adoptive homes from consideration because they are headed by same-sex couples? How do practitioners reconcile conflicts of interest created by concurrent planning efforts and pressures for permanency planning?

JUVENILE JUSTICE

In the United States, the criminal court system is designated to handle adult offenders, and the juvenile court is responsible for underage youths. Over the course of their history, both systems have realized significant changes in philosophy, but there remain differences of opinion regarding rehabilitation and punishment models, and which is more effective. On one hand, an emphasis on the rehabilitation of the offender encourages individualized assessments and careful case dispositions. On the other hand, high rates of recidivism promote more generalized and punitive measures. These alternating cycles of confidence in rehabilitation versus punitive "get tough" sanctions have influenced juvenile justice practices in the past and continue to do so (Bernard, 1992; Merlo & Benekos, 2003; Urban, St. Cyr, & Decker, 2003).

During the late nineteenth and early twentieth centuries in the United States, industrialization, immigration, and urbanization contributed to social problems such as crime, disease, and pollution, which tended to be experienced most acutely in urban centers. During this period, there was a belief that government involvement was necessary to remedy social evils, and the child-saving movement emerged as part of a larger reform effort that assumed that American ingenuity and spirit could solve many social problems. Through their affiliations with philanthropic and religious organizations, these early social workers endeavored to prevent children from leading corrupt, criminal lives. In doing so, they advocated the establishment of a separate judicial system for children accused of criminally delinquent activity. In the midst of these widespread efforts, reformers helped create the first juvenile court in Cook County, Illinois, in 1899. The idea of using juvenile courts to deal with youth crime spread rapidly, and by 1925 all but two states had juvenile courts. The courts followed closely the model developed in Chicago, achieving their goals of assisting and controlling youths while emphasizing informal processes for intake, adjudication, and case disposition; utilizing separate facilities for adults and for youths; and preferring probation to incarceration. Among the disadvantages of the informality were lax or missing records of proceedings, little due process, excessive judicial discretion, and the high potential for abuse. Probation (the supervised release of an individual) became one of the most important components of the new court. The primary goal of the court was rehabilitation of children and youths in their own homes, or foster homes, rather than institutions. In the nineteenth century, the monitoring of youths on probation was done largely by private citizen volunteers and volunteer societies, but by the early 1900s it had become the domain of trained professionals.

In the 1950s and 1960s, many began to question the ability of the juvenile court to succeed in rehabilitating youth offenders. Treatment techniques available to juveniles never achieved the desired effectiveness, and professionals were concerned about the growing numbers of juveniles institutionalized indefinitely in the name of treatment. In a series of dramatic decisions beginning in the 1960s, the U.S. Supreme Court required that juvenile courts become more like adult criminal courts. Formal hearings were now required in situations in which juveniles were being considered for transfer to adult criminal court, and delinquents facing possible confinement were given protection against self-incrimination. They also attained the rights to receive notice of the charges against them, to present witnesses, to question witnesses, and to have an attorney. Proof beyond a reasonable doubt rather than mere preponderance of evidence was now required for adjudication. The Gault case, described in chapter 3, was instrumental in extending constitutional due process protections to minors. As we shall soon see, along with the criminal protections afforded adults came greater potential for youths to be sentenced to criminal sanctions previously reserved for adults.

In 1974 Congress passed the Juvenile Justice and Delinquency Prevention Act. In combination with amendments passed in 1980, this act required the deinstitutionalization of status offenders and nonoffenders, as well as the separation of juvenile delinquents from adult offenders. Community-based programs, diversion, and deinstitutionalization became the cornerstones of juvenile justice policy in the 1970s. During the 1980s, the belief that serious juvenile crime was increasing and that the system was too lenient with offenders became widespread. Although this was not an accurate reflection of reality, many states reacted by passing harsher laws carrying more punitive consequences. Some laws removed certain classes of offenders from the juvenile justice system and handled them as adults. This trend continued as states passed laws designed to crack down on juvenile crime. These laws made it easier to transfer or waive juvenile offenders from the juvenile justice system to the adult criminal justice system. They gave criminal and juvenile courts increased sentencing authority and options and modified or removed traditional juvenile court confidentiality provisions by making records and proceedings more open. Often we think of youth offenders as "little criminals" rather than teenagers who have committed crimes. However, the intense focus on crime in recent years seems to obscure important aspects of youth mental health and psychosocial development that contribute to juvenile delinquency.

Rehabilitation versus Retribution

As we can see from this brief historical review, several philosophies have guided the development of the juvenile justice system since its inception. The first was a rehabilitation philosophy that emphasized protection of the youth's best interests. The second, which became influential in the 1960s, has been a due process philosophy emphasizing individual rights. The third, a radical nonintervention theory, emphasized diversion and the reduction of the harmful negative effects of the system on youths. While affording minors many of the due process rights of adults provided a certain level of protection from unfair decisions and consequences, it also granted minors corresponding responsibilities regarding sanctions and sentencing. The 1980s and 1990s brought significant changes as the system began to treat more juvenile offenders as adult criminals, a movement characterized by the mantra "If you're old enough to do the crime, then you're old enough to do the time."

Today the core tension between rehabilitation and retribution remains. Does the court decision-making process emphasize what is in the best interest of the child or the need to protect the community and society? Public opinion may hold that crime should result in certain and swift punishment in order to deter future crime. The public may believe that youths should be rehabilitated, although it also wants to be protected during the time it takes to complete rehabilitation. The well-intentioned privileging of the best interest of the child is still important, but it fails to address the concerns raised by victims and communities about the juvenile justice system. Both the therapeutic intervention and punishment models of justice appear to be inadequate and in constant conflict. Individually, neither rehabilitation nor a punishment orientation serves all stakeholders in the system.

More recently, restorative justice models are gaining popularity. The balanced and restorative justice model (BARJ) attempts to address the conflicting interests of community protection, system and offender accountability, and offender competency development (Bazemore & Umbreit, 1995). The restorative justice aspect of the model derives from the ancient notion that when a crime is committed, the offender incurs a debt, an obligation to restore the victim, and by extension the community, to his or her original state prior to the offense. The "balance" in the model proposes that the justice system should give equal weight to each principle. First, in the best interest of the child, youths need to develop competencies so that they are more capable when they leave the system than when they entered it. The needs of crime victims (accountability) must be central; this often involves some type of apology to the victim along with compensation for damages. Since crime affects the quality of life in communities, communities too become stakeholders in the juvenile justice system.

The BARJ model is part of a comprehensive strategy for addressing juvenile crime and victimization, emphasizing prevention, early intervention, and a series of graduated sanctions that holds youths accountable and protects communities. As such, it can be used to ground and guide ethical decision making in juvenile justice. However, the model's framework is much more likely to be successful in addressing minor crimes, and while appealing, it is difficult to operationalize and implement.

Ethical Dimensions

The juvenile justice system has long been a mixture of contradictions and competing concerns. While the BARJ model provides one strategy to alleviate the tensions that arise from these competing interests, ethical dilemmas remain. For example, what degree of risk should a community tolerate in order to maximize the rehabilitation potential of a young offender? How should justice and mercy be reconciled? How do issues of race and social class influence entry into and adjudication within the criminal justice system? Do punishments for youthful offenders deter future crime or ensure it? To what extent should developmental deficits in judgment, described in chapter 3, be considered in the assessment of juvenile crimes and consequences?

SUMMARY

Schools, shelters, clinics, and the various other systems from which minors voluntarily or involuntarily receive services all have their own idiosyncratic histories, philosophies, and tensions. These give rise to unique ethical dilemmas and particular preferences for resolving them. The three systems described in this chapter demonstrate how the evolution of services, competing frameworks and priorities, and shifting social policies lead to contemporary ethical and practice tensions. In practice, these considerations must be incorporated into ethical decision making when we explore practice standards and case information in making solid decisions.

Chapter 5

Short-Term vs. Long-Term Dilemmas

Short-term vs. long-term dilemmas pit immediate benefits and risks against more distant problems and prospects. These dilemmas typically deal with consequences and thus might be thought of as falling within the scope of utilitarian ethical theories. Competing goods are obviously involved when one must choose between urgent needs or desires and future aspirations or possibilities. Because it is easier to anticipate immediate rewards or harms, the particular risk in such dilemmas is that the decision maker focuses solely on the short term while ignoring impacts that may arise in the future.

These types of dilemmas are of special concern in practice with minors, in that maturity and sound judgment are predicated on the ability to plan ahead, anticipate implications, and temper the desire for immediate gratification. As you may recall from chapter 3, these capacities evolve during the developmental process and are necessary for competent decision making. As youngsters are invited to provide input and assent in solving ethical dilemmas, their guardians and helping professionals must be mindful of the challenges they may face in adequately weighing the effects of their decisions over a lifetime.

A similar challenge faces parents and other adults who make decisions for children without adequately considering the impact that those choices will have as the child ages into adulthood. One powerful example is gender assignment surgery for infants born with ambiguous genital characteristics. Conventional practices suggest that surgery performed at infancy is less traumatic for youngsters and creates a clear gender definition with which children will identify. "Assignment should be made as quickly as thorough diagnostic evaluation permits" (Houk, Hughes, Ahmed, & Lee, 2006, p. 755). Anecdotal accounts sometimes contradict this wisdom and indicate that strong biological preferences for one gender or the other cannot be quelled or remedied by surgery in infancy. Migeon, Wisniewski, Gearhart, Heino, Meyer-Bahlburg, Rock, et al. (2002) found that thirty of thirty-nine adults (77%) born with a range of intersex conditions were comfortable with the sex of rearing chosen by their parents and physicians, while the remaining nine (23%) were dissatisfied. Some advocates suggest that children with disorders of sex development should be allowed to mature and allow the gender with which they most naturally affiliate to reveal itself before undergoing corrective surgery. The decision to forego short-term certainty about gender for long-term compatibility with the child's tendencies and wishes is difficult, particularly for family members and others whose style of relating to infants is predicated on gender-based assumptions.

While some decisions can be deferred until the child is old enough to competently or legally take charge of the choice, others cannot. For example, the human papillomavirus has been linked to the risk of cervical cancer. The vaccine for the virus must be administered before young women become sexually active. This sets the stage for a conflict, in that the optimal time for receiving the vaccine is before one reaches the age of majority. Parents, however, may be reluctant to allow their daughters to be vaccinated due to skepticism about the medical establishment, fears about the safety of vaccines, naïveté about the age at which sexual activity might commence, or the belief that the vaccine will lead to promiscuity (Lopes, 2007). Whatever the reason, refusal to vaccinate in the short run can have long-term consequences for the young woman involved. Clearly, it is good to have positive immediate outcomes and avoid immediate harms, but it is also good to achieve long-term positive outcomes and reduction in harms. The fact that these goods cannot be reconciled is a common source of ethical difficulties.

IGNORANCE IS BLISS

Ruby is six. She has been in state custody since the age of two, when her father was imprisoned for murdering her mother. She is currently in a stable foster home and is eligible for adoption. Ruby is HIV-positive but asymptomatic at this time. There is disagreement within the treatment team regarding who should be told about her illness. While all the adults involved agree that potential adoptive families must be told of her status if they are seriously considering adopting her; they disagree about whether Ruby herself should be told, and whether other children in the foster home, her teachers, and other school personnel should be notified.

Those in favor of telling Ruby feel that she has a right to be told, in proper developmental terms, that she has an illness so that she can take precautions to protect herself and others. They feel that her foster siblings, teachers, and classmates should know for the same reasons. Ruby's CPS worker, Drew, and others opposed to telling believe that it is not their right to tell her—that that should be left to her adoptive family. They also feel that it would be burdensome and self-limiting information for a young child to carry, and that the damage would be greater than the good resulting from precautions that might be taken should her illness be revealed.

Tremendous gains in the understanding and treatment of HIV/AIDS have altered the course of the disease and the life expectancies of those who are diagnosed with it. This good news does not obscure the fact that it is a communicable, fatal illness that still carries tremendous stigma for those who are diagnosed, their families and friends, and society at large. Ruby's case demonstrates the intersection of these concerns as some helpers want to protect her from the harms that might arise from the release of her medical information, and others want to protect her and others from harms related to the spread of HIV/AIDS.

Assess Options

Ultimately, a decision as significant as this will be made by a team of representatives from the child welfare agency and other people with expertise regarding her situation and concern for Ruby. For the purposes of the ethical examination, though, we'll situate the decision with Drew. His choices boil down to the following:

1. He can tell Ruby about her illness and inform others with whom she has frequent interaction. (Related decisions involve who would be the best person to tell Ruby and which people should be told of her illness.)

2. He can continue to withhold the information from Ruby and others and let her adoptive family make the decision about what she should know and when. In the event that a permanent placement is not forthcoming, he can determine a developmental point (or a point in her illness trajectory) when she will be informed.
3. He can tell Ruby that she has an illness that requires her to take certain precautions but avoid telling others, such as her teachers and foster siblings.
4. He can tell relevant others (Ruby's teachers and foster siblings), but not Ruby herself.
5. He can notify parents that a member of the school community has HIV and educate them and their children about precautions they should take to avoid spread of the disease.

Evaluation must consider the long-term and short-term consequences of selecting or rejecting any of the options. For the options that involve telling Ruby, the long-term or short-term dilemma is largely a matter of *when* she should be told, rather than *whether* such a disclosure should take place. For the options that involve notifying those around her, the question is whether such disclosures should ever take place. Let's critically weigh the choices.

Ethical theories and principles. In addition to the long-term and short-term considerations in the case, Ruby's situation also requires us to differentiate between what patients have a right to know about their own conditions and what others have a right to know. The rules and practices in health care would tend to favor patients' rights to information and to privacy, encouraging disclosure to the person most directly involved and discretion in disclosures to others. At times, family members and professionals might be reluctant to fully inform a patient about his or her condition in the belief that dire diagnoses or poor prognoses can become self-fulfilling prophesies. That inclination appears to be dissipating thanks to increased appreciation of individuals' rights.

While it is fair and ethical for people to know their diagnoses, is it helpful? This is a clinical question. There are clear advantages in knowing what one is dealing with and what to expect for the course of the disease and treatment. Not only is this information an essential element of informed consent, but it allows patients to regain an element of control in a situation in which they are often powerless. With knowledge, patients can seek out support and information on treatments. It is unclear whether minor patients as young as Ruby would accrue the same benefits as adults from forthright conversation about their health status. However, from a rules-based perspective, we must ask which is preferable as a universal law, candor or obfuscation? Regardless of the patient's age, the clinical, practical, and ethical preferences would appear to support the patient's right to information.

We can also use a rules-based perspective to examine the other core ethical issue in the case, the permissibility of sharing medical information with others. Health data enjoy significant protections in our society. While there are certain situations in which people are expected to disclose their own conditions (infectious diseases) or when they may be disclosed without their consent (meningitis, tuberculosis, or other public health emergencies), they are the exceptions. One rule therefore is that people have a prevailing right to maintain their privacy. A related rule is that citizens have a right to information regarding threats to their health. The core question then is the degree to which HIV status poses a threat to the health of others. To the extent that it does pose a risk, deontological considerations would support actions that focus on the protection of others without revealing Ruby's particular status.

An ends-based analysis of Drew's various choices reveals other considerations. Despite Ruby's young age, if she is told, she can likely take measures to care for herself, such as adhering to a medication regimen, identifying troubling symptoms, or becoming involved in support groups. If Ruby is told of her illness, she might also be able to limit the possibility of incidental transmission to others, though this is a greater concern as she ages and possibly engages in high-risk behaviors than it is in elementary school. Knowing about her condition may alleviate confusion stemming from physicians' visits and medical tests, or from her illness itself.

There could be negative consequences when she learns of her illness. The revelation of her disease may raise questions about how she became ill, the answers to which may be troubling in and of themselves or lead to the disclosure of other information that has been kept from her. Knowing she has a serious illness, whether or not it is identified as HIV, may make her feel vulnerable and overly sensitive to symptoms that her body is betraying her. The knowledge may contribute to feelings of hopelessness or depression or life-limiting and self-destructive activities. Rather than encouraging her to act with caution as she ages, such knowledge may lead her to throw caution to the wind.

Of course, at some point Ruby will learn of her diagnosis, so whatever positive or negative outcomes might result can never be totally ruled out. It is wise, then, to focus on differential outcomes if she is told sooner rather than later. If she learns of her disease when she is older, she may be better able to use the information constructively and take the hoped-for steps in protecting herself and others. She may also feel angry, confused, or betrayed by the fact that she wasn't told sooner, and the erosion of trust in her caregivers and treatment team may have cascading negative effects. Alternatively, with greater maturity, she may be better able to put the information in context rather than allowing it to be self-defining. Maturity will increase her ability to use the information to engage in preventive activities and regulate her own disclosures about the illness.

Notifying others about Ruby's illness has implications for her and for those who are notified. The risks for Ruby include ostracism by classmates and their parents, her foster siblings, or school personnel based on stereotypes and fears of transmission. Other possible effects include gossip and prejudice about how she came to have the illness. The diagnosis will also affect the way people relate to her. For example, it may lower adults' expectations of her and limit the educational and recreational opportunities she is offered. Conversely, her family and caregivers may indulge and overprotect her to compensate for presumed health deficits. Clearly, any of these reactions may cause reverberating negative effects for Ruby's well-being, self-concept, and social supports.

On the other hand, notifying others about Ruby's illness may enable them to take action to avoid contracting the disease. If Ruby's teachers knew, they might take special precautions to protect her classmates in the event of a playground accident or a bloody nose, though even in those events, the risk of transmission is not significant. In fact, it should be noted that no cases of HIV transmission in schools or child care settings have been documented. Of course, school personnel should routinely use universal precautions, which dictate that *all* individuals should be assumed to have an infectious disease. In this sense, it is the school's responsibility to ensure safety, irrespective of an individual student's condition.

Could these positive consequences be achieved without disclosure about Ruby? Would a general communication about the presence of an HIV-infected student be sufficient? Would an even broader announcement about the importance of precautions achieve the same ends? The more general the warning, the less likely people are to take it seriously. While this is bad for safety compliance, it is good for protecting Ruby and avoiding the possibility of a witch hunt fueled by gossip and speculation about who carries the disease. Perhaps pairing a nonspecific warning with educational programs for parents, students, and teachers would achieve the positive consequences and limit the harmful ones.

We typically associate the possession of information with the capacity to exercise autonomy. Therefore, transparency is essential so that patients can choose how to manage their illnesses and live their lives in spite of their illnesses. The principle of autonomy implies that there is a fundamental right to know. However, autonomy is also reflected in a right not to know (Freundlich, 1998). In that personal freedoms might be constrained by the knowledge of a terminal illness, a patient would seem to have the privilege to say, "I choose not to know." The key is that the decision rests with the patient, not with others acting paternalistically on the patient's behalf. Since Ruby is not old enough to be granted autonomy, her guardians must make decisions for her, though they can choose to do so in a way that maximizes her right to self-determination. Parents (or Drew in this case) exercise substituted judgment on behalf of the minors for whom they have a responsibility. They effectively put themselves in the child's shoes to "make the decision the child would be expected to make were he or she competent" (Koocher & Keith-Spiegel, 1990, p. 13). The adults' understanding of Ruby's capacities and interests will have to serve as a guide in their decision on when and how much to tell her about her illness. Overall, of the choices available to Drew, Ruby's autonomy is maximized by those that inform her in an age-appropriate manner of her condition and limit disclosure about her condition to others.

Following the same principle, those who are put at risk by Ruby's condition cannot exercise their own autonomy if they are uninformed of the hazard. As with many threats to public health and safety, the decision must balance Ruby's interests with those of her community (classmates) and family (foster siblings). When it comes to HIV/AIDS, this tension is resolved by the leveraging of individual rights and the expectation that educated carriers of the disease will take precautions to protect others from transmission. It is also resolved through public education efforts that empower non-carriers to make responsible decisions about the risks inherent in certain activities. Individual autonomy is overruled, though, when it is misused and others are put at risk. The result would be intervention by health authorities to notify partners or other specific people at risk. It does not warrant the wholesale rejection of autonomy, empowering authorities to put up billboards or take out advertising announcing one's HIV status, for example.

Fidelity or trustworthiness is advanced when people act according to the expectations and agreements they have created. For trust to be violated, there must be an explicit or assumed obligation to behave in a certain manner. Ruby may feel betrayed if her condition is withheld from her and if it is shared with others. The parents of her classmates may feel betrayed as well if they presumed that the school or other authorities would alert them to the presence of health risks (even remote ones) in the school. Ruby's foster siblings might have similar expectations. While these reactions are understandable, whether they are reasonable or avoidable will depend on the nature of the trust obligations among the various parties. Trust is often linked to truthfulness, as the expectations above indicate. In this case, the challenges involve when information should be shared, how much should be shared, and with whom. All the options generated for Drew are truthful, though some could argue that withholding significant information from Ruby or others is not wholly honest. Obviously, any decision *not* to share information must be made in order to satisfy other competing principles (autonomy) or goods (the right to privacy).

Laws and policies. There may not be laws or policies that entitle Ruby to her health information, but there certainly are rules about how others can share it. The most obvious regulations in this case pertain to medical privacy. The Health Insurance Portability and Accountability Act (HIPAA) of 1996 places strict protections on the distribution of medical data by health care professionals. It also requires that patients (in this case, their guardians) be informed about the limits of privacy protections and afforded the opportunity to waive confidentiality for certain purposes, such as medical consultation and insurance claims. HIPAA defers to state privacy standards when those are more stringent than HIPAA, so it is difficult to examine the specific implications without knowing the jurisdiction of Ruby's case. We can assume, though, that the mental health and medical providers in Ruby's case are constrained by HIPAA from sharing information about her condition with others.

Ruby's status as a ward of the state introduces some interesting regulatory implications for her case. In most instances, parents have a right to their children's health information, especially when the minor child is Ruby's age. As proxies for their children's health decisions, parents are entitled to share their children's health information as they see fit. Interestingly, as a child in state custody, Ruby may enjoy greater protection from disclosure of her health information than she would in the custody of her parents. Drew, her CPS worker, and other professionals involved in the case may not be covered by HIPAA, but certainly other privacy regulations related to the treatment of HIV/AIDS patients and the protection of information in child welfare agencies, schools, and other settings apply. Despite these measures, disclosure might be beneficial in Ruby's case. If her teachers know she is immunocompromised, they can help protect her from exposures that may exacerbate her condition. For example, if she is exposed to measles or the chicken pox, she should immediately receive post-exposure protections to limit the impact of the exposure.

While statutes and agency policies restrict the information that can be shared with others about Ruby's case, they also set forth parameters about what information can be shared to protect other individuals at risk of infection. Conditions that warrant disclosure to the school are those that pose a direct threat to other students, such as TB, which is transmitted through the air. Conditions that do not pose a risk through incidental contact are not reportable. HIV/AIDS would fall into the latter category. Parents may elect to inform schools, day-care centers, and summer camps of their child's condition, but they are not required to do so, even when they are asked (Parents of Kids with Infectious Diseases, 2006).

Agency policies may also help with process issues in this case. For example, CPS procedures may indicate how decisions should be made, what information child clients should receive, and which decisions are at the discretion of the foster family and which fall to the CPS staff. School policies may specify how outbreaks of infectious or communicable diseases can be prevented and addressed. For example, school procedures for dealing with lice infestations and influenza, meningitis, or TB exposures could be applicable to Ruby's case.

As noted earlier, the use of universal precautions can greatly reduce the risk of HIV transmission. Public health authorities or the school system may have policies about the use of such precautions. These may include training requirements for all school personnel, informational resources, and guidance about how to carry out the precautions themselves.

Values. Drew and the rest of Ruby's team seem to value her privacy and her well-being. They value her right to know about her condition but are at odds regarding the proper timing for such a disclosure. The team may also value mitigating risk. They may be concerned about their culpability if teachers, parents of Ruby's schoolmates, or her foster siblings complain or, worse, if someone contracts HIV from contact with Ruby. This sensitivity to public perceptions and liability is probably heightened because of the nature of Ruby's disease. Unfortunately, the fear that HIV/AIDS engenders also gives rise to the bigotry that the helpers want to avoid by keeping Ruby's HIV status secret. Some members of the team may be more willing to endure the risks involved in breaking Ruby's confidentiality than they are the risk of angry parents, a lawsuit, or the spread of disease, even though the damage of the revelation is immediate and certain, and the risks of not telling are remote and slight. Social work values suggest that professionals "elevate service to others above self-interest" (NASW, 1999,

p. 5). A preoccupation with mitigating the risks to oneself at the client's expense might be interpreted as violating that value.

Other values of the social work profession apply in this case. The value placed on social justice would urge social workers to address threats of discrimination directed at Ruby and others with HIV. Enhancing dignity and worth means supporting individuals' autonomy in balance with the needs of society. It would suggest that any efforts to prevent the spread of HIV should afford Ruby the maximum level of privacy and respect. The value placed on human relationships would mean taking care not to alienate Ruby from her peers, her foster family, or her treatment team. These bonds are particularly vital in her case, given the early and significant losses she has already endured.

Information. Some of the information we already possess is significant as we weigh out the options. Foremost is Ruby's age. It clearly limits her decision-making capacity and thus her ability to express a preference for any of the choices under consideration. Depending on her functioning, her age may be indicative of her ability to properly inform others if they are at risk or to take precautions to ensure her own and others' well-being. Another consideration is her custody arrangement. Because her parents' rights have been terminated and her custody has been assigned to state welfare authorities, the individuals in charge of her care must take particular effort to ensure that her long-term interests are guarded in the same manner they would be by a parent protecting the interests of his or her child. We don't know about the makeup of the team or their familiarity with and concern for Ruby, yet that information plays an essential role in the determination of whether they can adequately act on her behalf.

It would be helpful to have other information about the case to weigh the choices at hand. In crafting the options, we are presuming the foster parents know about Ruby's HIV status and are accepting of it and comfortable in managing her illness along with her other needs. We are also assuming Ruby has a doctor with expertise in infectious diseases who is providing ongoing care in the case. His or her appraisals will be important in setting priorities and balancing the various demands in her case.

It would be helpful to know how Ruby is functioning. Tenuous peer and school relationships, emotional fragility, and cognitive deficits might all suggest waiting to disclose her disease until she is better able to deal with the information. It would also be helpful to know how imminent a permanent placement might be, given some of the team members' belief that notification should be postponed until she has an adoptive family. Related to this, it would be helpful to know what evidence there is to indicate that waiting to tell Ruby is better than telling her now and that hearing it from her new adoptive family is better than hearing it from her long-term care team.

Standards. Practice standards in HIV/AIDS services reveal little consensus about the appropriate age at which children should be informed of their HIV status (Wiener, Mellins, Marhefka, & Battles, 2007). Nor is there agreement regarding the psychological outcomes of disclosure. However, in a study of seventy-seven children living with HIV, Mellins, Brackis-Cott, Dolezai, Richards, Nicholas, and Abrams (2002) found that children who knew their HIV status did not have increased mental health problems. Nevertheless, when the decision is made to inform Ruby of her condition, it will be important for the foster family to attend to potential negative outcomes. Any concerns should be brought to the attention of Ruby's caseworker (if not Drew, then his successor) as well as her medical team. To assist in the adjustment process, the foster parents may seek out support groups for children who are HIV-positive or have other chronic health conditions.

Several ethical standards have particular significance for Ruby's case. "In instances when clients lack the capacity to provide informed consent, social workers should protect clients' interests by seeking permission from an appropriate third party, informing clients consistent with the clients' level of understanding. In such instances social workers should seek to ensure that the third party acts in a manner consistent with clients' wishes and interests. Social workers should take reasonable steps to enhance such clients' ability to give informed consent" (NASW, 1999,1.03c). As the person with decision-making authority (Drew) might be a social worker, he should be alert to the possibility that his roles as Ruby's custodian and a representative of the agency might be blurred. That is, things that might be viewed as wise or expedient from the agency's perspective might be unacceptable acts by a guardian, who should be alert to long-term effects on the client. "When social workers act on behalf of clients who lack the capacity to make informed decisions, social workers should take reasonable steps to safeguard the interests and rights of those clients" (NASW, 1999, 1.14). In consenting to decisions made on Ruby's behalf, Drew must put her interests before the agency's interests. This is in keeping with the NASW Code's provisions on conflicts of interest as well as those on informed consent.

The hazards of Drew's dual role are revealed again in regard to possible disclosures about Ruby's health status. The Code states, "Social workers may disclose confidential information when appropriate with valid consent from a client or a person legally authorized to consent on behalf of a client" (NASW, 1999, 1.07b). The Code and his position may permit Drew to reveal Ruby's diagnosis, but the responsibility to share information only for "compelling professional reasons" (NASW, 1999, 1.07c) should act as a constraint on that freedom.

Be Mindful of Process

A key in resolving short-term and long-term dilemmas is deciding how to maximize positive outcomes now and in the future and minimize negative ones. For Ruby, the beneficial or deleterious effects of knowing about her disease may depend on how she is told. The risks of disclosure can be minimized if the person telling her is able to time the conversation appropriately and explain it in a way Ruby can understand. This individual should be familiar *to* Ruby, and also familiar *with* her, so that he or she is able to read her nonverbal cues, her level of understanding, and her readiness to learn more. Perhaps most importantly, the person who has this conversation must be comfortable doing so, well informed on the issues, and prepared for the array of reactions the news might generate. There is substantial guidance available for family members and caregivers delivering developmentally relevant explanations about HIV and related issues. Ruby's team can preview books and resources they might suggest for Ruby to learn more about HIV, adoption, parent death, and other issues relevant to her needs. The advantage of such resources is that they are available whenever Ruby is ready to learn more.

Whenever possible, an attempt to gain the child's assent to all decisions regarding of his or her care should be obtained, and dissent should be honored. The providers should solicit Ruby's willingness to participate in her own care. An HIV-positive child with a high viral load may require a series of carefully scheduled doses of anti-retroviral medications and prophylactic antibiotics, and understanding and assent may enhance compliance and efficacy (Behrman, Kliegman, & Jenson, 2004).

The process for disclosures to others will be equally important. Given the low risk of transmission for Ruby's age group, primary prevention activities would appear sufficient to offer the class, Ruby's foster siblings, and others protection from HIV. Such broad-based efforts protect Ruby as well as the communities of which she is a part. HIV prevention would ideally be a part of health and wellness programs offered as an intrinsic part of public education. However, community sensitivities about sex education (even education addressing disease prevention) and federal funding preferences for abstinence-only education programs mean that special efforts may be required to deliver prevention programs in Ruby's school system.

Consult

Consultation should be facilitated by the fact that a team of providers is already assembled to assist Ruby. Still, service fragmentation is possible due to staff turnover, busy schedules, narrowly defined roles and funding streams, and a host of other causes (Indyk, Belville, Lachapelle, Gordon, & Dewart, 1993). Drew is in an ideal position to call a meeting of those most directly involved in wraparound service provision to Ruby. That session can be used to share information about her history and functioning and the service plans in place to meet her needs. The meeting can identify gaps in services that can be filled and can serve as a forum for the team to consider the questions related to revealing her diagnosis. It may be an opportunity for the team to identify missing information and to think through the process and timing for discussing Ruby's diagnosis with her.

If the group cannot come to a consensus about how to handle the disclosure, they must discuss how to handle the impasse. As Ruby's guardian, Drew and the CPS staff have the ultimate authority for determining what is in her best interest. The group should be mindful of this authority and explicitly agree to defer to it in matters such as the revelation of Ruby's diagnosis.

Document

Hopefully, each of Ruby's providers is keeping records of their services to her and their observations of her functioning. If a case conference regarding disclosure of her HIV status is held, each participant is responsible for recording the meeting in their respective systems. Some such meetings result in a summary of the points discussed, the sources of data reviewed, and the decisions made, in which the client is referred to in general terms and his or her initial is used instead of his or her name. Since he bears special responsibility as Ruby's guardian, Drew must take special care to detail the choices made in her case, the rationale for those decisions, and the results.

Evaluate

All the adults involved in Ruby's life must be attuned to the impact of both continued silence about her disease and disclosure. Should the team decide to defer telling her, special attention should be paid to signs indicating when she is ready to receive the information. These signs may emerge in her play, in questions she asks of those around her, in statements she makes, and in her behaviors. If she is told, her reactions will materialize in the same ways. The team should be alert to detrimental reactions, either by Ruby or to her, and prepared to respond. As indicated earlier, they should also be prepared to capitalize on positive reactions and to provide information commensurate with Ruby's readiness to receive it.

Evaluation must also be employed regarding prevention efforts with Ruby's classmates, playmates, and foster siblings. What new knowledge was acquired and what myths were dispelled? How durable was the knowledge acquisition? Can those who attended prevention information sessions identify the risk factors of transmission and demonstrate the proper steps to take in responding to those risks? Did the sessions reduce the likelihood that participants will stigmatize people with the disease? Were participants able to effectively engage in the sessions in the absence of the identification of a specific or immediate threat?

Case Conclusion

Medical and scientific advances have given rise to an array of clinical, ethical, legal, and social issues as new knowledge is applied to the detection and treatment of disease. Professionals of all disciplines must be well versed in the concepts and current findings in health care in order to contribute meaningfully to the interdisciplinary teams that characterize effective patient care.

A number of variables affect the advisability of health status disclosure for children, including the nature of the condition, the age of the child when he or she contracted the condition, the potential for a cure, and transmission to others, and the effects of the discovery on the child's self-concept, life planning, and relationships. Ruby's history of traumatic losses, her guardianship, and her lack of permanent placement all present additional considerations for appraising the long- and short-term implications of her case. Fortunately, her involvement in multiple service systems means she has a team of providers who may share information and collaborate in decision making in her case. Because there are a number of options for educating Ruby about her illness and preventing transmission to others, Drew and the other providers are spared an either-or choice in resolving the matter. The use of an ethical decision-making framework helps workers articulate the apprehensions they may have regarding disclosure or maintaining silence in the case. The framework also helps to identify the immediate and long-term consequences of various choices, so that positive results can be optimized.

KRAMER VS. KRAMER

Mike K is nine. He likes soccer, word games, and reptiles. He is in the gifted and talented program at school and is likely to skip a grade next year. His parents divorced two years ago and share custody: he resides with his mother and sees his father several times per week and on alternating holidays and school vacations. Mrs. K is a real estate agent and Mr. K is a furniture woodworker. Recently, Mrs. K announced plans to marry a stockbroker whose house she had once listed and relocate to a city 3,000 miles from where she and Mike currently reside. She has filed papers for sole custody of Mike, contending that she and her future husband can best provide for Mike's needs, particularly his educational advancement. Mr. K is countersuing for custody, contending that uprooting Mike will disrupt his ties with friends and family and effectively deprive Mr. K of contact with his son. Mr. K maintains that it would be financially more feasible for his ex-wife to travel for visitations than for him to do so. Mrs. K counters that Mr. K's schedule makes it easier for him to do so.

The court has appointed a social worker, Beth, to make recommendations in the case. In her assessment, she learns that Mike's fondest wish is for his parents to get back together. He is apprehensive about the move and about his mother's future husband, who has never had children. Beth finds that Mrs. K evokes strong negative feelings in her, yet in terms of their abilities as parents, she concludes that each of the Ks has flaws and strengths, though clearly Mrs. K has the greater socioeconomic capacity. When both parents are good enough, how can she determine which placement is in Mike's best interests?

Approximately half of all marriages in the United States end in divorce, affecting over a million minors per year (Divorcemagazine.com, n.d.). Not all dissolutions are contentious, but in those that are, child custody rights and arrangements often become a major source of friction. As a result, an abundant body of literature exists across disciplines examining the effects of divorce on children, their rights in custody decisions, and the ways that their best interests can be determined (see, e.g., Braver, Ellman, & Fabricius, 2003; Kaltenborn, 2001; Kelly & Lamb, 2003). While the court will make the final decision about Mike's custody, Beth's opinion may carry great weight in the outcome. She might also be capable of crafting an acceptable compromise that meets the needs of all members of the family in the immediate future and over their lifetimes. Unfortunately, such outcomes are more elusive than they appear. It can be difficult for parents to look past financial interests, entrenched positions, old hurts, and win-lose mentalities to negotiate a successful option. Children's confusion, loyalties, hurts, and developmental capacities can affect their ability to determine and articulate their preferences. In addition, the biases, experiences, and inclinations of the professionals involved can diminish their capacity for crafting objective interest-based solutions.

Let's review Beth's options in light of these variables and in recognition that her actions are but one element of the decision concerning Mike's future.

1. Beth can support Mr. K's position in her work with the family and in her report to the court.
2. Beth can support Mrs. K's position in her work with the family and in her report to the court.
3. Beth can encourage the Ks to come up with their own solution and accept it regardless of her preferences.

On the face of it, the third option is the simplest, fairest, and perhaps most ethically sound. Why bother to go through the decision-making process if a de facto preference emerges? Several reasons support the use of a decision-making model to explore or affirm a choice. First, the fact that an answer is clear doesn't mean it is comforting. In this and other cases, the dilemma may reside not in reconciling competing standards, but in reconciling rights and standards with the worker's own beliefs. A decision-making model should help Beth avoid inappropriately biased choices and build her confidence in the suitability of the option she decides to pursue.

In this case, Beth must choose a course of action that takes into account the needs of each member of the family system, now and in the future. Absent an effective decision-making process, professionals might focus too narrowly on one individual or one moment in time, rather than the big picture. And because custody disputes are high-stakes decisions, they can present the workers involved with heightened liability. A decision-making model helps ensure that the right decision emerges for the right reason. If Beth ultimately chooses option 3, it should be because she believes it is the best option, not just the easiest or the safest.

Assess Options

Let's start by examining the rationales for and consequences of Beth's various choices. Supporting Mr. K would allow Mike to stay in the community in which he has grown up. He apparently has a good relationship with his father and is well connected to recreational, educational, and social networks there. He has voiced a slight preference for that option. Beth might infer that Mr. K's occupation would allow him more time with Mike. Beth might also sympathize with Mr. K. After all, Mrs. K's remarriage and relocation have given rise to the suit and disrupted what was apparently a workable arrangement of shared custody. It is Mrs. K's choice whether or not to move. If she does move, she and her new husband have sufficient financial means to visit Mike on a regular basis, facilitating their ongoing relationship.

Most of these positive consequences for placement with Mr. K are short term in nature. Beth may be concerned about the long-term implications of the move. Some research suggests that residential instability has deleterious social, behavioral, and educational consequences and may even lead to suicide attempts though the effects of a single move are less clear (Adam, 2004; Sommer, Bravender, & Hogan, 2004).

Alternatively, Beth might be inclined to side with Mrs. K because she and her new husband can provide Mike with a higher standard of living and greater access to educational and enrichment activities. Placement with his father might mean Mike is stuck in a school system that is incapable of meeting his educational needs. This could negatively affect his educational attainment in both the short and long term. If Mike is placed with Mrs. K, she can probably afford to send him for regular visits with his father, facilitating the relationship between the two as well as Mike's ongoing connection to his old friends and classmates.

The choice to try to get the Ks to work out an agreement or compromise is preferable in that it may increase the family's ownership of the choice, and thus their compliance with it. They know Mike best and presumably can act in his interests. Generating a solution rather than having one imposed on them is likely to reduce their animosity toward each other, to Beth, and to the process as whole. A successful outcome may create a feeling of unity as they move into the next phase of life post-divorce. This is preferable to the divisiveness and partisanship that may result if one parent's request is favored over the other's.

The problem with this option is that the parents are already in an adversarial proceeding. If they were capable of crafting a compromise, it is likely that they would have done so by now. A further risk in high-stakes negotiations is that power dynamics related to gender, money, personality, and other factors can powerfully advantage one party over another. The result is nominal or begrudging agreement rather than a fair and mutually acceptable outcome. The risk is that compliance in the short term may lead to sabotage, dissatisfaction, and continued strife over time. While this option is certainly an acceptable starting place for Beth's work, a prolonged and unsuccessful effort at compromise may further entrench the parties and estrange them from each other. At some point a partisan decision might be preferable to continued destructive interactions in the name of negotiation.

Ethical theories and principles. From a utilitarian perspective, the compromise option, if successful, should yield the most benefits for all parties and diminish the possibility of negative outcomes. The other two options clearly disadvantage one parent. Options 1 and 2 also hold positive and negative short- and long-term outcomes for Mike. At the very least, different custody arrangements may mean trading comfort and familiarity for opportunity and socioeconomic advantage. And either of those choices may put him in a partisan position with one parent and distance him from the other. That is an undesirable outcome, now and in the future.

A deontological framework would encourage Beth to look at the rules embedded in her choices and determine whether they would still be desirable if translated into universally applicable laws. If the choice is between showing preference for one party and encouraging both to come to an acceptable agreement, clearly the latter is more acceptable. If the choice is between imposing a solution rather than letting the parties work out their problems, the latter would also seem to be better. Beyond these obvious distinctions, it is not easy to discern what rules are reflected in the choices laid out earlier. For example, is staying with Mr. K preferable because kids should not have to move when their parents do? Should Mike be with Mrs. K because she is the wealthier parent? Even if these were fine rationales in Mike's case, they have little appeal when universalized. Unless other prevailing rules or laws become evident, the deontological perspective would apparently support option 3. Beth should act in the way that is fairest to all three parties, that gives them the greatest opportunity to solve their problems, and that best supports their autonomy.

Beyond considering philosophical positions, Beth must utilize ethical principles for selecting her course of action. The first two choices effectively limit the parents' autonomy by removing decision-making power from them and giving Beth a greater say in the outcome. The third choice situates the power for problem solving with the parents and in that way is supportive of their autonomy to address their own problems. Mike's self-determination may be best supported by options 1 and 3, though as noted earlier, his ability to assert his autonomy (or render his own consent) is limited by his age, his loyalties, and the magnitude of the decision under consideration.

The impact of the principle of justice is more difficult to discern. One could say that Mrs. K's decision to move is an unjust disruption of an existing agreement, and therefore the decision should default in favor of her ex-husband. Others might argue that resources (financial capacity) would be more fairly distributed if Mike were placed with Mrs. K rather than his father. This would be an alternative interpretation of justice. Some might argue that option 3 best meets the standard of justice if it results in a compromise acceptable to both parties that fairly distributes the advantages and disadvantages between the two parties.

Laws and policies. The judge in the Ks' case will apply the relevant legal principles to the decision. Hopefully the referral for Beth's services specifies the expectations (or policies) governing her work on the case. Her agency policies may also provide direction for her work. For example, does she have the liberty to encourage and assist the parents in reaching an amicable solution? If she is expected only to conduct an evaluation and render an opinion, what elements of the case must she review? Should she do home visits? Interview teachers? Assess the new husband? Is she required to render an opinion or simply summarize her finding? Is she working under a clearly understood standard of what constitutes Mike's best interests? These elements play an important role in structuring her options. They should also frame her initial conversations with the Ks so that they know what to expect and the ways in which their statements may be used in her evaluation.

Values. Custody decisions and the people who make them are laden with judgments and values. Some that might be at play in this case include:

- Children belong with two parents.
- Boys need to be raised by their fathers.
- Smart students need to be challenged in school.
- Mothers shouldn't move away from their children.
- Women shouldn't be so career oriented.
- A new couple needs time to develop their relationship without the intrusion of a child.
- Mrs. K works hard and shouldn't be penalized for her financial success.
- People marry and divorce too easily.
- Divorce is selfish.
- Mrs. K is selfish for wanting to uproot Mike.
- Mr. K is selfish for wanting to hold Mike back from the opportunities his new life could provide.
- Mike should get to decide.

The list could go on and on. Beth's work with the family will require her to uncover and address the values embedded in each member's contentions and positions. She must also be mindful of her own values. Empirical evidence may lead her to favor the suitability of one parent over another, but her personal biases should not.

The social work values regarding the dignity and worth of people, the importance of human relationships, and integrity should inform the process by which Beth carries out her role. Despite her antipathy toward Mrs. K, she must be respectful in order to be effective in her role and to avoid distressing or harming Mike. Recognizing that the family's relationships transcend her time with them, she should be mindful of the power of her role and assiduously work for an agreeable and constructive outcome, and a process that minimizes the friction within the family.

Information. How effective are custody evaluations? Emery, Otto, and O'Donohue (2005) challenge the current practice of child custody evaluations, claiming that evaluations utilize instruments that have not been scientifically validated and that they misuse validated instruments. Other common elements of evaluations, such as how much weight to assign a child's preference, have not been studied. Indeed, Emery et al. (2005) assert that the process itself is counterproductive since evaluations, by their very nature, create an adversarial relationship between parents that is detrimental to the process. In regard to children's preferences and their capacity to assent to placement, Emery (2003) notes that in his own experience as an evaluator, it was far more common for children to request that their parents stop arguing than for them to express a preference about whom they wished to live with.

The vignette provides some information about each family member's wishes and issues regarding the custody decision. Other information would help Beth decide how constructive problem solving will be and how likely it is to lead to a satisfactory outcome. For example, are the parents' parenting styles and philosophies similar? Is one home more conducive to Mike's well-being? If they are not similar, is this another area of contention between the parents, and another rationale for recommending that one parent be granted exclusive custody?

What evidence is there that the Ks are capable of effective problem solving? The original custody arrangement may provide clues about their communication skills, their flexibility, and their willingness to put Mike's interests before their own. If the crafting and execution of the shared custody was fraught with conflict, it doesn't bode well for the negotiated option now. Prior to the filing of the respective motions to change custody, did the couple try to work it out amicably? What were the sticking points? Will the impetus of the judge's order help Beth's work with them to succeed where other efforts have failed?

The vignette provides some information about Mike's interests and wishes. It would be helpful, though, to know more about his functioning. Is his preference that his parents reunite understandable wishful thinking, or is it the result of mixed messages he has received, immaturity, or difficulties with reasoning? How might Mike adapt to the move and to a long-term change in households? How does he get along with Mrs. K's fiancé? Is his discomfort with his future stepparent merely apprehension about the unknown, or is there a reason to conclude that the placement might not work? And how does the fiance feel about parenting a nine-year-old?

What do kids who have been in Mike's situation think? As adults, what advice might they offer Beth and other helpers? Ahrons and Tanner (2003) interviewed 173 adult children of divorced parents twenty years post-divorce. Most participants reported that their relationships had either improved or remained stable after the divorce, regardless of custody arrangements. Factors such as parental conflict and low paternal involvement shortly after the divorce were associated with less satisfactory relationships.

Standards. Practice standards can guide Beth's actions in carrying out her evaluation. While some researchers are skeptical about the adequacy and validity of custody evaluation procedures, they do outline a few noteworthy ideas about how Beth might approach the case. Ideally, custody arrangements would be negotiated out of court by the parents themselves (with assistance from relevant professionals), and the arrangements would mirror the involvement that each parent had before the divorce; for example, if Mrs. K carried 60% of parenting responsibilities during the marriage, she might be entitled to 60% of Mike's care after the divorce (Emery et al., 2005).

Ethical standards guide Beth's decision and the way she carries it out. Informed consent is particularly important so that the Ks understand her role and goals and can determine the extent to which they are willing to cooperate with her efforts. Informed consent requires clear and understandable explanations of costs, alternatives, rights, and consequences (NASW, 1999). Since the Ks were ordered to see Beth, they can be presumed to be involuntary clients, in which case additional standards apply: "In instances when clients are receiving services involuntarily, social workers should provide information about the nature and extent of services and about the extent of clients' right to refuse service" (NASW, 1999, 1.03d). This would be an opportunity for Beth to clarify that bad-faith efforts at problem solving might lead her to make an independent recommendation. She might also talk about other potential long-term consequences for Mike if his parents' animosity continues.

The NASW Code provides guidance on managing informed consent and conflicts of interest in services to multiple-client systems:

> When social workers provide services to two or more people who have a relationship with each other (for example, couples, family members), social workers should clarify with all parties which individuals will be considered clients and the nature of social workers' professional obligations to the various individuals who are receiving services. Social workers who anticipate a conflict of interest among the individuals receiving services or who anticipate having to perform in potentially conflicting roles (for example, when a social worker is asked to testify in a child custody dispute or divorce proceedings involving clients) should clarify their role with the parties involved and take appropriate action to minimize any conflict of interest. (NASW, 1999, 1.06d)

As Beth assesses her options, she should consider whether she can fairly combine the options she is considering. Specifically, can she urge the family to come to an agreement and still have the option of writing up a report in favor of one party or the other if the negotiation fails? On one hand, the possibility of a negative evaluation might be the leverage needed to make the parents work seriously toward an agreeable outcome. On the other hand, it may be perceived as a threat, leading to posturing by the couple instead of cooperation. Or it might lead one of the parents to capitulate to an unacceptable agreement rather than risk an adverse appraisal. Beth has to consider whether these two roles are incompatible and whether she can reconcile her responsibilities without a conflict of interest. If she cannot, perhaps another worker should take over the job of evaluation and custody recommendation if the negotiations prove to be unsuccessful. If one has not been assigned already, perhaps the identification of a guardian *ad litem* can ensure that one individual speaks exclusively to Mike's interests.

Be Mindful of Process

Some process issues are evident in the informed consent explanations and other efforts Beth makes to set the stage for the therapeutic relationship. In addition, in order to ensure that her decisions are made both effectively and ethically, Beth should be candid, and her process transparent, so that the Ks know what she is looking for and what she will say when asked to render her report. She should endeavor to appreciate each family member's perspective, recognizing there is no objective standard for the ideal parent. In her interactions with the family, Beth should attempt to determine each parent's capacity for a relationship with Mike and each one's ability to anticipate and appreciate his needs in adjusting to whatever life changes result from this process. She should also use the process as an opportunity to educate the Ks about the short-term and long-term implications of their choices. She can explain the prevailing research about what happens when parents refuse to come to an agreement or refuse to disengage from their conflicts. In short, the Ks may win the battle but lose the war if the custody decision ruins their long-term relationship with Mike and diminishes Mike's capacity to build trusting intimate relationships in adulthood (Emery et al., 2005).

If the Ks perceive Beth to be an objective, caring, and competent individual, they may be amenable to her advice and suggestions for an acceptable compromise. For example, she may encourage them to consider a graduated arrangement, wherein Mike spends school vacations with his mother to work on developing a relationship with her husband and get a better sense of what life in that household and community might offer. Incremental change might help all parties appreciate the advantages of changed arrangements rather than simply the losses and disadvantages. For option 3 to work, Beth must take an active and helpful role in the family's problem-solving process.

Consult

Beth's consultations should help her solve her ethical dilemma and competently conduct her sessions and evaluations with the Ks. Given Beth's assignment to the case, we can presume that she has sufficient expertise and experience to work effectively with conflict in custody cases. Within that specialty area, the Ks' situation seems fairly customary, except perhaps for Beth's aversion to Mrs. K. Still, Beth should access assistance as needed to reinforce her fairness and competence in the case. For instance, if Beth has questions, the judge can clarify his or her expectations. Beth's supervisor or consultants can help her prepare for the negotiation sessions and assist her in examining her countertransference with Mrs. K. It is especially wise to seek professional input in contentious cases such as this. Custody matters seem particularly prone to generating malpractice complaints, so careful, confidential assistance will do much to support, inform, and protect Beth ("Practice Basics," 2005).

Document

Careful, thorough, and timely documentation will ensure Beth's command of the case facts and preparation of her report for the court. Unbiased and comprehensive record keeping will also serve Beth well should her competence or fairness in the case come into question. In terms of risk management, Beth should be certain that confidentiality waivers, informed consent agreements, and other forms are properly completed and stored.

Whatever the nature of her written report to the court, she should clearly describe the data and process she used to come to her conclusions and the basis for those conclusions. She and her supervisor or consultant should review the report for accuracy and to eliminate any pejorative descriptions or inflammatory language (Reamer, 2005).

Evaluate

The wisdom of her decision will be revealed in the process of carrying it out. If Beth decides to encourage the parents to negotiate an acceptable compromise, she will be able to determine their capacity for doing so fairly early on and make adjustments if needed. If she recommends a particular custody arrangement, she will observe the immediate impact on the family members and on the judge's decision. Her role, though, does not allow her to see the eventual implications of her efforts. This is common in the helping professions, wherein workers' efforts are of a short-term nature, but the outcomes (positive or negative) are long lasting. This may serve as a reminder to professionals to consider the long-term view, even in short-term work. It is also a reminder to use the available literature to develop as full an understanding as possible of the enduring effects of particular choices. While Beth may not know Mike as an adult, the literature in her field will help her anticipate longitudinal outcomes for youths like him.

Case Conclusion

Social workers and other helping professionals may become involved in custody disputes through a variety of mechanisms. Because such situations are typically contentious, the professionals involved must have absolute clarity about roles and expectations prior to commencing the work. In Beth's case, the judge's referral of the case structured her tasks and authority. On the other hand, a professional who is hired by one party or another must be alert to the role he or she is expected to play and the potential for conflicts of interest in carrying it out.

Like other long-term and short-term dilemmas, custody decisions involve numerous facts, beliefs, and intentions that must be balanced as workers seek solutions that are in the child's best interests. Workers in this field must be aware of their biases and preconceptions and effectively manage countertransference reactions. They must use the research literature to evaluate long- and short-term consequences and their clinical skills to help clients reach a decision. Consultation is essential for sound, defensible decisions, and courage is required in crafting and forthrightly advancing unpopular opinions.

SUMMARY

Short-term and long-term dilemmas involve not only competing goods but anticipation of possible effects that may or may not come to pass. Professionals can consult the available literature for guidance on prospective outcomes for their interventions. But even the best-established research will only provide an approximation of what might accrue for a particular case. Therefore, it is vital to maximize client input and autonomy in these types of dilemmas. Ultimately, the client will live with the decisions long after the worker's job is done. These situations deserve the utmost levels of integrity, humility, and honesty so that positive possibilities are maximized and harms minimized.

Chapter 6

Justice-vs.-Mercy Dilemmas

Dilemmas that involve the enforcement of policies usually come down to tensions between justice and mercy. Policies specifying processes, consequences, requirements, and eligibility standards exist to ensure that decisions are standardized according to certain criteria, rather than left to the whims of an individual. Such rules are intended to guarantee due process, ensuring that relevant facts and qualifications are taken into account and irrelevant variables are not. Thus, if a school has a zero-tolerance policy for alcohol, tobacco, and drug use, the presumption is that the criteria and consequences are handled consistently regardless of what substances are being used, where they are being used, or who is using them. However, the application of rules and policies is not always so clear cut. Because policies are imposed on humans by humans, other considerations exist in tension with justice. Compassion, empathy, extenuating circumstances, harsh consequences, leniency, and a host of other rationales can interfere with the implementation of just policies. Is it ethical for a teacher to report a teen caught smoking behind the gym, when he or she knows that doing so might result in grave consequences for his participation in extracurricular activities, which are essential for his college applications? How can it be unethical to give this student a break when one is familiar with the power of second chances and lessons learned from close calls? Such rationales have clear appeal. Yet justice has appeal as well. Would the teacher in this scenario give every student a similar break? Would every teacher be similarly flexible about the policy? And does giving a warning in this case teach the teen a lesson about forgiveness and that actions have consequences, or does it teach him that he can subvert rules and get away with it? As may be evident in this example, justice-vs.-mercy choices often have a greater impact than simply the decision itself. In that the purpose of any policy is to ensure fair and consistent treatment, the abrogation of the policy in one instance may lead to injustice in others.

TOO LEGIT TO QUIT

Alice is the director of a subsidized after-school program. To be eligible for the program, youths must carry an Axis I mental health diagnosis, such as ADHD or bipolar disorder. Tim and Victor have been in the program for a little over a month. Alice met their mother during enrollment and sees her occasionally when she comes to pick up the boys. On those occasions, she seemed harried, irritable, and depressed. Other staff members who are familiar with the family from other service settings have suggested that she has a drinking problem and a history of neglecting the boys. Her children, however, seem peaceful, pleasant, and well adjusted. Staff members report that despite the boys' ADHD diagnosis, they appear capable of great concentration and are able to stay on task when working on projects and with other children.

Alice suspects that Tim and Victor's mother has manufactured their symptoms to access free after-school care. Is it better to look the other way and allow them to stay or pursue the matter so that other more deserving kids can benefit from the program?

This case raises numerous questions about the program's practices as well as the core ethical dilemma. The answers to these questions will shape Alice's options. For example, how is eligibility determined? Are there processes in place to reevaluate admissions and admission criteria? Is there a waiting list for the program? How significant are the signs of incongruence between the boys' behavior and their diagnosis? Could the difference be explained by medications and treatment (or is it perhaps the result of the after-school program itself)? Is it possible that the boys' are indeed eligible and there is no fraud at play? How do Alice's impressions of the mother affect her concerns about the case? Do they make her inclined to believe the mother had bad intentions in placing the boys in the program? Do they feed Alice's desire to hold the mother accountable if the boys' diagnosis is indeed a fabrication? Or do they make Alice sympathetic to the boys and eager to keep them in the program and away from such an unhealthy caretaker?

Assess Options

Alice has several options, some of which will be contingent on the questions above and some on the outcomes of other options. She can:

1. Review the program application for any errors or omissions and act according to her findings
2. Require additional documentation or testing to determine Tim and Victor's eligibility and act based on her findings
3. Accept the application as it stands and take no further action
4. Review Victor and Tim's admissions and change practices to ensure that applicants' eligibility is more carefully determined in the future, while allowing them to remain in the program

Ethical theories and principles. Justice-vs.-mercy dilemmas align nicely with the two principle philosophies for determining right and wrong. A deontological or rule-based perspective would support the justice stance, presuming that policies are structured as they are for a reason and are intended for universal application, regardless of extenuating circumstances. A utilitarian or ends-based philosophy would affirm merciful responses made in consideration of the effects of the decision. Alice's first two choices follow a justice framework and are appealing from a rules-based perspective. They would have her review the information she has or gather further information and apply her findings to the existing policy, regardless of the consequences. One perhaps unsettling rule issue is the appropriateness of reexamining admissions after they have occurred, if that is not a standard program policy. Would we want every program to retroactively review—and perhaps dismiss—participants based on observations of them following their admission? The process of periodically evaluating eligibility is a common one, but the issue here is what prompts the review. The practice is ethically sound when done regularly, based on pre-stated criteria such as specific time periods or as required by client accomplishments or milestones. A decision to review Tim and Victor's case or demand further evidence of their condition becomes ethically questionable when it is done solely because of suspicions staff members have about their mother. The principle of fairness would ask us to consider whether we would review other kids in the same circumstances if we are going to review Tim and Victor. Perhaps the agency has a policy of revisiting admissions when a child's presentation is at odds with the eligibility criteria. If that is the case, a review of their admissions is sound and proper from a deontological perspective.

A rules-based perspective would be less supportive of letting the case stand (effectively, the third and fourth options). These choices seem to endorse looking the other way when evidence might suggest services and resources are being misdirected. Alternatively, options 3 and 4 suggest that once decisions are made, they should never be revisited. While the choice to leave the case alone may be understandable in Tim and Victor's case, it is not a practice that we would want to propagate.

This is an apt point at which to address the ethics of rationing. Rules and policies are instituted to ensure the fair and appropriate allocation of services: Medicaid guidelines specify enrollment qualifications, special education is reserved for students with certain intellectual or medical needs, and so forth. Such criteria are not bad, in and of themselves. They ensure that the programs and funding are used as intended, and as such, they are in keeping with the ethical principles of justice and communitarianism. Justice does not require that people be treated equally, because individual needs and conditions are not equal, but it does mean that they should be treated equitably and evenhandedly (Beauchamp & Pinkard, 1983; Gutman & Thompson, 1984). Communitarianism suggests that any individual's right to resources is limited by concern for the needs of others. When social workers participate in the allocation of services, they are acting as stewards of resources, simultaneously caring for individuals and for the interests of the individuals who fund the services or those who may also need the services in the future. We saw examples of this in chapter 4 with the cost-saving mechanisms employed in managed care. Communitarianism requires that those pooled resources be used wisely.

While there is ethical support for rationing, vigilance is required to ensure that the processes for prioritizing access to services and for informing recipients are also ethical. Such processes should be rational, explicit, and transparent and offer broad opportunities for various sources of input (Boyle & Callahan, 1995). Once the basis for rationing is determined, fairness and informed consent are required so that those who receive services and those who do not understand their options, the limits, and their right to appeal.

Each of Alice's choices has advantages and disadvantages when viewed through an ends-based perspective. Reviewing Tim and Victor's admission may affirm their appropriateness for the program. This would be good in that it would put to rest apprehensions about their mother and concerns about the possible misallocation of services. Conversely, a review may reveal that the information in their case was skewed or inaccurate. Alleviating them of stigmatizing diagnoses and referring them to more appropriate services could be positive results of such a finding. Programmatically, this finding could reveal flaws in the admissions screening process that should be remedied. Perhaps the program relies entirely on parents' self-reports instead of independent diagnostic evaluation or mandatory physician referrals that would confirm the child's condition. A finding that Tim and Victor are inappropriately enrolled in the program may lead to an audit to ensure that similar mistakes are not made in the future. This may be unflattering for the agency and a lot of work for the staff, but it has the advantage of ensuring that the program is serving those for whom it was intended, which is both a resource allocation concern and a practice issue. Also within the agency context, Alice may experience backlash from staff members, who may be sorry they ever shared their observations about the boys. Workers may focus on Tim and Victor's interests at the exclusion of other considerations and wonder why Alice couldn't leave well enough alone rather than digging around in eligibility determination processes.

Less positive consequences are also possible. Asking for more information to substantiate their eligibility may unfairly single the boys out. It may aggravate and alienate their mother and lead her to withdraw them from the program if providing the additional information proves too troubling. Requiring a review of Tim and Victor may set an unfortunate precedent that any time a child does not appear to fit in, his or her eligibility is rechecked. Other parents could learn that such activity is going on and begin to feel either judgmental toward the boys or insecure themselves. If Tim and Victor were enrolled inappropriately, some of the options would require terminating them from the program, which could have a detrimental effect on their well-being, opportunities, and social supports. Tim and Victor may feel hurt, confused, or rejected if they are required to leave the program. Depending on the funding for the program and the nature of the error that led to Tim and Victor's enrollment, it is possible that financial penalties or other repercussions might accrue for their mother or the program. If Tim and Victor are allowed to stay in a program for which they are ineligible, they are taking the places of other deserving youths. Further, their mother's difficulty in meeting their needs goes unaddressed, as does her (potentially) deceptive behavior.

When she weighs the choices based on the goal of maximizing positive consequences (beneficence) and limiting negative ones (nonmaleficence), the last of Alice's choices seems the most sound. Good things may happen if the admission policies and processes are reviewed and necessary changes are made, but the benefits that Tim and Victor are deriving from the program are not disrupted, if in fact it is found that their admission was inappropriate. Yet this solution still means they are in a program for which they are ill suited, they are taking the place of qualified children, and their mother's deceit is being rewarded. Perhaps a new option can be formulated to address these remaining troubling outcomes; for instance, Alice might discuss the boys' assets with their mother and explore other programs or afterschool activities for which they are eligible. Involvement in afterschool sports teams, clubs, or other activities may ultimately be more fulfilling and less stigmatizing than the program in which they currently participate and may help them to build new strengths and social networks.

Ethical principles would endorse any of the options that involve reexamining the admission criteria and Tim and Victor's particular eligibility. Specifically, fidelity would compel Alice to be trustworthy in her administration of the program and to ensure that she does not shirk her responsibilities to be a careful steward of scarce resources. Justice supports the fair and transparent use of services, ensuring that they are distributed equitably. Veracity supports truthfulness, requiring Alice to be candid in explaining her motivations for reviewing admissions or in terminating Tim and Victor from the program. Veracity might also encourage truthfulness in others. As such, ignoring signs that the youths are misplaced could be a form of complicity with fraud, and thus a violation of the principle of honesty.

Laws and policies. In weighing her choices, Alice should look into several regulatory issues. The funding that supports Tim and Victor's participation in the program and that specifies the eligibility criteria would be an obvious place to start. Alice needs to find out whether the agency's screening process conforms to the funding agency's expectations and what penalties there might be for improper enrollments in the program. If the program is funded under a contract, there may be benchmarks Alice needs to meet for the program to be eligible for continued funding. Depending on what the benchmarks are, Tim and Victor's enrollment may positively or negatively skew the program's eligibility. It will also be helpful to know if funding policies allow or require periodic review or continuous authorizations for services. Such stipulations would facilitate a reexamination of Tim and Victor's participation as well as that of all other enrollees as a matter of policy.

Alice should familiarize herself with the criteria for entry to the program as well as the criteria for continued participation. For example, there are likely policies and procedures that dictate types of behavior that are grounds for dismissal from the program (fighting, etc.). Is it possible that continued need is one of the specified criteria? If so, Alice would probably want to check to ensure that Tim and Victor's good performance in her program is not anomalous—perhaps symptoms of their ADHD are more severe in the classroom and their classroom performance indicates that they *do* actually need after-school services.

But what if program policies do not specify criteria for continued participation? Alice could suggest that certain policies be implemented to address this and similar cases. For example, would the funder allow diagnoses to be only a part of the eligibility criteria? It could still be weighted more heavily than other factors, giving precedence to those with diagnoses, yet also consider other needs. Such a broadening of the eligibility criteria may permit the continued participation of children like Tim and Victor, who, despite having relatively mild ADHD, nevertheless have other risk factors that may be addressed by program participation. Allowing Tim and Victor to remain in the program while Alice works with the school or funding agency to improve standards may be a win-win scenario—she is being honest with funders about needed changes, thereby honoring her responsibilities as steward of the limited resources, and in the meantime, Tim and Victor continue participating as long as their diagnoses are accurate and sustained.

Values. Alice can draw upon her values and those of the profession in choosing a desirable course of action. If Alice's value system places a high premium on honor and her personal and professional reputation, as well as that of her agency, she will likely embrace a strategy to ensure that Tim and Victor's participation is legitimate. Values that emphasize harmony, championing the underdog, or not tinkering with the status quo would suggest that she take no further action. The values of the staff; the program's board of directors, advisory committee, or parents' council; or another entity may also influence Alice's decision. Any of these groups might embrace punitive or inclusive action, depending on their perspectives and relations with the boys and their mother.

The social work profession's values appear to encourage Alice to act to uphold the just use of agency resources. The value of integrity would specifically require action to support ethical practices. The value placed on social justice means ensuring access to "needed information, services, and resources" (NASW, 1999, p. 5). The value placed on individual dignity and worth distinguishes socially responsible self-determination from fraudulent or inappropriate choices that clients might make. Therefore, the value does not compel workers to unilaterally accept clients' behaviors, but it does require that people be treated with dignity and that individual interests be properly reconciled with societal interests. In this last element, we can see a parallel with Alice's responsibility to ensure that services are available to those for whom they were intended.

Information. Further case information will be essential for Alice's decision making and the steps that follow. For example, have the boys' diagnoses been verified? On what basis were their diagnoses given? Can anyone explain the apparent discrepancies? What is the status of their father? Who else is part of Tim and Victor's family or support system? Are other agencies or health care providers involved? Do others note the discrepancies between their behavior and diagnoses, aside from the staff in Alice's program? If, by chance, the diagnoses were inappropriately rendered or fraudulently obtained, are other forms of misconduct involved? Is it possible that the boys have been inappropriately placed in other programs, such as special education? To what extent is it proper or necessary for Alice's investigation to extend beyond the limits of propriety for her program alone?

It would be helpful to know more about Victor and Tim's mother and her needs, beliefs, and motivations. If Alice and her staff knew more about the issues behind her presentation, they might be better equipped to reach out to her respectfully and constructively. For example, if the mother misconstrued her sons' behaviors in order to use the program as free after-school care, could Alice's program assist her in finding a more suitable arrangement? If the mother is depressed, using substances, under stress, and in need of respite care, are there resources to help her and ensure that the boys are not in a precarious situation? If she is angry and resistant to help and the boys have few other supports, the after-school program, appropriate or not, might be a valuable lifeline for the perilously isolated brothers.

Standards. Standards in the NASW Code of Ethics address both the decision that must be made and the considerations for carrying it out. Their applicability will depend on the ways that the facts of the case evolve and shape Alice's decision. For example, the NASW (1999) Code forbids social workers to "participate in, condone, or be associated with dishonesty, fraud, or deception" (4.04). If Alice decides to look further into the boys' suitability for the program and discovers fraud, she may need to take action to ensure that she and the agency are not complicit in any wrongdoing in allowing the boys to continue participating in the program. Similarly, if her review reveals unethical behavior on the part of staff or another professional in misdiagnosing the boys, the Code may offer guidance. For example, the Code states that "Social workers should take adequate measures to discourage, prevent, expose, and correct the unethical conduct of colleagues" (NASW, 1999, 2.11a). They should be familiar with policies and procedures for dealing with unethical behavior and, if feasible and constructive, discuss their concerns first with the colleague involved. The Code does not specify who counts as a colleague, so Alice might seek consultation to determine whether this is intended to apply only to colleagues within her agency, within the social work profession, or across disciplines. However, in that the intent of these provisions is to protect vulnerable consumers from unscrupulous practices, it is probably wise to interpret the mandate as broadly as possible in an effort to thwart wrongdoing. As such, "colleague" may mean any helping professional with whom one is acquainted. However "colleague" is defined, the decision to report one for inappropriate conduct or offer him or her a chance to improve practice without reporting is, in itself, a justice-vs.-mercy dilemma.

Other relevant sections of the Code apply to Tim and Victor's needs if they are ultimately terminated from the program. Specifically, "Social workers should take reasonable steps to avoid abandoning clients who are still in need of services. Social workers should withdraw services precipitously only under unusual circumstances, giving careful consideration to all factors in the situation and taking care to minimize possible adverse effects. Social workers should assist in making appropriate arrangements for continuation of services when necessary" (NASW, 1999, 1.16b). They should also "notify clients promptly and seek the transfer, referral, or continuation of services in relation to the clients' needs and preferences" (NASW, 1999, 1.16e).

Be Mindful of Process

As noted earlier, Alice's decision and processes will be more acceptable if they meet the principle of fairness. That is, whatever standard or review she requires for Tim and Victor and whatever consequences follow should be employed for all others in the same circumstances.

The most delicate process issues arise if Alice decides to seek more information and, based on that, must dismiss the boys from the program. The first process consideration is to ensure that her decisions aren't based on rumor, stereotypes, or conjecture. Approaching this task with objectivity, transparency, and respect for the parties involved, including her staff, Victor and Tim, and their mother, may diminish defensiveness and suspicion. The key is not to alienate Tim and Victor's mother, as she is a necessary partner in their well-being, whether they remain in the program or not. If Alice decides to follow up on the suspicions and indeed finds that the boys were inappropriately placed in the program and cannot stay, she must carefully manage their transition so that expulsion from the program does not harm the boys. Proper timing, age-appropriate explanations, available alternatives, and sensitive termination processes will all be essential in mitigating damage to them.

Consult. Being an administrator can be an isolating position. To whom can people without supervisors turn when they have ethical dilemmas? Hopefully Alice has colleagues and mentors within and outside her agency whom she can contact for confidential problem-solving assistance. In this case, they can help her with the philosophical, legal, and policy-related dimensions of her decision. Hopefully, they can also offer support should she endure backlash or entreaties from her staff to reconsider her decision in Tim and Victor's case.

Other consultation may address the clinical and regulatory aspects of the case. The agency attorney or the project officer from the funding source can help Alice translate admission guidelines. Alice may know administrators in programs receiving similar funding and turn to them for feedback on the ways they have interpreted the guidelines. The key in these consultations is not to discuss her concerns about Tim and Victor specifically, but simply to ensure that Alice's program is using the best practices possible in eligibility determination.

Consultation with agency staff would help Alice explore the consequences of various options and obtain missing information about Tim and Victor. For example, direct care workers can provide input about the boys' behavior and its congruence with their stated diagnosis. Staff discussions might reveal more information on their situation, referral options, or constructive linkages with their mother.

Another source of assistance for Alice may come from her program's board of directors or advisory committee. Leaders in nonprofit organizations routinely consult with members of the board, based on their positions (e.g., president, treasurer), expertise (e.g., accounting, personnel), and trustworthiness. Alice's dilemma does not seem worthy of sharing on the basis of a board member's need to know, but she could share it to get the views of a reliable confidante as she selects a plan of action.

Finally, there may be additional people available for consultation regarding Tim and Victor's situation if Alice and her staff have permission to reach out to these individuals. For example, contact with the boys' diagnostician, doctor, and teachers and other social workers might help Alice fill in some of the blanks in their histories and their family dynamics.

Document

The existing program records for Tim and Victor's case will be important sources of information regarding their original eligibility and their behaviors once they entered the program. Alice should be certain that the observations that led to her dilemma are well documented. Her consultations and considerations in solving the dilemma should be spelled out as well, along with the rationale for her final decision. If she decides to review Tim and Victor's appropriateness for the program and, as a result, act on it, the process for notifying the family, seeking alternative arrangements, and any other consequences of the decision should be recorded.

Evaluate

The clearer Alice is on her objectives, the easier it will be for her to evaluate the effects of her decision. If her intention is to help Tim and Victor's continued growth by allowing them to stay in the program (with or without a review of their eligibility), she should be alert to signs that their participation has had a positive effect in that regard. If her objective is to ensure the propriety of the program's processes, she should determine whether the review of Tim and Victor's case helped to meet those ends. Of course, she must also be alert to the unintended consequences of her decision. Did her decision not to review Tim and Victor's case (or in allowing them to stay when they were ineligible) mean that other qualified children were turned away or kept on a waiting list? If the decision involves revisiting the brothers' admissions, does she find that they have been harmed, either by the process or the outcomes? Can steps still be taken to mitigate those harms? Could such situations be handled differently in the future?

A different level of evaluation asks, "What should be done to avoid such problems entirely?" Sometimes a blend of justice and mercy can be achieved when systems allow for proportional justice. That is, in apportioning punishments or consequences, contextual or mitigating factors are taken into account so that the result is not a one-size-fits-all response. Thus, for example, Tim and Victor's participation in the program might be reduced to evaluate their capacity to function without the program, rather than discharging them entirely.

Case Conclusion

The ethical decision-making process should help Alice arrive at a sound conclusion, both for the program and for Tim and Victor. It might keep Alice from making a decision that is easy in the short run (ignoring the concerns) but is troubling in the long run, for the boys or for the program. The process may or may not help Alice address a question underlying the entire dilemma: How far does she want to go in pursuit of justice? Is her goal simply to ensure that the boys are not in her program by mistake, and the services are reserved for those who properly qualify? Is it to rectify a wrong that may have been done to them in misdiagnosis? And is all of this worth it?

Too often the default in ethical dilemmas is mercy, not out of good intent but out of pragmatism. The red tape, research, deliberations, and communications necessary to enforce policies or rectify errors may seem too cumbersome, or the outcomes too insignificant, to warrant the effort. To use a highway patrol analogy, is it more trouble to write a ticket than issue a warning? The answer in the short run is that it probably is. However, before we are too hasty to default to mercy simply on the ease of it, we should be alert to long-term or cumulative considerations. In Tim and Victor's case, for example, what are the cumulative effects of administrators refusing to adhere to eligibility criteria or explore possible errors in admissions? In this example we have focused on the deleterious effects of misdiagnosis or misplacement on Tim and Victor as individuals, but there are profound consequences for resource allocation and fairness when the individual decision is multiplied over an array of programs and services. Were such programs to be audited, what would be the cumulative financial impact of intentional or accidental impropriety?

We can also predict potentially problematic long-term effects of inaction by referring back to the highway patrol example. Repeated acts of mercy, such as issuing warnings when tickets are called for, may leave the perpetrator emboldened rather than chastened. News broadcasts regularly cover cases of motor vehicle accidents or violent assaults in which the person responsible received a trail of second chances in the form of warnings, suspended sentences, plea agreements, or reduced charges. There are many reasons beyond mercy for these accommodations, yet they demonstrate how repeatedly favoring mercy over justice can have substantial negative long-term effects. An ethical decision-making model can help Alice look beyond the immediate concerns to the large-scale and long-term impact of enforcing program policies.

SECONDHAND CLOTHES

Lilly is an elementary school social worker. Many of her clients come from impoverished families, and she uses a wide array of charitable resources to help meet the children's basic needs. One child, Zeke, particularly tugs at her heartstrings. His hair is greasy, and he often wears clothes that are ill fitting and unfashionable. Despite the school's rules regarding civility, the other kids tease him, calling him "Zeke the Freak," which he appears to endure with stoicism.

Lilly has spoken to Zeke's parents to find out how she can help with food, heat, clothes, and other needs, but they have flatly refused on the basis that their culture fosters self-sufficiency and forbids them to accept charity. Lilly is discouraged by their resistance and feels that their pride is leading them to put their needs before their son's. Lilly's son is two years older than Zeke, and she would like to give him clothes that her son no longer uses. She often buys him a box of milk and sits with him when she sees him alone at a table by himself in the lunchroom. Can she reconcile her sympathies and responsibilities in this case with his parents' clear refusal of her overtures?

In this dilemma, justice and mercy come not in the form of policies and exceptions but rather in the tension between expectations and compassion. Zeke's parents have clear beliefs (family policies, if you will) about accepting help from others. Lilly's sympathy for Zeke compels her to seek exceptions to those family norms so that he can be spared hurt and derision. Her dilemma is whether she will abide by the parents' wishes, subvert them, or try to find some method of compromise. Perhaps there are other ways to help Zeke that conform with his family's rules, in effect blending justice and mercy.

Assess Options

Lilly's options might be seen as spanning a continuum from avoiding any activities that the parents may construe as charity to working collaboratively to come up with compromise measures to channeling resources to Zeke without his parents' awareness or permission. The options may also be ordered sequentially, in that Lilly could try to bridge the gulf with the parents and arrive at a mutually acceptable alternative and, failing that, retreat to either of the more extreme options. Strategy will also be a question in this case. Might Lilly involve child protective services in an effort to improve Zeke's living conditions? Is such a referral just and appropriate, or would it be an artifact of aggravation with the family? Is a caring family with insufficient resources to buy new clothes or pay for hot water going to be a priority for child welfare authorities? And what effect would that referral have on Lilly's ability to work constructively with Zeke and his family in the future? What role does Lilly's obvious affection for Zeke have on her decision making in the case? Is countertransference constructive in her efforts to help Zeke, or does it hinder her effectiveness? Does it blind her to the similar needs of other children whom she might view less favorably? The answers to these and other questions offer a foundation for understanding Lilly's motivations and interests in pursuing an ethical conclusion to this dilemma.

Ethical theories and principles. Of the following choices, which would we prefer if it were rendered in the form of a universal rule—honoring parents' wishes in regard to their children, working with parents to help them meet their children's needs, or helping children, even against the parents' wishes? Clearly the middle choice has the most universal appeal, as there are exceptions in the other two options. We would not want always to be bound by parents' wishes, for example, in cases of abuse, but we should also be reluctant to usurp parents' rights by siding with their children when the parents' prerogatives are causing no harm.

What consequences must we weigh in looking at Lilly's choices through a utilitarian lens? Following the parents' wishes would honor their position and demonstrate respect for their culture. It might help Lilly develop a constructive relationship with the family, which might generate benefits in the long run. However, there is a limit to supporting their position. If their resistance to outside intervention extends to other areas of child care (they fail to access proper health and medical care or cannot properly heat their home or provide adequate nutrition), then Lilly cannot simply acquiesce to their wishes. Absent any improvement in the family's capacity to help Zeke bathe and dress appropriately, he will probably continue to be the subject of his classmates' derision. His staid response to their taunts may be a sign of strength and inner confidence, or it may mask profound hurt, shame, or anger. His current cognitive and emotional responses, of course, can lead to long-term consequences, more likely negative than positive (Rutter, 1990).

Acceding to the parent's wishes may prove difficult for Lilly, given her emotional reactions to them and her compassion for Zeke. Yet working cooperatively with the family may improve Lilly's appreciation of their culture and make her more sensitive to the various ways that charitable impulses are experienced by recipients. It may foster a positive and trusting relationship between the family and the school. To the extent they are able to craft one, an agreeable solution may help improve Zeke's comfort at school and his short-term and long-term well-being. Perhaps some resources can have reverberating positive effects for other members of the family system as well.

A variety of consequences could result from a decision to overrule the family's wishes by surreptitiously providing clothes or money or by colluding with Zeke to keep secrets from his parents. While the assistance may help Zeke fit in with his classmates, he may pay a price in confusion, discomfort, or divided loyalties in hiding the gifts from his parents. Encouraging dishonesty, even to provide assistance that the family has declined, reflects negatively on Lilly, perhaps even putting her position or reputation at risk. It also sends a negative message to Zeke. If his parents find out, they may feel angry or betrayed, and they may generalize their ill will to the whole school system, which Lilly represents. Both Zeke and Lilly may pay a price for the deception. It is not guaranteed that these acts of charity will help Zeke fit in, given his history with the class. As such, of the three options, the last option represents the greatest risks with the least assurance of benefits.

The principle of autonomy would support the parents' rights to their beliefs and require Lilly to respect those beliefs. While Zeke may wish for appropriate clothes, toys, and other goods, his age precludes his autonomous choices, subjugating them to his parents' will. The principles of justice, fidelity, and veracity also support the choices that honor the parents' rules or include them in coming up with a mutually acceptable decision. These principles would rule out false promises or deceptive acts by Lilly. The principle of justice in particular would also question the appropriateness of taking Zeke on as a special cause over other children with similar needs, with or without his family's consent.

Laws and policies. As discussed in chapter 3, parents are granted wide latitude to make decisions on behalf of their minor children, particularly those as young as Zeke. The expectation, then, would be that Lilly should respect those decisions, unless they are putting Zeke's health or well-being at risk. An open question in this case is whether Zeke's condition meets the threshold for neglect, which would warrant a referral to child protective services, or is simply an unfortunate artifact of poverty and parental choice, which would not. Neglect, in the legal sense, must be serious enough in nature to cause harm to the child, either physically or emotionally. Not enough food, inadequate clothing for the weather, a failure to obtain medicine to ameliorate a medical condition, and insufficient attention to develop reasonable attachment would all be prevailing issues in distinguishing a neglectful family from a merely poor or peculiar one. Lilly will need to be familiar with the laws in her state before she can conclude which situation characterizes Zeke's family. In deference to her responsibilities as a mandated reporter, Lilly might simply refer the family to child protective services so that they can make the determination of Zeke's risk.

Lilly should also consult school policies regarding the rights of parents to provide or withhold permission for various services and referrals and also in regard to staff responsibilities in singling out individual students for assistance. The latter query is really about the basis for Lilly's decision to focus her charitable efforts on Zeke. If she is doing it on the basis of his need and would do so for other youths, that would seem consistent with her job responsibilities and with basic human kindness. However, if her particular affection for Zeke has compelled her to help him, even despite his parents' wishes, she may be overstepping her boundaries and those set by school policy. Whether or not policies address this dilemma, consultation with other professionals will help her sort out her motivations and determine whose interests she is advancing by her actions.

Values. Fundamentally, this case represents a value clash between Zeke's parents and his social worker. Rooted in their culture and perhaps religious traditions, Zeke's family values self-sufficiency and thus rejects acts of charity, government assistance, and social services. Embedded in these values may be other beliefs—that it is wise not to be beholden to others, that charity should be reserved for those who are in greater need, or that accepting gifts is a sign of weakness. Understanding the values that underlie the parents' position will be important if Lilly is to pursue option 2 and craft a mutually acceptable alternative with the family.

Clearly, Lilly's values differ from the family's. She may value nice clothes and material possessions. She may value sharing her abundance with others. She may believe that students need social supports and that parents who are iconoclasts may not appreciate the damage their children experience. As noted, Lilly must be aware of her motivations in her compassion for Zeke and her efforts to help him. She must also be aware of the ways in which her judgments about Zeke's parents may alienate them and ultimately harm her efforts to help Zeke.

The values of the social work profession have merit in a consideration of Lilly's choices. Her instincts to help Zeke are rooted in the value of service, providing assistance to people in need, and perhaps even fighting injustice, in light of his poverty and his treatment by his classmates. While she may see her efforts at securing resources for him as bolstering his dignity and worth, she cannot do so at the expense of the family's self-respect or their relationships with her, the school, or their son. Her actions must be in keeping with the value of integrity, and with appreciation for cultural differences that shape the family's beliefs and self-determination.

Information. Zeke's case brings to mind a number of questions that may shape Lilly's decision-making process. Clearly his age is a relevant factor, as is the nature of the dispute with the family. A teenager whose family wishes to prohibit him or her from receiving needed benefits might have the maturity and competence to decide independently whether to comply or rebel. A social worker in that case would be able to contrast the youth's rights with the family's rights and engage the student in a conversation about the relative risks and merits of particular choices. Since Zeke is an elementary school student, such an option is ruled out. The effect of the family's beliefs on Zeke is another relevant consideration. Refusing assistance to improve his appearance or wardrobe is different from refusing a medical intervention or organ donation to save his life. The magnitude of the intervention and the impact of refusal are a significant consideration. In Zeke's case, the issue would not seem to warrant formal or informal steps to overrule the parents' prerogatives.

The nature and origin of Zeke's deficits are relevant in Lilly's decision whether or not to refer the case for a child abuse investigation. Perhaps she knows enough about the family and understands their objections to services sufficiently to assess that he is not at risk of neglect and that a child welfare referral would be fruitless and perhaps harmful. If she does not have this information, it may be wise to refer the case for a specialized assessment by child protective authorities.

It would be helpful to have more information on the family's cultural and religious background so that Lilly can better understand the basis for their position and the possibilities for compromise. Lilly might contact indigenous leaders from their culture or faith community, who could help her understand the family's position or perhaps be developed as allies in meeting Zeke's needs. They might be able to broker an arrangement whereby Zeke could "work" around the school in exchange for clothes, books, and other needed items. These leaders could also enhance Lilly's cultural competence in her work with other youths at the school.

Finally, it would help to know about the family's relationship with the school and other social institutions. Is this an isolated family, suspicious of and at war with the world? Or is the family connected to but wary of social institutions? Is the family confident in their beliefs but defensive about their poverty and weary of do-gooders like Lilly? This historical case information would expand Lilly's understanding of the parents' position and whether or not their resistance to her overtures is indicative of other possible hazards for Zeke.

Standards. Several standards in the NASW Code of Ethics have bearing on Lilly's decision. The Code states, "Social workers' primary responsibility is to promote the well-being of clients. In general, clients' interests are primary. However, social workers' responsibility to the larger society or specific legal obligations may on limited occasions supersede the loyalty owed clients, and clients should be so advised" (NASW, 1999, 1.01). While the first part of this standard might be construed as supporting Lilly's efforts for Zeke at all costs, the last sentence may be presumed to qualify her actions, in light of his parents' legal rights.

Further, the NASW (1999) Code requires social workers to "have a knowledge base of their clients' cultures and be able to demonstrate competence in the provision of services that are sensitive to clients' cultures and to differences among people and cultural groups" (1.05b). This would endorse Lilly's search for information and understanding before she passes judgment on the parents' beliefs or acts to undermine them. The standard that forbids social workers from participating in, condoning, or being associated with dishonesty, fraud, or deception would also clearly preclude collusion with Zeke against his parents' values and preferences (NASW, 1999).

Social work standards are also relevant to the possibility that Lilly may refer Zeke's case to child protective services. The Code states, "Social workers should inform clients, to the extent possible, about the disclosure of confidential information and the potential consequences, when feasible before the disclosure is made. This applies whether social workers disclose confidential information on the basis of a legal requirement or client consent" (NASW, 1999, 1.07d). Thus, this standard would suggest that Lilly talk with Zeke's parents about her concerns and her rationale for referral. The presumption here is that such a conversation would be respectful of the parents and help Lilly preserve a working alliance with them, in spite of the report, and that discussing the referral with a parent won't inappropriately skew the investigation, if one is pursued by CPS. It is entirely possible, however, given the family's feelings about any form of assistance, that they will not respond favorably to the referral, with or without forewarning by Lilly.

Be Mindful of Process

Conversing with the family prior to making a CPS referral is one example of a process consideration in this case. Lilly should anticipate the ways in which she might carry out her other choices, as this preparation may shed light on the viability of her options. If she decides to acquiesce to the parents' wishes, can she do so in a respectful fashion? Can she involve herself in other strategies to bolster Zeke's self-esteem and improve the climate in his classroom? Are the school's policies on civility and bullying being properly enforced (a justice-vs.-mercy issue)? What interventions might Lilly and the faculty use to improve the ways that Zeke and other students are treated? As these options suggest, the decision to honor the parents' beliefs need not mean that Lilly has to abandon all efforts to help Zeke. In fact, it may force her to look at other more comprehensive change efforts targeted at more significant issues than simply Zeke's clothes.

If Lilly decides to pursue plans to give Zeke hand-me-downs and other goods, she should think through how exactly that could be done without his parents' knowledge. Would he change clothes at school? Shower there? Would doing so lead to less ostracization than what he experiences now? How would his borrowed clothes be stored and cleaned? Would Lilly's kindnesses run the risk of leading to more compromising boundary crossings? How would she explain the donations (or other charitable acts) to Zeke?

Lilly's ability to craft a compromise with Zeke's parents will depend on her history with them, the nature of their objections, and her therapeutic skills. Do they share Lilly's concerns about the way Zeke is treated by his classmates and the effects it may have on him? If they refuse material gifts, would they object to favors—allowing him to shower at school, if facilities were available? Would they allow him to participate in clubs or other extracurricular activities that might help him to express himself in a positive way and develop a group of social supports? Perhaps the parents have suggestions about what they and the school can do to address the difficulties Zeke is facing.

Lilly may draw on her clinical skills in developing a constructive process with Zeke's parents. De Jong and Berg (2001) outline how solution-focused interviewing can be used to engage reluctant clients in treatment. This approach emphasizes client strengths and the "co-construction of cooperation" (De Jong & Berg, 2001, p. 361). Techniques such as this (and others to address resistance) may be useful in this case. Ultimately, the compromise option may not be successful, but it is more likely to prevail if Lilly or some other person can forge an honest and caring relationship with the parents as well as with their son.

Consult

As suggested earlier, Lilly should discuss her concerns with other school personnel to get guidance on organizational policies and their ideas about addressing Zeke's situation. Lilly's supervisor and a CPS representative can address the advisability of a CPS referral in this case. Zeke and his parents can also be a source of assistance in acquainting Lilly with the tenets of their belief system and the ways she can be of help to them. They may also link her with other resources from their faith community or cultural group to learn more.

Consultation will also help Lilly look at her motivations in helping Zeke, and in apparently singling him out for assistance. It may also be beneficial for her to think more deeply about the nature of charitable intent. Because it feels good to be a giver, and donations and other charitable efforts fill an apparent need, the presumption is that receivers should be grateful. Yet being on the receiving end of charitable efforts is undoubtedly more complex than that. While people may appreciate receiving a gift or having their suffering alleviated, charity reinforces power and resource differentials. It may highlight the fact that a person is unable to meet his or her own needs and thus diminish the person's sense of dignity and self-worth. When we think about it this way, it does not seem so unreasonable that some people would rather go without than be diminished in the process of receiving (Cleveland, 2005). Thoughtful, trusting discussions will sensitize Lilly to these value differences and to her judgments in this case and others.

Document

As in any case, documentation should begin with the needs that gave rise to Lilly's concerns. She should note her conversations with the parents and their position on her offers of help, preferably using verbatim quotes. Her records should reflect her consultations, the information received on the case, and her efforts to create change for Zeke, whether directly on his behalf or via improvements to the school environment. Given her responsibility as a mandated reporter, Lilly should clearly note the suspicions and observations that led her to make a CPS referral or the rationale and assessment for her decision not to do so.

Evaluate

With an open mind and sufficient information, Lilly may be successful in cooperatively crafting an intervention with Zeke's parents. But whether or not she is able to achieve her objective of making Zeke's school days easier, she can learn from the experience, reassess her strategies, and consider other options. Two of her original options may be defaults for the compromise effort, though the weight of evidence would seem to be against violating the parents' wishes. If Lilly makes a referral to CPS, she should be alert to the family's response and the degree to which the referral was warranted and effective in changing Zeke's circumstances. At any point in the change process, bridging the differences with Zeke's parents will require considerable effort and goodwill on Lilly's part and probably on the family's as well. The support Lilly receives throughout may enhance her effectiveness in the case and her ability to objectively evaluate the results.

Case Conclusion

Children's cruelty toward each other can be heartbreaking. For the victims, taunts can create personal resolve and fortitude or personal pain that lasts a lifetime. It is the stuff of novels, music, newscasts, and film. When students retaliate with violence to mockery and bullying, psychologists, criminologists, teachers, social workers, and others weigh in on interventions that might have prevented such carnage. Lilly's compassion for Zeke is understandable, and her desire to reach out to him may be appropriately intended to avert an array of harms. Nevertheless, Zeke's family has well-established rights to raise him as they see fit. Overruling those rights requires a compelling case and evidence of substantial harms. It involves significant risks and carries a questionable probability of success. It also focuses intervention efforts on changing the family or the child, instead of changing the environment that is hostile to the child's appearance and the family's values. Resolving the tensions in this case requires a search for compromise, for creative alternatives, and for a true understanding of the concept of charitable intent.

SUMMARY

Justice-vs.-mercy dilemmas challenge our heads and tug at our heartstrings. Justice requires rational, transparent, and fairly applied policies—a hard standard in a world where interpretations and circumstances can vary. Take a moment and imagine yourself in private practice, and try to come up with a policy for selecting pro bono (free care) cases. Every scheme has its flaws. You set a firm income limit, but then how is the case of a family with eight children weighed against that of a single parent or a couple with three children in private school? Should an apparently well-to-do woman qualify when her abusive husband controls her through a meager allowance? The more sophisticated the policy, the more data and investigation are required and the more time is diverted from services to screening. Clear policies are not easy to create, and even when we have them, our human instincts and compassion tempt us to make exceptions in the name of leniency or benevolence.

Reconciling these two tensions requires an appreciation of the consequences of strict adherence to either position. Too strong a focus on justice may fail to account for harsh or unintended outcomes. Such an outlook may fail to appreciate extenuating circumstances and other contextual factors, and it may preclude the benefits that can come from teachable moments and second chances. Overreliance on mercy may mean that rules and regulations are flouted or become irrelevant. It can mean that policies are unevenly, unfairly, and perhaps prejudicially enforced, and the intentions that gave rise to the policy are never fulfilled. Weighing the considerations and facts for each dilemma will reveal the particular constellation of risks and benefits for the individual case and for others who may be in the same circumstances.

Thoughtful decision making about justice and mercy may reveal acceptable compromises in the form of proportional justice. In fact, planners, policy makers, and administrators can incorporate the consideration of mitigating circumstances in the criteria and guidelines they create, thereby reducing the likelihood of dilemmas involving choices between adherence and exceptions. Yet even with incremental rules, policies, and punishments, and even with the clearest of lines drawn, there will always be discomfort with compliance and temptations to cross it.

Chapter 7

TRUTH-VS.-LOYALTY DILEMMAS

Truth-vs.-loyalty dilemmas are a common feature of practice with minors. At their essence, the dilemmas in this category involve the conflict between the need to share information and the value of upholding implicit or explicit promises to do otherwise. All dilemmas involving the right to privacy fall into this category. Conflict-of-interest dilemmas often do as well. In practice with children and adolescents, the common standards of confidentiality are challenged by the rights and interests of parents and the social institutions that limit minors' rights.

Helping professionals are entrusted with an array of information that minor clients might wish to be held in confidence. This includes information about thoughts and feelings (for example, of despair or suicidal ideation, or regarding sexual orientation or views about family members), experiences (abuse, substance use, sex), and intentions (to run away, to choose a vocation at odds with family wishes, to terminate a pregnancy). As these examples illustrate, in some instances telling the truth about minors' secrets may be necessary to avert harm. Yet not all secrets rise to that level.

Truth-telling dilemmas may also arise when parents or institutions wish to withhold information from minors, but the clinician's loyalty to the minor suggests otherwise. Examples might include family history, diagnoses, treatment options, or information about sex, contraceptives, religion, or other controversial topics. As a result of these conflicting obligations, helping professionals must decide whose loyalty to honor (the wishes and expectations of the minor or those of the parent, guardian, or other authority) and what truths are worthy of telling.

The confidentiality concerns inherent in this type of dilemma are also linked to informed consent. That is, what were the various parties' expectations regarding privacy at the outset of the relationship? The more explicit the agreement, the easier it is to determine the respective obligations as the case unfolds. Some might suggest that it would just be easier never to promise a minor privacy, in recognition of the statutory and parental prerogatives incumbent in minors' care. Yet such dictates are clearly antithetical to the helping process and, at times, to the health and safety of young clients. Clients of any age have the right to privacy, though for minors this right is circumscribed by legal, clinical, and ethical considerations. Denying youths the right to privacy is not an acceptable mechanism for avoiding the complexity of truth-vs.-loyalty dilemmas.

TOP SECRET

Ben works in a child guidance clinic. One of his clients is fifteen-year-old Sid D, who was referred for counseling as part of a diversion program after he and his friends were found joyriding in a stolen car. It is Ben's practice to meet with the parents of child clients to gather their views on the case, assess the family's interpersonal functioning, and establish parameters for service, including those involving the sharing of information.

During his session with Sid's parents, Ben learns that Sid's mother and father were in their early forties when Sid was born, and that Sid's other sibling is now in his thirties and living in another region of the country. Ben perceives that the parents have very different levels of involvement with their son: Mrs. D seems preoccupied by his every move, and Mr. D shrugs and says, "What can you expect from teenagers?" During the session, the parents reveal that Sid is not Mr. D's biological son, but rather, was conceived in an affair Mrs. D had. The parents explain that Sid is unaware of this, and they have no intention of telling him. They also make it clear that they expect Ben to respect their privacy in the matter.

As Ben commences his work with Sid, he finds a young man confused by his father's distant and laissez-faire parenting style, and chafing under his mother's excessive involvement. Ben comes to regret the promise he made to Mr. and Mrs. D and wonders if the family secret is at the core of Sid's identity and behavioral issues.

The treatment of family secrets is a complex clinical and ethical dilemma. Some suggest that the secrets are, indeed, the family's—to share or not, as they see fit. Because they ultimately must live with the consequences of the revelation or the continued silence, it is presumed that the family knows better than the clinician which choice is best for them. A contrary position would suggest that secrets have a destructive effect on all members of the family system, and that those who are invested in keeping the secret may be doing so against the interests of unknowing family members. When this point of view is taken, it may be the clinician's responsibility to reveal the secret or persuade others to do so in order to get the family "unstuck" from its present pathology and to prevent the problems arising from the secret from perpetuating themselves. The presence of family secrets is not necessarily associated with psychological problems (Kelly & Yip, 2006). The weight of a secret may simply be a heavy burden that clinicians can be instrumental in easing.

Workers in clinical practice are privy to all kinds of secrets—about adoptions, parentage, out-of-wedlock births, alcoholism, abuse, causes of death, and so on. Some secrets are benign, reflecting family lore more than an unwillingness to confront difficult truths (Uncle Jimmy was a war hero, not a draft dodger). Some are simply a matter of personal privacy with no reverberating implications for the family system (Aunt Sally had an abortion when she was fifteen). Some secrets, though, involve information to which the unknowing family members involved have a legitimate claim (Jeff was adopted or Juanita's twin died at birth). The nature of the secret, the way in which the social worker came to possess the information, and the effect on the client are significant considerations in the resolution of dilemmas involving truth telling.

Though it is unclear why they shared the information about Sid's biological father, Mr. and Mrs. D were unambiguous about how they expected the information to be treated, and Ben clearly agreed to respect their privacy in the matter. No doubt he made that agreement without considering the ramifications it might have for his work with Sid. As his work has progressed, Ben's clinical judgment suggests that knowing the secret might demystify for Sid Mr. D's remote behavior. In this, Ben appears to believe that it would be helpful for Sid to know (as opposed to believing that he has a right to know, on the basis of honesty, trust, the potential need for an accurate medical history, etc.).

While Mr. and Mrs. D may wish to keep their secret to protect Sid from troubling information or to conceal unflattering information about Mrs. D, the secret is likely to have additional significance for Sid. The information would shatter long-standing beliefs about his parentage, give rise to questions about his "real" father, and undermine his trust in his family as he looks back at their lives in light of this information. Do the advantages of knowing outweigh the disadvantages? Is a revelation in service of Ben's treatment goals? Are there other ways to meet the treatment goals without violating the parents' wishes? Who will help the family address the consequences if the secret is revealed?

Assess Options

Reflection on the issues generates three options for Ben:

1. He can ask Mr. and Mrs. D to reconsider their position and tell Sid or permit him to tell.
2. He can tell Sid without the parents' permission.
3. He can adhere to the parents' wishes and maintain the secret.

Each option involves particular risks and benefits that must be weighed and considered through the decision-making model.

Ethical theories and principles. Ben's struggle fits neatly into a utilitarian framework. Do the ends (of silence or disclosure, voluntary or otherwise) justify the means? According to the vignette, Ben is focused on the advantageous consequences that might accrue if Sid is told about his father. He presumes that knowing would help Sid make sense of his relationship with Mr. D. Yet revealing this truth might require him to breach the parents' trust and privacy. Even with their consent, it would come at the cost of disrupting the family's equilibrium. If there are negative consequences to Sid's continued ignorance in the matter, are they worth the price of maintaining the parents' privacy and the status quo? In a utilitarian framework, Ben must weigh the consequences of his decisions. In doing so, he must take care to consider the array of possible outcomes, not simply the hoped-for outcomes. What risks and costs are incurred in the pursuit of a particular benefit?

The deontological framework would require examination of the rules embedded in his choices. A core issue here is privacy and promises. Should social workers uphold the promises they make to clients? Should social workers maintain the confidences shared with them by clients? The answer to both is yes. Except in extraordinary circumstances, professionals would agree that privacy and trustworthiness are essential to practice in the helping professions. A deontological perspective, then, rules out Ben's option of telling without the parents' permission and supports the option of remaining silent. A rules-based perspective would encourage Ben to share his dilemma with the parents and ask them to reconsider, though it would rule out the use of pressure or threats to secure their agreement.

When examined in light of ethical principles, Ben's options reveal a similar dilemma. To reveal the secret without the parents' permission would violate the parents' autonomy and Ben's responsibility for fidelity and veracity. Determining which choice meets the spirit of beneficence or nonmaleficence (ensuring benefits or averting harms) would depend on the predicable outcomes. Clearly, breaching the parents' privacy creates harms for them, for Sid, and for Ben that are not justified by the possible benefits. That is, the harms are more likely, immediate, and predicable than the benefits. Whether it is more beneficial for Ben to remain silent or seek the Ds' approval to reveal their secret should be determined through a frank examination of the likely effects of the revelation on Sid's mental health, behavior, and self-concept, and on the family as a whole. Put simply, is he better off knowing or not knowing? Determining the benefits of these choices is a clinical as well as ethical exercise.

Laws and policies. Certainly, Ben's agency has policies on the disclosure of confidential information and on the use of informed consent. These constitute an important resource to guide his decision making, as violations of policy would likely engender serious consequences in terms of both his employer and the wronged client. On a larger scale, state and federal laws on patient privacy would apply to this case. HIPAA (1996) provides minimum protections of privacy but allows disclosures for numerous circumstances such as health oversight, and coordination of care. HIPAA also requires all relevant disclosures about a client's case to be documented in the record. State laws may be more specific; for example, they may allow the agency provider to withhold Sid's records from him, even once he is eighteen, if the information contained in them could be injurious to his mental well-being.

Values. The key values for consideration in this case are those of the client system, the social worker, and the profession. Since Sid is clueless about the controversy, there is no way to gauge what his values or perspective might be. While we may know little about the D family and the values that are driving Mr. and Mrs. D to keep the truth about Sid's parentage from him, we might consider a few possibilities. The Ds may place a high value on monogamy and marital fidelity. That these values were breached may be a source of shame for them and thus give rise to the desire to keep the breach secret. They may feel that this was an aberration in an otherwise long and satisfactory marriage, and that the revelation could overshadow the positive aspects of their union. Alternatively, their reluctance to reveal the secret may come from concern for Sid. They might be afraid of how he will react and how he will view them and the integrity of the family. They might worry that this will push him further away from them, a concern exacerbated by the tenuous stage of adolescence and his recent run-in with the law. Perhaps they believe that the revelation will give rise to questions that neither they nor Sid are ready or able to address. Amid the speculation about the values underlying their choice, we can be clear that Mr. and Mrs. D value their privacy in the matter and have been led to believe that that value will be honored.

We must also speculate about Ben's values. Perhaps his inclination to reveal the secret is driven by more than his clinical impression that the information would benefit Sid. Ben may value honesty and transparency in family communications and wish that the behavior and actions of the D family could reflect that value. He may value minors' rights and believe that Sid should be told on that basis. He may simply feel that it is unfair of the parents to withhold such significant information affecting the life of their child. All these values are understandable, and Ben would be well advised to consider their role in his decision making. However, he should also be mindful of his responsibility not to put his values before those of his clients or those of his profession. Even the option of seeking Mr. and Mrs. D's consent to reveal the secret may reflect Ben's beliefs about what is best more than the clinical and case knowledge regarding what is best for Sid and his family.

Ben might construe social work values regarding social justice, human dignity, or the primacy of human relationships as supporting his inclination to tell Sid about his birth father. It is not apparent, though, that this is an accurate application of those concepts. Consultation would allow Ben to gauge his interpretation against that of his fellow social workers. One social work value with clear application to the case is that of integrity—the expectation that social workers will behave in a trustworthy manner. While Ben may feel that keeping a secret from Sid challenges his integrity, he has made an explicit promise to Mr. and Mrs. D to maintain their privacy. Breaching that would actively violate the social work value of integrity.

Information. It is not clear from the vignette how Mr. and Mrs. D came to believe that Sid is not Mr. D's child. The basis for their belief will be significant in the decision regarding whether or not Sid should know. It is possible that they have presumed something for years that may not in fact be true. Perhaps Ben took Mr. and Mrs. D's report at face value. If so, he needs to revisit the issue with them. Uncertainty about the accuracy of their claim would tip the scales of ethical decision making toward continued secrecy.

Some crucial information in the case is embedded in the values and beliefs that underlie Mr. and Mrs. D's decision not to tell Sid. If they are silent because they fear his reaction or regret that he has spent so many years in ignorance, they may be more amenable to attempts by Ben to encourage them to reveal the truth at this point. On the other hand, if their position is based on shame or guilt, they might find a revelation at this point too threatening to accept.

Other significant information involves Sid's maturity and emotional health, and the family's functioning. That is, would revealing the secret with or without the parents' consent have a positive effect on Sid's well-being and on the family as a whole? Can Ben and the parents fully anticipate and appreciate the effects of the revelation or the ramifications of maintaining the secret? What does the practice literature indicate about these matters? An unknown at this point is the status of Sid's older brother. Does he know the secret? Is he estranged from the family? Could he provide insight about the impact that revealing the secret may have? Could he be a support to Sid and his parents at this difficult time?

Some information will be helpful as the question of whether the revelation should be made at all or whether is it necessary to do so at this time is revisited. In particular, how germane is the issue of Sid's birth to the problems for which he is seeking treatment? And how relevant is it that this information would be revealed unbidden? Sid is unaware that information is being withheld from him, and he is not asking for the information. Thus, Ben is not being put in a position of having to lie if he keeps the secret (in contrast to the case of Leticia in chapter 2). And, while the information may be significant in shaping Sid's views of himself and his family, it is not a matter of life and death (as it might be if the biological father were known to have a condition that might put Sid's health at risk). These facts call into question the necessity and urgency of the revelation.

Standards. The NASW Code of Ethics has an array of standards on confidentiality with clients. Taken as a whole, they require discretion on the part of social workers. For example, workers are not expected to dig for extraneous information irrelevant to the case, and they are not expected to share information with others without valid consent from the client or someone "legally authorized to consent on behalf of a client" (NASW, 1999, 1.07b). Disclosures without consent should be made only for compelling professional reasons, when necessary to prevent harm, or when required by law. Even in situations in which a social worker is permitted or compelled to breach privacy, discretion is still required in what information is shared and with whom. For example, reports of suspected child abuse required of mandated reporters do not authorize a worker to share with child welfare authorities everything he or she knows about the case, nor do they permit discussion of the suspected abuse with other parties, such as teachers, family members, or neighbors. The Code recommends that clients be informed in advance, when possible, of unapproved disclosures. It also requires that clients be informed about the limits of confidentiality early in the helping process. This would include informing clients in family counseling about agency and worker policies on disclosing information to members of the client system.

In Ben's case, the Code would clearly suggest seeking Mr. and Mrs. D's permission before sharing their secret and, absent that, would expect fidelity to the agreements regarding privacy laid out in the informed consent process. It is unlikely that the disclosure Ben is contemplating meets the ethical standard of "compelling professional reasons" or averts harm in such a way that the Code would endorse a decision to tell Sid about his birth father against Mr. and Mrs. D's wishes.

While no apparent practice standards apply specifically to Ben's dilemma, guidelines about revealing adoptee status might be generalized to the case. There are two conflicting beliefs about the optimal time to disclose to a child that he or she was adopted (American Academy of Child & Adolescent Psychiatry, 2002). Some argue that the child should be informed early in life. This up-front approach is thought to reduce the secrecy and shame associated with adoption. Additionally, informing the child early in life may allow for a gradual incorporation of adoptive status into a child's identity development. Others, however, argue that disclosure should occur at a time when the child can fully comprehend the information. By either of these standards, Sid should probably be informed that Mr. D is not his father.

Be Mindful of Process

The sensitivity of the information involved is an indicator of the care with which Ben must approach each of his choices. Should he decide to ask Mr. and Mrs. D to revisit their decision, he might start by inquiring about their choice to withhold the information, the benefits they perceive in doing so, and any concerns they have about the secret and its impact. He might then share his perceptions about the deleterious effects that keeping this secret may have on Sid and offer his assistance if they wish to reconsider their decision to keep the identity of his father a secret. The parents may regret that they did not reveal their secret earlier in Sid's life. Doing so might have prevented the possible repercussions of delivering such startling news in a single jarring conversation with an already vulnerable adolescent. Given the challenges that are certain to accompany this process, Ben can make a strong argument that there is no time like the present. Sid is already in a trusting therapeutic relationship. Although there is no ideal way to facilitate the disclosure, having an established support system is a certain benefit.

Ben might also explore whether the parents have considered how Sid might respond if he discovers the truth on his own. Who is listed as the father on his birth certificate, and what happens when he needs a copy of it? What if he is contacted by a sibling from his biological father's side of the family? The Ds would likely agree that disclosure under such circumstances would be less desirable than telling him now within the context of the therapeutic relationship. At present, Mr. and Mrs. D have the opportunity to share the secret on their own terms, though there is no guarantee that it will always be so.

Whatever strategy he takes, Ben must be careful not to coerce or badger Mr. and Mrs. D into agreeing to reveal their secret. If his beliefs about the case are strong, it would be easy to apply undue pressure on the couple. This could harden their position and alienate them as trusted elements of their son's care. Alternatively, Ben might obtain their reluctant agreement or deference to his appeals, which is not a sufficient foundation for so profound a decision.

If Mr. and Mrs. D agree authentically and knowledgeably to share their secret with Sid, they and Ben should negotiate a careful plan for doing so, being mindful of the timing, setting, and content of the disclosure. They should anticipate the questions that may result and prepare to answer them in a way that is respectful and supportive of all the parties involved. That is, the discussion should strike a balance between Sid's desire for information and his parents' comfort and ability to provide it.

Ben is in a very tenuous position if he decides to reveal the secret against the family's wishes. He is on shaky ethical, legal, and clinical ground, so guidance on how to proceed may be lacking. And in breaching the Ds' wishes, Ben would alienate the very support system necessary to address the emotional and behavioral repercussions that disclosure may have for Sid. How can Ben tell without the parents' willingness to participate in the process, answer questions, and support their son as he grapples with this new knowledge? Proactively imagining this prospect may dissuade Ben from pursuing the option of telling.

Process also matters in the option of not telling. How will Ben carry out the decision to respect the parents' privacy? He should be vigilant to ensure that he doesn't drop hints accidentally in his work with Sid. He should also consider how he can help Sid with the dynamic issues of the case without telling him about his father. There are numerous reasons why parents can be perceived as distant and unloving, just as there are numerous ways to overcome those hardships. In fact, one of those reasons might be more germane to Mr. D's behavior and Sid's problems than the secret. In keeping his promise of silence, Ben may utilize clinical tools to help Sid accept *what is* rather than try to answer *why it is* this way.

Consult

Fortunately, Ben's dilemma is not urgent and does not require speedy resolution, which allows him to seek advice about his choices. One important area for consultation involves the possible legal and regulatory ramifications of a decision to breach Mr. and Mrs. D's privacy without their consent. It is likely that an attorney from his agency or counselor from his professional association or licensing board would caution against this choice and articulate the possible penalties for such action. These resources might also inform him of any risk in withholding information from Sid.

Social workers do not always act in accordance with the advice of attorneys and others who would mitigate their liability. In fact, the NASW Code notes that when laws and ethics conflict, professionals may take actions that go against the law, in the belief that they are doing so to uphold a higher good or avert a harm. An example would be refusing to report a client's status as an undocumented worker in the belief that doing so might discourage the client and others from seeking needed services. Any decision to engage in civil disobedience or otherwise subvert the law should be consciously made with full appreciation of and willingness to endure the consequences for the sake of principle. In Ben's situation, it appears that neither the law nor his code of ethics endorses violating the parents' confidentiality. Further, it is unclear what principle he would be advancing in doing so. One could say he is standing up for honesty or transparency, but he is doing so at the expense of other principles such as the parents' self-determination and trust. As an employee of the child guidance clinic, Ben's actions take on greater significance and create liabilities for the organization. In this case, he is wise to abide by the advice of legal experts and regulatory authorities and avoid breaching the Ds' privacy.

The other crucial consultation for Ben will be with a trusted supervisor or colleague. In that Ben's supervisor is responsible for his actions and his interface with agency policies, he or she has a right to be informed about the dilemma. The supervisor and other colleagues can also help Ben explore his inclination to tell Sid, his judgment that Sid will benefit from knowing, and practice strategies for helping Sid, whether or not the secret is revealed. Such discussions will be useful not only for the current decision, but for future practice situations when Ben is ill at ease maintaining clients' privacy.

Document

The clinical information in the case (Ben's session with the parents, Sid's behaviors and issues, Ben's assessment of the case) should be documented in the case file. Assuming Ben's session with the parents was as an adjunct to Sid's care rather than service to the parents themselves, the question arises as to how their secret should be handled in the record. On one hand, it is significant information that is germane to the case. Clinical records often contain intensely private information recorded for the purposes of accurate documentation and continuity of care. Therefore, there is no basis for leaving secret information out of the case file. Ben should consider, though, Sid's right to review his records and the possibility that it might inadvertently reveal his parentage. The NASW Code of Ethics and HIPAA both support the right of clients to review their records, though both could allow for confidential information from other sources to be withheld or redacted. In light of these provisions, it is clear the Ben should be thorough in his case documentation, but prepared to protect the information recorded, should it become necessary to do so to protect the parents' privacy. Ben should also seek advice about how to handle Sid's eventual right to his personal health information once he reaches the age of majority. Information gathered at his family intake may not be adequately obscured or protected in the file, and when he is an adult, his parents would no longer be able to restrict his access to it (U.S. Department of Health and Human Services, 2007). Under that interpretation, Ben should be circumspect about what he reveals about the parents' secret, lest it is disclosed inadvertently at a later date.

Beyond the case documentation, Ben should record in a personal journal or log his efforts to resolve his dilemma, including data on his consultations and the results of those conversations. Here too, though, he should be careful about how explicitly he details the secret in the event that those materials are discoverable in a legal proceeding or other action.

Evaluate

Whatever path Ben chooses, he should examine the effects and discuss them in supervision. Did his decision have the expected and desired effects? If not, can something be done to rectify the situation? If so, could improvements have been made to the decision or the way it was carried out? For example, if Ben decided to ask the Ds to revisit their decision regarding the secret, did he handle it in a sensitive and effective manner? Did their reaction indicate they were offended or troubled by his queries? If so, can he remedy these effects to salvage his relationship with the Ds and assure them of his fidelity to the promise of privacy? Overall, what lessons can be taken from the decision and the decision-making process? How might these apply to future cases?

Another area for evaluation would involve determining whether the dilemma could have been averted in the first place. For example, what would have happened if Ben had refused to make a promise to Mr. and Mrs. D that he might not be able to keep? Could the informed consent in the parents' session have been structured in such a way to provide Ben with latitude to share with Sid whatever he felt was clinically important from the session with his parents? If those had been the ground rules, Mr. and Mrs. D might not have revealed their secret. So, in the end, would it have been better for Ben to know something he could not share or remain ignorant about this piece of family history? Evaluation, even after the fact, is crucial for the purposes of altering practices and policies or sustaining their merit.

Case Conclusion

While Ben might be tempted to reveal to Sid his family's secrets, it is clear that doing so would breach Mr. and Mrs. D's right to privacy and the assurance Ben gave them that he would protect that right. Whether it is wiser ethically to keep the secret or to ask Mr. and Mrs. D to reveal it depends largely on the effects all members of the family would experience in either case. Ethical analysis supports the decision that it is the parents who can and must make a decision whether or not to tell Sid. Ben can play a helpful role, not as a partisan in that choice, but as an educator and facilitator as they consider the pros and cons of each alternative and the ways that they might handle this momentous decision now or in the future.

THE RIGHT TO REMAIN SILENT

Vilma is a social worker at a community mental health agency. Her fourteen-year-old client Rosa was referred by her family after their pastor expressed concerns that she seemed despondent and thin. The agency strictly adheres to a brief treatment model, however, Vilma was able to secure service extensions in order to give herself time to better understand Rosa's situation. Today Rosa revealed that the precipitant to her current condition was a sexual assault by her brother's sixteen-year-old best friend. She reported that the assault was an isolated incident. She does not appear concerned about further risk, though she has regular contact with the boy since he lives in the neighborhood and the two families are extremely close. As Vilma attempts to learn about the incident and the aftermath, Rosa becomes reluctant to say more. She states, "It is in the past," and adamantly refuses Vilma's suggestions that the police or her family, be informed or that she seek health care or rape crisis services.

Like Ben, Vilma is torn between competing imperatives: to honor Rosa's wish that she not disclose the sexual assault or to encourage Rosa to tell someone about the incident. Vilma must decide whether there is merit in abrogating her client's wishes, or in encouraging her to rethink her position. In contrast to Ben's case, this secret involves a recent event and is being maintained *by* the minor client, not kept *from* her. An additional feature in the present case is the role of the agency's philosophy in Vilma's decision making. Does Vilma feel pressure to record and reveal Rosa's sexual trauma in order to forestall pressure to close the case? If she must close the case, should she be venturing clinically into the sexual trauma that she will ultimately be unable to address?

A final distinction between this case and Ben's is the lack of clarity about who should be told and to what ends the disclosure would be made. For example, Vilma may feel that the parents, as Rosa's caregivers, have a right to know, and that withholding that information might create an unwanted liability for herself and her agency. A different reason for telling the parents might be so that they can protect Rosa's safety. This relies on the assumption that the parents would indeed have the desire and ability to do so and that Rosa's assurances that she is already safe cannot be trusted. Vilma's desire to tell the police might also stem from a concern about safety—both Rosa's and other women's, if this young man is a predatory sex offender. Alternatively, the desire to involve law enforcement may stem from a desire to avenge the harms, without an appreciation for the victim's wishes in the case.

In this, as in many ethics cases, intention matters. Vilma must be certain of what she wants to achieve, so that in seeking consultation and assessing her options she may find more acceptable (less harmful) strategies for accomplishing those ends. Similarly, she and other decision makers must be alert to their motivations. It is more defensible for Vilma to breach Rosa's privacy in order to help Rosa than it is to breach it to relieve her own distress over the situation or to advance her own cause. How will ethical analysis view these various circumstances in weighing truth and loyalty?

Assess Options

At first glance, Vilma has several options to consider in resolving this dilemma:

1. She can honor Rosa's decision to keep the rape a secret.
2. She can encourage Rosa to tell her parents and let the parents decide what further action is needed.

3. She can share Rosa's disclosure with the police as a matter of public safety.
4. She can share Rosa's disclosure with the girl's parents, in the belief that they are responsible for her well-being and thus have a right to know, even if she wishes otherwise.

Other options, motivations, and combinations may come to light as we examine the four most obvious choices.

Ethical theories and principles. The deontological view in this case is represented by the fundamental expectation that clients' privacy will be protected. The recognized exceptions to this universal law are in place to avert significant and impending harms—to children (in the case of child abuse), to all clients (in the case of planned suicidal acts), and to others (in the case of homicidal or public health threats). This is a fairly high bar, set intentionally because the success of the helping relationship is believed to rest on the foundation of privacy. Helping professionals, clergy, and attorneys may struggle with this imperative but recognize that to act otherwise would cause greater harm.

The utilitarian perspective on Vilma's choice depends on what outcomes she foresees and thus is trying to encourage or avert. This perspective might endorse telling the parents or police if doing so is necessary to protect Rosa's safety. This would require Vilma to find in her evaluation that Rosa is at risk of self-harm or harm from her reported assailant. Other ends such as easing Vilma's mind might not justify the disclosure.

The principles of beneficence and nonmaleficence also require explication of the expected outcomes of the decision. The benefits to be derived from telling might include the ability to involve caring persons, such as the family, health care experts, rape crisis workers, or law enforcement, in Rosa's case. Each of these entities might be able to offer assistance for support, safety, healing, justice, or recovery, all of which are desirable ends. Not telling would deprive Rosa of these resources and supports. However, telling against her will might yield the same result, should she prove unwilling to talk further about her assault or cooperate with authorities. Further, a confidentiality breach against her wishes may lead her to regret her candor, alienate her from Vilma, and destroy her trust in all helping professionals. These would clearly be undesirable outcomes.

Analysis using the ethical principle of autonomy supports a decision to seek Rosa's consent. Allowing her to tell or getting her to permit Vilma to tell would respect her autonomy. Conversely, telling despite her protestations may in effect revictimize her as her will and wishes are again disregarded by someone able to exercise power over her.

The principles of fidelity and veracity would, respectively, support acting in a trustworthy and honest manner. Vilma's choice should be congruent with statements she has already made and her agreements with Rosa and her family. If, in the informed consent process, Rosa's parents were led to believe that they would be entitled to any information shared in the counseling process, they and Rosa might reasonably expect the assault to be disclosed. Vilma's decision to do so, with or without Rosa's consent, would be true to those expectations.

These principles highlight the importance of paying careful attention to informed consent processes. If Vilma skimmed over her responsibilities when orienting Rosa or her parents to the therapeutic process, her choices in handling the disclosure of the assault are further complicated. For example, if she led Rosa to believe that she would only reveal information regarding suicidal or homicidal risk, and she led the parents to think she would reveal anything that might cause them to be concerned about their daughter's safety, she is now caught between conflicting expectations. As a result, any choice she makes violates her fidelity, either with the parents or their daughter.

Laws and policies. Vilma should consider whether her responsibilities as a mandated reporter apply in this dilemma. Several elements of the case might affect whether or nor there is a need for a referral to child protective services in any given jurisdiction, so she would be wise to seek CPS consultation about the general principles in the case. For example, if the alleged assailant is not a family member and is a peer of the victim's, would her assault fall under CPS jurisdiction? Does the fact that the sex was not consensual make it reportable? Vilma should be clear that even when there are CPS reporting obligations, they may not require or entitle other disclosures. For example, in California, Vilma would not be required to notify the parents (or Rosa) that she has made the report (though she may see clinical benefits in doing so, and it would be congruent with the guidelines of the NASW Code) (California Department of Social Services, 2003).

Vilma might also look into state licensing laws regarding her responsibilities and liabilities around disclosure. For example, such regulations may offer her immunity for her from allegations of a breach of privacy, presuming that Vilma made the disclosure in good faith. The regulations might also permit disclosure if it is needed to prevent the possible commission of a felony or violent misdemeanor. If Vilma determined that the assailant posed a continued threat to Rosa or others, she might contact the authorities to forestall further damage. She should note that the language doesn't compel her to break Rosa's privacy, but it provides protections if she does.

Agency policies may be relevant to this case, dictating how the case should be handled, how much time Vilma will have to treat Rosa, and how disclosures should be handled. Vilma's supervisor is best positioned to help her understand the policies and navigate them in light of the dilemma at hand. For example, what are her choices if the policy for case extensions requires written appeals and Vilma is concerned that in justifying an extension based on Rosa's assault she may have to reveal her secret?

Values. Let's imagine the values of the various actors in this case. Rosa clearly values her privacy. She may value control and feel that if the assault is revealed, she will no longer have power over what happens. Rosa's parents may value her safety and their inclusion in matters affecting her well-being. They may also value virginity or sexual abstinence and, as a result, may place particular significance on the assault. They may value their son's happiness and friendships and their family's relationship with the assailant's family. Such a stance might raise concerns about whether they would use knowledge of the assault to Rosa's benefit.

Vilma's values may include self-preservation and an avoidance of risks. She may be a parent herself and value the parents' perspective and rights. Or she may value victims' rights and empowerment, which might lead her to take Rosa's report of an assault at face value. Those values could alternately lead Vilma to respect Rosa's position or push her to take action when she is not ready to do so. Vilma's agency clearly values brief treatment. It may also place a premium on mitigating risk, which may mean its stance is to avoid angering the parents by withholding this information from them.

The values of the social work profession must also be considered here. Integrity would encourage Vilma to behave in a way that is consistent with the promises made to Rosa and her family. Competence would encourage her to use consultation to get the information she needs to help Rosa. The value placed upon human dignity and worth would suggest that she honor Rosa's wishes.

The value placed on human relationships is operationalized as follows: "Social workers understand that relationships between and among people are important vehicles for change. Social workers engage people as partners in the helping process. Social workers seek to strengthen relationships among people in a purposeful effort to promote, restore, maintain, and enhance the well-being of individuals, families, social groups, organizations, and communities" (NASW, 1999, p. 6). Thus the value would seem to apply differentially to Vilma's choices. It could be interpreted as supporting Rosa's preference not to discuss the assault, thus honoring the helping relationship. Or it might suggest that Vilma tell Rosa's parents out of respect for the family's relationships. The value on human relationships might also encourage Vilma to link Rosa with other providers so that she might access needed care and support. The value's merit for any of the choices seems to depend on which relationship Vilma is concerned with enhancing or preserving.

Information. Information, particularly regarding Rosa, her family, and the assault, will have bearing on Vilma's decision. First, it will be helpful to know when the assault took place and what steps, if any, Rosa has taken to secure medical attention. This is particularly important so that it can be determined whether she is pregnant or has contracted a sexually transmitted disease. If Rosa has not seen a health care professional, this must be added to Vilma's list of concerns. It is likely that Rosa can seek STD and pregnancy testing without parental notification if Vilma can persuade her to do so (Parsons, 2001). If Rosa seems reluctant to seek health care, Vilma may feel the tests are sufficiently important to tip the scales of decision making toward telling her parents so that they can ensure she gets care. On the other hand, Vilma may feel that by honoring Rosa's privacy she will eventually be able to convince the girl to seek care. Either way, the health needs add another pressing dimension to an already vexing case.

Knowing about the nature of the assault, how it happened, and the meaning it has for Rosa is also important. Some basic information could help Vilma determine the veracity of Rosa's account. The intent here is not to put Vilma in the role of investigator or judge, but rather to secure enough information to decide how appropriate referrals to law enforcement or others might be. In further assessment, Vilma may also want to know if the assault was Rosa's first sexual experience, if she blames herself for the encounter, and whether the circumstances under which it took place (e.g., drug use) put her at continued risk. These facts and others serve two purposes. They will help Vilma determine whether she is the most appropriate person to help Rosa in the wake of the assault or if specialized victim services are called for. Rosa's answers to these questions will also help Vilma assess her client's judgment and the accuracy of her claims that she is in no further danger from her assailant. As noted in chapter 3, a careful and individualized assessment is required to determine whether a minor has sufficient developmental maturity to make decisions about matters such as privacy, risk, and service needs. In this evaluation, Vilma's overall assessment of Rosa is significant. For example, does her cognitive functioning demonstrate acceptable levels of insight, reasoning, problem solving, and judgment? Does she display signs of coexisting mental health or substance use issues, which could be exacerbated by the assault? Does she have a history of self-destructive or self-injurious behavior? How is she functioning socially and educationally? Does she demonstrate maturity, self-control, and self-awareness appropriate for a fourteen-year-old? Preparation and consultation will ensure that Vilma seeks the proper information and synthesizes it appropriately. The intent is to determine whether Rosa has sufficient maturity to make a sound decision about revealing her rape, and whether she has the capacity to evaluate the risk of further harm.

While Rosa's maturity is key to Vilma's decision making, so too is information about her family. Vilma must rely on her observations and interactions with the family and on Rosa's reports to determine whether their response to Rosa's rape will be in the client's best interests. In other words, if Vilma breaches Rosa's privacy so that the parents can provide her with support, services, and protection, is it likely that these will be the result? How might the family's beliefs, culture, and faith shape their response to the assault? Does their willingness to bring Rosa in for care at the pastor's behest demonstrate a positive relationship with her and a concern for her well-being that indicates they'll handle the disclosure in a positive manner? Or does their failure to seek help until the pastor pushed for it signify inattention toward Rosa or the devaluing of therapeutic services?

Finally, it will be helpful to know why Rosa is reluctant to tell anyone. It may be that she blames herself, having internalized messages that girls "ask for it" through the way they dress or behave. Perhaps she feels her family will blame her. It may be that she fears losing the love and companionship of her brother. Maybe she just wishes it would all go away and thinks that putting it behind her is the best way to deal with it. Unless Vilma is willing to take the time to understand the nature of Rosa's resistance, she will be ill equipped to overcome it. This process may require her to respect Rosa's wishes as she builds trust and learns more about her concerns. Trust will also be essential if she is to deal effectively with Rosa's fears with education, support, assessment, and empathy. This process might resolve Vilma's ethical dilemma if it softens Rosa's refusal to tell or if it reveals other options, such as Rosa telling her parents, with Vilma's support and assistance.

Standards. NASW ethical standards would have required Vilma to inform her client system about the limits of confidentiality to ensure that all parties knew upfront what could be shared and with whom. Regarding confidentiality, the NASW (1999) Code commands that information be protected, except where there are "compelling professional reasons" (1.07c). Professionals are allowed to break confidentiality to protect the client or others from "serious, foreseeable, and imminent harm" (NASW, 1999, 1.07c) or when compelled by laws or regulations. Vilma's consultation and legal research will help her determine if such conditions apply in this case. Breaching Rosa's privacy to protect her from greater harms (to her health or safety) would likely constitute compelling professional reasons. Breaching it to ease Vilma's apprehensions about the parents' reaction would not.

Practice standards in the rape crisis field would typically take a client-centered approach, placing a premium on the right of the victim to direct the helping process. This means respecting the victim's rights to privacy and confidentiality and to freedom from the imposition of the worker's values or preferences. Specific to Rosa's case, applicable standards state, "Services provided to victims and significant others are not counter to interests of the victim or the victim's recovery process. With child victims, services are provided in the interest of the child, as expressed by the child and assessed by the sexual assault staff" (Illinois Coalition Against Sexual Assault, 2004, p. 5-3) and "At times, with the client's consent, center staff may need to talk with nonoffending parents, guardians and other significant others regarding a client being served by the center. The purpose of this contact may be to inform the significant other about counseling goals, progress toward goals, ways in which the significant other can support the victim and the victim's progress and other similar issues" (p. 5-19). The emphasis on client discretion and empowerment offers an important perspective. Although Vilma does not work in the rape crisis field, these guidelines would still suggest that she honor Rosa's wishes to every extent possible.

Be Mindful of Process

Vilma must consider in advance how she would carry out various decisions. For example, if she decides to tell anyone without Rosa's consent, she should take pains to explain to Rosa why she feels disclosure is in her best interest. In doing so she may continue to offer Rosa the opportunity to tell, to participate in the conversation, or to dictate what Vilma will tell. For example, is it possible to tell the parents that Rosa was assaulted, but not give the details or identify the assailant? This might achieve the end of securing care and bringing her family into the information loop without exposing an excessive amount of information against Rosa's will. This allows her a measure of control while satisfying some of Vilma's concerns and meeting the parents' expectations. However it occurs, Vilma must consider the timing and mechanisms by which she will tell the parents, and what questions, needs, and concerns might result.

If Vilma decides to keep Rosa's secret for the time being, she should consider the focus for their continuing relationship. For example, is her plan to address the assault within the context of their work? Is she allowed to do so, given the constraints of her agency's philosophy? Is her plan to focus on the presenting problem instead? Does she intend to give Rosa the space to develop trust in Vilma so that eventually she will reveal her secret to relevant others? Or is she simply trying to buy time to pursue other tactics to get Rosa to tell? The way in which Vilma handles either acquiescence to or refusal of Rosa's request will require careful application of social work skills and clinical acumen.

Given her agency's emphasis on brief intervention, Vilma may not be able to provide services for the duration that Rosa's situation requires. It may be advisable that she assist Rosa in establishing a relationship with a provider who can see her over an extended period of time or in specialized services for sexual assault. Vilma's efforts should promote continuity of care, as Rosa may be more likely to pursue treatment if the referral comes from a trusted source.

Consult

Throughout the analysis, we have emphasized the benefits for Vilma of consulting with her supervisor, rape crisis specialists, child protective services, and law enforcement personnel. Supervision is an accepted process to ensure that client needs are met, and therefore it is not viewed as a violation of clients' rights to privacy. The other consultations do not have the same protections, and thus Vilma should avoid revealing her clients' name and age and specifics about the assailant as she seeks specialized advice. For example, she might ask, "What would you suggest if a teenager reports being sexually assaulted by an acquaintance but is reluctant to report it?" or "Are you aware of any policies or statutes clinicians should know about for a case like this?" Keeping the discussion on this general level, Vilma can seek assistance without putting Rosa's confidentiality at risk.

Another possible resource for consultation would be Rosa's pastor. Confidentiality would prohibit Vilma from conversing with him without Rosa's consent, but given his apparent position of respect and his evident concern for Rosa, his input might be helpful in a number of ways. He might be able to shed light on ways that culture, faith, and family dynamics may affect how the family receives news of Rosa's assault. He could provide input on Rosa's history and capacity to make independent decisions regarding privacy and safety. He might become an additional trusted adult to whom Rosa can turn with the assurance of privacy. Perhaps he might accompany her and provide support when she tells her parents about the assault. Note that even with the client's permission, social workers seeking consultation should reveal as little information as is necessary to achieve their aims. Thus Vilma should ask for the pastor's input and/or involvement without revealing the name of Rosa's assailant or other unnecessary details.

Document

Rosa's report of the assault should be recorded in the case record, as it is significant information that is germane to her care. Vilma may have concerns about doing so, in light of Rosa's parents' right of access to the files. She may also be concerned that the documentation required to persuade the agency utilization reviewers to approve extended care will require her to reveal excessive information about Rosa's history. Clinical records often contain intensely private information, which is recorded to substantiate services. Hopefully, Rosa and her parents understood that records of their case would be kept. Vilma would have been required by legal and ethical standards to provide them with information on privacy rights and limitations. The issue of Rosa's parents' access to these records is more complex and troubling. They have a right to see her records, though they may not realize they have that right or choose to exercise it. If Vilma omits reference to the assault in the clinical record, she could be falling short of accepted professional and agency standards regarding documentation (Houston-Vega et al., 1997). If she includes it, she may be creating a mechanism by which the parents can learn of the assault and, presumably, more of their daughter's secrets. Rosa should be aware of this possibility as a result of informed consent, but Vilma should reiterate this information as they weigh the pros and cons of disclosure about the assault.

Vilma should provide thorough and timely documentation of her options, consultations, and considerations in her decision-making process in Rosa's case. It will provide important substantiation of a thoughtful and thorough consideration of the pros and cons, concerns, and intentions in the case.

Evaluate

Documentation will not end when Vilma makes her decision. Regardless of whether she reveals information about the assault without Rosa's permission, reveals it with her permission, or keeps her client's secrets temporarily or in perpetuity, careful attention to and documentation of the effects of her decision on the client and others involved will be essential. Vilma must be especially alert to any untoward effects of her decision. That is, if she decides to abide by Rosa's wishes but observes an increase in depressive symptoms, continued weight loss, or the emergence of suicidal ideations or health problems, she may decide that family involvement is necessary, not optional. If the family is informed and embraces the assailant instead of Rosa, other sources of support must be quickly mobilized.

Case Conclusion

Many experiences in the lives of minors fall in the gray area where parental interests and client interests are in conflict. The younger the client, the easier it is to default to the parents' prerogatives on the basis of the youth's incompetence to render decisions and the parents' legitimate rights in regard to their children. The issues are muddied by the minor's maturity, the nature of the secret, and the risks involved in revealing it. In Rosa's case, the social worker's decision will be significantly shaped by the case information and the recommendations made in Vilma's consultations. Ideally, Vilma can use her skills and relationship with Rosa to encourage her to involve other caring adults for short-term and long-term support and assistance. Alternatively, if Rosa refuses to tell, we must hope that Vilma knows Rosa and her family well enough to be confident that the decision is in her best interests.

The analysis reveals that all choices carry risks, benefits, and uncertainties. It also helps Vilma formulate additional strategies for maximizing the success of her decision.

SUMMARY

Truth-vs.-loyalty dilemmas pit two valued principles against each other: the pressures to be honest and forthright yet honor agreements that might command silence. When these dilemmas occur in service to minors, they require consideration of other actors, in particular the minor's parents or guardians. Thus, truthfulness with one party may conflict with promises made to another party. Consultation, careful review of the case facts, and appraisal of the risks, benefits, and alternatives can help practitioners rule out options and give weight to some over others. Even when conclusions are not wholly supported or satisfying, the decision-making process puts the worker in a position to defend his or her choice, respond to any negative outcomes, and build on the experience in preparation for future dilemmas.

Chapter 8

Individual-vs.-Community Dilemmas

Individual-vs.-community dilemmas are in essence conflict-of-interest problems. These dilemmas pit the well-being of one person against that of a collective (a family, class, or community, for example). This category can also include situations in which the decision maker is torn between one person's needs and interests and those of another individual. As such, it can also involve dilemmas in which the decision maker's own interests are part of the equation.

A common theme in individual-vs.-community dilemmas is the issue of distributive justice. At a recent meeting I attended, a philanthropist mused about the ethics of her donating practices, wondering if she should give to the poorest of the poor instead of established and well-to-do institutions like foundations and universities. As is common in right-vs.-right dilemmas, neither choice is unethical. That individual's funds could clearly make a difference in the life of a poor family or people in a village without potable water. But, combined with the funds of others, her money might fund research or education that will help vast numbers of people, perhaps including the same villagers, who will ultimately be assisted, albeit in a different and less direct manner.

In decisions such as these we are reminded of utilitarian philosophies, which focus on consequences, asking which choice creates the greatest good for the greatest number. As noted earlier, different definitions of "good" and different degrees of responsibility make the utilitarian principle complex in practice. For example, a high school student writes gory scripts in English class and is referred to the school social worker. The worker must be able to distinguish the next Quentin Tarantino from the next Dylan Klebold. The worker must also balance the rights and needs of the individual with the interests of the school and community. It is not proper or fair to restrict an individual's right to free speech or creative thought or to institutionalize a budding screenwriter. However, it is also improper and unfair for others to be placed in harm's way when risks are apparent.

This calculus of whose needs merit attention is particularly challenging in the helping professions. People who seek out or are referred for counseling often reveal their most intimate and troubling thoughts and experiences as part of the process. Their trust that those revelations will be handled with discretion is the bedrock of the helping relationship. Social workers and other professionals are allowed, and in fact required, to break confidentiality in certain situations, most notably those involving serious, imminent, and foreseeable risk and those in which child maltreatment is suspected. However, there are many other situations in which the worker is the repository of troubling information that he or she cannot divulge, but that others might legitimately want or need to have. Consider, for example, the following client revelations: a real estate agent reports engaging in deceptive business practices, a prominent pastor reveals multiple adulterous affairs, a legislator vocally opposed to gay rights provisions is himself a closeted homosexual, a school bus driver fears an escalation in his debilitating panic attacks, a politician admits taking bribes, a restaurant inspector describes grotesque discoveries that are "all in a day's work," a teenager tells of widespread cheating on end-of-grade tests. In each of these scenarios, it is easy to see that other people might have interests in learning the information that the worker possesses. Yet given the conditions under which the information was received, the worker has a particular responsibility to place the client's interests above others'.

Decision making in this category of dilemmas, then, requires more than just selecting which individual one will favor. It requires discretion in upholding professional responsibilities to clients and evaluative prowess in determining when, where, why, and how one individual's preferences will be favored over those of another.

TROUBLE WITH A CAPITAL B

Kelvin is a social worker in an urban police department. He and his social work interns provide an array of services to crime victims, grieving families, and young offenders. One of their roles is to provide intensive case management and group therapy for youths convicted of drug crimes, theft, and assaults. Typically, the young people referred to this service are first-time offenders whom the judge determines are likely to benefit from rehabilitative versus punitive services. Youths who successfully complete the program have their records expunged when they reach the age of eighteen.

Kelvin has mixed feelings about the program. He notes a distinct racial pattern wherein white youths are overwhelmingly referred for services, while black and Hispanic youths are disproportionately excluded. Kelvin also worries about the efficacy of the program, as he believes that some teens' success in the program is due more to their charm and apparent compliance than remorse or rehabilitation. One such client, Bennett, is about to graduate from the program, pending Kelvin's letter of recommendation. Kelvin, however, has an instinctual concern that behind Bennett's genial exterior is a cunning sociopath. How can Kelvin ethically address his concerns about the program and about Bennett?

Not only does Kelvin feel tension between Bennett's interests and the community's, but he may also be concerned about his own well-being in speaking out about the program and the racial disparities he observes. In the latter, he must consider his interests along with the interests of those who are unfairly excluded from the program. Ultimately, this dilemma may be as much about the courage to take action as it is about deciding what to do.

Assess Options

Although Kelvin's concern about Bennett focuses on a micro-level client system and the concerns about the program are macro-level matters, Kelvin's choices in both boil down to two options: he can speak up or remain silent. Of course, there are complexities within these two extremes and nuances in how they might be carried out, but at this point the two extremes are sufficient for the purposes of ethical analysis.

In order to assess these choices, we must understand the basis for Kelvin's concerns. Is there data to support Kelvin's impression that youths of color are being disproportionately screened out of the program? On what basis was the department's intervention selected? How is it evaluated? Is there an empirical basis for the belief that it should work? Is there data to indicate that it does not? And what foundation does Kelvin have for his apprehensions about Bennett? Do the client's actions, independent evaluations, or other legitimate processes support the suspicion that he is a sociopath?

Gut instincts about a client's capacity, about racial disparities, or about a program's efficacy are not illegitimate sources of concern. But as we weigh the risks and benefits of action and the impact of misdirected action, we want to go forward on as solid a basis as possible. A first step, then, before Kelvin decides to speak up or remain silent about any of his concerns, is to bolster his impressions with facts. They may not be conclusive, but they will help ensure that his instinctual reactions are not themselves artifacts of stereotypes, biases, and misunderstandings. The stronger the support for Kelvin's concerns, the more likely others will find them legitimate and cooperate with him to effect change.

Ethical theories and principles. In addition to balancing the needs of various constituencies, Kelvin's dilemma can also be seen as a short-term vs. long-term problem. Acting (or failing to act) will have immediate and enduring repercussions for those same constituencies. What consequences should be considered when we employ a utilitarian lens to view the merits of speaking up or staying silent? In regard to Bennett, speaking out may mean speaking to the referring judge or writing frankly about his concerns in his letter of recommendation. Or it might mean withholding the recommendation entirely. If Kelvin's concerns are well founded, his actions may prevent future harms that Bennett could commit, but more likely they will simply lay a paper trail that can be utilized should Bennett run afoul of the law in the future. Speaking up will probably ease Kelvin's conscience if he does all he feels he can do to express his reservations about the young man.

Kelvin's actions could also have negative effects. They could stigmatize Bennett and single him out unfairly if positive recommendations are routinely issued for all participants and his is withheld. His actions could result in a backlash from Bennett, his family, and others who want to avoid interpersonal conflict or negative publicity about the program. These consequences are avoided if Kelvin decides to go along with the status quo rather than express his concerns. However, doing so may mean that Bennett goes into adulthood with a clean record and the confidence that he "got one over" on the authorities.

In regard to Kelvin's concerns about the efficacy of the program, speaking up may result to improvements to the interventions which will advantage the program and the youths referred to it. At the very least, his actions should lead to efforts to measure the program's efficacy. Kelvin's peers, superiors, and community leaders may be grateful for the effort if they share his apprehensions, or they may be angered that he is calling the program's utility into question. In an environment of tight budgets, mere questions of efficacy can lead to discontinuation of funding. That might be bad for the program and its employees, but it is ultimately good if the resources go to efforts that yield better results, and the community and clients are no longer misled about the program's worth. Kelvin's efforts would be in vain, though, if the program survives intact despite examinations revealing that it is ineffective. As evaluations of the DARE drug prevention program have demonstrated, popular programs often have staying power despite research that suggests they should be discontinued or changed (Jarlais, Sloboda, Friedman, Tempalski, McKnight, & Braine, 2006; U.S. General Accounting Office, 2003). If Kelvin's call for evaluation is unpopular with his colleagues, he may face personal consequences, including alienation, poor performance ratings, and perhaps even dismissal. These repercussions may not be fair or warranted, but they are the reality often faced by whistle-blowers, regardless of setting (Schulman, 2007).

Kelvin's concerns about the racial disparity in referrals may be met with less animosity. If he is successful, raising these concerns will provide immediate and perhaps long-lasting benefits for youths who are allowed to attend the program and graduate with clean records. Depending on the capacity of the program, opening it up to more youngsters may mean that others are still excluded. In that case, the program and the referring agencies will need to allocate the spots on some rational basis rather than the racial profiling that is done now. An influx of new referrals may mean that previously eligible youths will not get in, but it will ensure that appropriate criteria are used to select those who do.

A utilitarian perspective would encourage Kelvin to speak up, assuming there is legitimacy to his concerns. While he may face personal harm in his activism, greater goods are achieved by his action than by his silence. Interesting variations emerge when a rules-based perspective is applied. Would we want people to remain passive when injustice is being done, for example, through racial profiling or the misuse of funds on ineffective (and perhaps harmful) programs? Hopefully, the answer is no! Nor would we want people to sacrifice these goods for the benefit of their own interests. Deontology appears to support activism in the macro-level concerns.

What about with Bennett? Presumably there are rules about what youths must do to successfully complete the program. If Bennett has complied with expectations, would we want Kelvin to withhold his recommendation because he distrusts Bennett? Would we want Kelvin to demand extra testing or evidence for Bennett when neither is required for other participants? These actions are unappealing both in Bennett's case and as a matter of routine.

Should workers who believe their clients are generally dangerous be able to have them incarcerated or identified as potential threats to public safety? Times of heightened insecurity make people wish for protections that are not feasible or that create other harms. Despite Kelvin's desire to alert the world to the danger Bennett may pose, there is no feasible mechanism to make that happen absent a specific threat. And without that threat, how do we distinguish Bennett from anyone who looks different, acts unconventionally, or in some way makes us ill at ease? People deserve to be safe, but safety means little if we can't be certain of the nature of the peril. However, if Kelvin's choice is to write an honest report about Bennett, we would applaud this as a universal rule, because the assumption is that it would then apply to all participants. If it is good to have truthful recommendations, Kelvin's recommendations for every client should be truthful. Whether Kelvin should speak up in Bennett's case depends, from a rules-based perspective, on how and why he means to do so.

Evaluating Kelvin's choices according to the principle of autonomy is complex. As is often true for individual-vs.-community dilemmas, the outcome depends on whose autonomy is given preference. Certainly Kelvin's choice to speak up or not speak up about any of his concerns would be an exercise in his own freedom. If he acts to ensure better access to the program, that would enhance the autonomy of the youths who will benefit from inclusion. If he chooses to withhold a recommendation from Bennett, write a negative one, or otherwise alert people to the risk he poses, he will impede Bennett's autonomy, which is entirely the intent of such actions. Facilitating Bennett's freedom, in spite of Kelvin's significant concerns about him, may ultimately impinge on the autonomy of others if Bennett brings them harm.

The principles of fidelity and veracity ask Kelvin to be trustworthy and true to his agreements. If he perceives flaws in his program, either in admissions data or interventions, those principles would place responsibility on him to act by calling others' attention to his concern and by being a constructive agent of change. Overlooking deficits or shirking responsibility because it is not his job violates the trust placed in him as a professional and a steward of scarce resources. Similarly, justice is served when the program's resources are fairly allocated and employed as intended.

Kelvin should also keep his promises in regard to Bennett. Fidelity, veracity, and justice are compromised if Kelvin holds Bennett to a different standard than other program participants, whether by withholding the recommendation, writing a negative one when positive ones are routine, or speaking out to others about Bennett's troubling profile. However, if such actions are in keeping with Kelvin's traditional role and with the expectations he set forth when Bennett joined the program, those principles are upheld.

Laws and policies. In a program that offers diversion from legal sanctions such as incarceration, there are likely supporting policies and regulations defining Kelvin's role. These should specify the referral criteria for the program, the services to be provided, and the expectations for participants. It is important for Kelvin to be familiar with all these elements before he proceeds with his decision making.

If those elements are undefined, an appropriate action step would be to develop and explicate them for clients, staff, and referral sources.

Privacy laws would be relevant should Kelvin decide to speak out about Bennett. The relationship between the program and the court probably permits communication between the two entities as a condition of a youth's participation. Thus, Kelvin would not be legally constrained from sharing his observations with court authorities, though he would not be at liberty to do so with other individuals or via public safety announcements. Once again, we must note that Kelvin should exercise discretion in what he shares. Observations, case information, Bennett's statements, and other facts are permissible, but Kelvin should be wary of sharing his gut reactions without the benefit of other supporting evidence, as laws about defamation protect people from injurious and unfounded comments by others.

Ideally, Kelvin's activism on behalf of program improvements would be protected from retribution. Statutes might provide protection in the case of fraud or civil rights violations. Unfortunately, whistle-blower statutes are narrowly drawn and poorly enforced. They might offer redress if Kelvin's reputation or employment is harmed by his decision to speak out, but it would be unwise to rely on that possibility.

Values. As noted earlier, in times of national insecurity, societal values tend toward enhancing safety even at the expense of abridging due process protections and individual freedoms. Thus community values would encourage Kelvin to take action, particularly if it is needed to neutralize a threat posed by Bennett. Citizens also tend to condemn wasteful spending, thus supporting Kelvin's efforts at improving program efficacy. Action is also in keeping with the social work values embracing social justice, integrity, and competence.

The value placed on people's dignity and worth has interesting applications to Bennett's situation and in fact all individual-vs.-other dilemmas. The NASW (1999) Code states that "Social workers treat each person in a caring and respectful fashion, mindful of individual differences and cultural and ethnic diversity. Social workers promote clients' socially responsible self-determination. Social workers seek to enhance clients' capacity and opportunity to change and to address their own needs. Social workers are cognizant of their dual responsibility to clients and to the broader society. They seek to resolve conflicts between clients' interests and the broader society's interests in a socially responsible manner consistent with the values, ethical principles, and ethical standards of the profession" (pp. 5–6). The value suggests that Kelvin treat Bennett and his other clients honestly and respectfully, giving them the chance to succeed but also holding them accountable if they fail. Responsibly reconciling competing interests might mean writing an accurate and thorough evaluation about Bennett, without either avoiding his concerns or rashly overstating and broadcasting them.

Since Kelvin's program is situated in a police department, the values of the host setting must be considered, as they will somehow influence or impede his actions. To the extent that the department emphasizes accountability for criminals, they may disdain Kelvin's program as an impediment to punishment. That might mean the department would support action to address Kelvin's concerns about Bennett and efforts to make the program more effective. Kelvin will need to be mindful of the setting's values and the ways those might be leveraged in as he pursues his strategies even as he gives precedence to the values of his own profession.

Information. As described earlier, an essential piece of information is the substantiation of each of Kelvin's concerns. Beyond that, his choices might be influenced if he knows how raising his concerns about Bennett might make a difference. That is, would a poor recommendation mean he would be remanded to complete his original sentence, or would he be enrolled in another program, or reenrolled in Kelvin's? We know nothing about Bennett's original crime, his family, or his social and educational functioning. More information about these would help in strategizing other avenues to monitor Bennett, help him, and hold him accountable after he leaves Kelvin's program.

It would help to know why the judges are differentially referring white clients to the program. Is it an artifact of institutional racism reflecting disproportional differences in the categories of crimes youths of color are charged with? Is it the result of individual biases and stereotypes? Is it due to insufficient information about the program or about enrollment patterns by race? Each of these causes would lead to different strategies for intervention should Kelvin decide to act.

A similar diagnosis is needed for the program itself. Are the shortcomings Kelvin notes reflective of fundamental flaws in the theoretical or empirical base for the interventions? Are the problems more about inconsistency or incompetence in how the program is carried out? Are there ethical concerns? Do poor boundaries or a default to mercy over justice mean that staff members inappropriately align with the clients and fail to hold them accountable?

It would also be helpful to be familiar with precedents in each of the areas of concern. Have the concerns been raised before? What change efforts were attempted? To what ends? Who else might notice or care about these issues? What power do they have to elevate awareness about the issues, attract allies, or generate resources for improvements?

Standards. As with social work values, ethical standards require decision makers to balance individual and societal rights. Specifically, a "social workers' responsibility to the larger society or specific legal obligations may on limited occasions supersede the loyalty owed clients, and clients should be so advised" (NASW, 1999, 1.01). The informed consent process should have addressed expectations for Bennett and other clients, their rights and responsibilities, and those of the staff. Confidentiality standards would also require the informed consent process to convey the circumstances under which information gleaned from the clients would be shared. This is particularly important in research and clinical services for clients involved in the correctional system, as workers may be compelled to share information on past crimes if they are revealed.

NASW (1999) standards clearly have a predisposition for action in regard to quality and fairness concerns at the agency:

- "Social workers should work to improve employing agencies' policies and procedures and the efficiency and effectiveness of their services" (3.09b).

- "Social workers should base practice on recognized knowledge, including empirically based knowledge, relevant to social work and social work ethics" (4.01c).
- "Social workers should not practice, condone, facilitate, or collaborate with any form of discrimination on the basis of race, ethnicity, national origin, color, sex, sexual orientation, age, marital status, political belief, religion, or mental or physical disability" (4.02).
- "Social workers should work toward the maintenance and promotion of high standards of practice" (5.01a).
- "Social workers should uphold and advance the values, ethics, knowledge, and mission of the profession. Social workers should protect, enhance, and improve the integrity of the profession through appropriate study and research, active discussion, and responsible criticism of the profession" (5.01b).
- "Social workers should monitor and evaluate policies, the implementation of programs, and practice interventions" (5.02 a).
- "Social workers should promote and facilitate evaluation and research to contribute to the development of knowledge" (5.02b).
- "Social workers should act to expand choice and opportunity for all people, with special regard for vulnerable, disadvantaged, oppressed, and exploited people and groups" (6.04b).

These actions are not only important for the betterment of clients, the program, and the profession. They are also important for the messages they send to aspiring social workers. The NASW (1999) Code notes that social workers "should provide instruction based on the most current information and knowledge available in the profession" (3.02a). Should Kelvin fail to act, the reverberating effects will include the impressions left on the students placed at the agency, who may leave without a proper appreciation for integrity, program quality, or equity.

As mentioned in chapter 4, society's response to adolescent offenders has vacillated between rehabilitation and retribution. The practice standards in Kelvin's department may fall anywhere along this continuum in balancing community protection, system and offender accountability, and offender competency. Which of these he emphasizes most heavily will depend on the nature and status of Bennett's original offense, Kelvin's role in influencing Bennett's sentence, and his assessment of how he can have the best impact on Bennett's behavior.

Be Mindful of Process

As noted earlier, how Kelvin decides to speak out about any of the matters before him will influence the success of his efforts. These are all, then, matters of process and strategy. Some choices are more ethical than others, and some are simply more likely to be effective. Inducing Bennett to commit another crime so he can be reapprehended might be effective, but not ethical. Sending a vague letter of warning to the court might be ethical, but it would not be effective. Writing a frank report of Bennett's conduct in the program with a sound assessment of his capacity for recidivism and forwarding it to the referring judge would be both ethical and effective. And so it is for each of Kelvin's concerns.

The literature on large-systems change will be able to guide Kelvin's decision-making process and outline the skills necessary to carry them out effectively (Frey, 1990; Kirst-Ashman, 2008; Kirst-Ashman & Hull, 1997). For example, Brager and Holloway's (1983) five-step strategy for instituting internal organizational change could inform Kelvin's process as he works to make the referrals less biased and improve the efficacy of his program. In brief, the model suggests beginning with an extensive initial assessment, which involves understanding where the proposed change fits with existing organizational values, whether it addresses a generally recognized problem, whether it can be implemented incrementally or reversed if it does not work, identifying the resources required to implement the change, and estimating how widespread its impact will be. This phase also requires the change agent to identify both pro-change forces and restraining forces and determine what forces will be amenable to change.

In the second step, pre-initiation, Kelvin would strategically build social capital (relationships and respect), develop legitimacy as a spokesperson or resource on the issues, increase awareness of the changes that are needed, and encourage others to take on leadership in the change efforts. Next, initiation involves developing a coalition that is committed to implementing the changes. Here Kelvin would shift the focus of his appeal from people who already care about the issues to key decision makers, developing communications about the proposed changes to reduce resistance to their adoption. Even if the proposals are adopted, resistance may reemerge as people experience the impact and discomfort of change. Therefore, in the implementation stage Kelvin and his allies should act when support is at its peak, identify obstacles in advance, set and achieve interim goals, and be open to feedback and transparent in their communications. The last step, institutionalization, involves standardizing the new procedures and linking them to established organizational elements, thereby minimizing the chances that the changes will be sabotaged or undone.

The strategies for large-scale change vary along a continuum ranging from collaborative efforts to adversarial or conflict-based tactics; like his options concerning what action to take in regard to Bennett these strategies vary in their efficacy and ethics. Kelvin's consultants can assist him in the formulation of change strategies that will maximize the possibility of good results and minimize the possibility of negative ones.

Consult

Hopefully, Kelvin has been sharing his observations and concerns with his supervisor since they emerged. If he has not, he should certainly do so as he contemplates action. The supervisor may not support and may even thwart any of Kelvin's choices, but the discussion between the two is important, and it serves as a demonstration of respect for the hierarchy in the change process and as a gauge for Kelvin to assess the degree of support or opposition he will experience.

Kelvin might also consult individuals with expertise particular to his areas of concern. An expert in criminal pathology might help him understand the features to look for and instruments that could substantiate or refute his concerns about Bennett. Colleagues in the field of criminal justice might help him strategize ways to get extra services for Bennett or mitigate the risks that his freedom might bring. These same colleagues might be able to help with evaluation and refinement of the interventions Kelvin's program uses. Researchers and state or federal juvenile justice officials might also be resources for program evaluation. A person familiar with the state judiciary and particular judges can advise Kelvin about the possible causes for racially disparate referrals and promising tactics for change. This is not to suggest that Kelvin has the right or responsibility to independently pursue program changes. Rather, consultation may help him assess how close his service is to demonstrated best practices and what steps and assistance might be accessed if program administrators wish to pursue change.

The challenges in this dilemma go beyond deciding what is right or best and making it happen. They also involve Kelvin's fundamental willingness to take on the problems and try to effect change, even without certainty of success. Moral courage, or the readiness to endure danger for the sake of principle, is never easy (Kidder, 2005). Kevin can benefit from both strategic assistance and more personal support. For the latter, he may turn to mentors, family members, friends, leaders in his faith community, and others who can offer him solace or inspiration.

Document

Precise documentation establishes a record of Kelvin's concerns and the outline of his ethical decision-making process and the resulting actions. Record keeping provides crucial support for his efforts at mitigating Bennett's potential for damage. It also helps him organize his efforts at system change. As a risk management device, Kelvin's record of his concerns and the related communications may be important should others attempt to punish him for his activism.

Despite his intense reactions to Bennett, Kelvin must be restrained and professional in his communications on the case. As the NASW (1999) Code of Ethics states, "Social workers should not use derogatory language in their written or verbal communications to or about clients. Social workers should use accurate and respectful language in all communications to and about clients" (1.12). This advice could be broadened to the macro-level aspects of Kelvin's dilemma. His documents and conversations about program shortcomings and racially skewed referrals should be descriptive and impartial, clearly addressing the issues without condemning the intent or character of those involved.

Evaluate

What is a successful outcome? Sometimes in individual-vs.-other dilemmas it is hard to tell, because one person's happy ending is another's undoing. This complexity is evident in some of the possible outcomes in this case:

- Kelvin acts based on his gut regarding Bennett, and his gut is wrong.
- Kelvin fails to act, and Bennett causes harm or is given insufficient punishment as a result of his clean record.
- Kelvin remains silent about the perceived flaws in the program. He keeps his job and avoids experiencing distress, but the youths who participate show little improvement.
- Kelvin tries to create change in the program but is marginalized by anti-change forces and fails to accomplish what he set out to do.
- Kelvin decides not to broach his perception of racial preference in referrals. He is still able to effectively work in the program. Vast numbers of otherwise eligible youths are sentenced to jail and accumulate criminal records instead of having the opportunity for rehabilitation and a fresh start.
- Kelvin raises large-systems concerns and is able to increase awareness about referrals and a commitment to ongoing program evaluation and improvements.

Success in changing systems and protecting the community is ideal. But if Kelvin falls short of that, has he failed? Evaluation of his decisions will help us identify the constructive elements within mixed results. It will point to tactics and techniques that might have been handled differently. And it will point out the damage that can occur when one fails to act. We have noted that Kelvin might pay a price for his activism, but we are less aware of the price he might pay for moral cowardice. John McCain says it best: "I can recall all too well those times I've avoided the risk of injury or disappointment by overruling the demands of conscience. . . . Remorse is an awful companion. And whatever the unwelcome consequences of courage, they are unlikely to be worse than the discovery that you are less a man than you pretend to be" (McCain & Salter, 2004, pp. 70–71). Effective evaluation must assess the road not taken, as well as the results of the choices made.

Case Conclusion

Because individual-vs.-community dilemmas always advantage one person's position or well-being over another's, decision makers must have well-substantiated foundations for action. There is no room for biases, presumptions, or knee-jerk reactions. Ethical decision making helps to reveal the presence of these flaws. It may also facilitate compromises that benefit both parties. The considerations and consultations in decision-making processes can also reveal strategies for maximizing the likelihood of success in any given outcome.

But no decision-making model is beneficial if the decision maker lacks the will to act. Someone once said to me, "When it comes to power versus principle, power always wins." The ultimate risk in individual-vs.-community decisions is that those without privilege, connections, money, or majority will never prevail, even when their cause is just. The willingness to stand up and speak out is not easy or painless. But standing up for strangers on the basis of principle sets a powerful example and lays the groundwork for change.

TODAY'S YOUR BIRTHDAY

Katie has been a child protective services worker for thirteen years. She lives with her new husband and his children in the rural community where she works. The seventh birthday of her oldest stepdaughter, Juli, is approaching, and there has been a lot of discussion about the theme for her party. As they work together on the guest list, Katie realizes that several of the children Juli has included are current or former clients of CPS.

Not all individual-vs.-community dilemmas involve vast social inequities played out on a global scale. Sometimes they play out in our living rooms. Katie must consider the needs of her stepdaughter, herself, and her agency's clients in coming to a decision regarding the birthday invitations. Her decision and actions in the case will be both professional and personal in nature as she chooses whether or not to invite the children and how to carry out her decision.The ethical considerations involve worker-client boundaries and the evaluation of whether inviting clients and former clients would constitute a problematic dual relationship or other conflict of interest. Confidentiality issues are also prominent in this case, as Katie must protect the children's privacy in her conversations regarding the invitations and the party itself. As a helping professional, Katie must anticipate how exclusion from the party, or inclusion, may affect the children with whom she has or has had a working relationship. While some of those relationships are ongoing and some have ended, it is likely that some are more contentious than others, as some children probably experienced her interventions as disruptive, and others as helpful.

In addition to her professional responsibilities, Katie must consider her personal needs. Her desire to throw a fun and memorable party for Juli takes on even greater significance in light of her role as a new stepparent. Parents in the helping professions often must juggle overlapping relationships between their family members and the clients they serve. Children often become attuned to those complexities and make adjustments to their requests and questions in respect for their parents' professional obligations. However, given Juli's age and Katie's recent marriage to her father, she may not understand or appreciate those distinctions. Katie may also be concerned about her own privacy and safety. Inviting the children may mean interacting with their parents, which would set the stage for boundary crossings as the families negotiate pick-up and drop-off times and locations, gifts, and other aspects of the event. She may also be uncomfortable with the families knowing the location of her home, and having the children in her personal space and interacting with her in a different capacity (as Juli's stepmom, not their worker).

Assess Options

In light of the various considerations above, Katie's choices appear to be the following:

1. Invite all the children on Juli's list, including the children with whom Katie has worked
2. Limit the guest list to children without a history as Katie's clients
3. Have a family-only party and invite none of Juli's classmates

Variations of options 1 and 2 include moving the party to a public site, such as a museum or park, and having Juli's father act as the designated host. Those options may remedy some of the challenges in the case, so we should take them into account in examining the possible choices.

Ethical theories and principles. Katie's dilemma rests in the possible consequences of her choices, none of which may be appealing at first blush. Let's start by illuminating the possibilities, as part of a utilitarian examination, and determining which choices best meet the principles of beneficence and nonmaleficence. If Katie invites all the children on Juli's list, Juli will be happy, and it will not be necessary to explain why some children can come and some can't. The children who are CPS clients will not be marginalized and may even benefit from inclusion in social activities with Juli and their other classmates. Inviting all the children, even to a party at a public site at which Katie plays little or no role, may lead to relationships between Katie's family and the families she is serving. In ideal circumstances, this would offer a means for Katie and the children she serves or has served to develop a deeper understanding and empathy for each other. In that she got to know the children and their families under the worst possible circumstances, there may be benefits in coming to know them in a different respect, as fellow parents and community members.

Unfortunately, given the nature of Katie's agency and her role there, the consequences could be less than ideal. Unless Katie and her husband are totally secretive about their relationship, the families will know (if they don't already) about Katie's connection to Juli. That is, Katie can remove herself from the party, but not the relationship. This connection might be a source of confusion or distress for the children and an opportunity for various forms of retribution by family members. In that party invitations often incur reciprocal invitations, it is possible that Juli will be invited to parties hosted by those families. Will Katie and her husband be comfortable having her attend? Will they be able to discourage her from doing so? Clearly, Juli may receive such invitations (or others for playdates or sleepovers) anyway if the children are friends, regardless of whether the children are invited to Juli's party. However, the party invitation opens the door to further boundary incursions in the future.

Both negative and positive consequences can be seen in the option of excluding the CPS clients from the invitation list. Doing so may unfairly isolate and stigmatize children who have already suffered sufficient degradation to warrant CPS intervention. It will, by default, identify them as Katie's clients and potentially send a message that they are unworthy of her stepdaughter's friendship or inclusion in activities involving their classmates. It will be difficult to explain their exclusion to Juli without inappropriately revealing private information or resorting to the typically unsatisfactory "Because I said so, that's why" dictum. On the plus side, not including them frees Katie to fully participate in her stepdaughter's party and to feel comfortable doing so. It would give the family more options about where to have the party, if they prefer to host it at home rather than at a public site. It avoids potentially messy and contentious interactions between the parents involved with CPS and Katie and her husband. Having a firm boundary between work relationships and home relationships may make it easier for Katie to manage both worlds and may prevent conflicts of interest from arising if Katie has additional roles or interactions with the clients who are Juli's friends.

A family-only party would allow Katie to avoid making distinctions in inviting some classmates and not others. As such, it would avoid complications of boundary crossings that may arise from including the children, and the hurts that may come from excluding them. It will likely be an unsatisfactory resolution for Juli and the cancellation of a birthday party with her peers may detrimentally affect her relationship with Katie. Ultimately, having a family-only party may only be of limited benefit, in that Juli will continue to be classmates and ostensibly friends with Katie's clients. Failing to negotiate acceptable boundaries around these unavoidably coexisting relationships doesn't mean they will go away.

The tricky part in weighing the consequences in individual-vs.-other dilemmas is deciding whose consequences have the greatest import. Katie should put the needs of her clients before her own, but the question is *which needs*—the need for children to feel included and valued or for them to have pure relationships with their social workers? And even if Katie's needs get factored in secondarily, which ones take precedence—her need for privacy and for boundaries between her personal and professional relationships or her need to be fully involved in Juli's life? The question then becomes which consequences one can live with, given the fact that not all of them (positive or negative) may come to pass. The most desirable trade-off between risks and benefits would appear to be those offered by option 1, providing that no child or family presents a significant threat to Juli or Katie's well-being. Having the party in a non-private setting and managed by Juli's father attenuates Katie's involvement with the kids but allows all of Juli's friends to participate without putting the clients' privacy or dignity at risk through exclusion.

A rule-based examination of the choices is less straightforward. What laws are embedded in the options, and which would we desire to view as universally applicable? One rule evident in all the choices is that workers should maintain proper boundaries, emphasizing their professional relationships with clients and avoiding private relationships. Clearly there are strong ethical and clinical reasons for such boundaries. They help structure the interactions between workers and clients, in that they create norms for behavior, roles, and expectations that guide the helping relationship. Boundaries protect clients from the inappropriate, confusing, or exploitive interactions that often arise when two types of relationships co-occur (friend and client, supervisee and client, intimate partner and former client). While boundary maintenance and boundary transgressions have received a good deal of attention (Reamer, 2001; Schank, & Skovholt, 1997; Strom-Gottfried, 1999), they are not without critics. Some suggest that boundaries create an artificial and unhelpful distance between helper and helpee and are antithetical to empowerment and feminist perspectives, which emphasize mutuality and equality in personhood regardless of the roles played in a particular interaction (Ebert, 1997; Lazarus, 1994). Whether or not one embraces the importance of therapeutic boundaries, the reality is that they can be difficult to maintain, calling the feasibility of our universal rule into question. Katie's dilemma is a fairly common example of the ways that overlapping relationships can emerge, whether people find them appealing or not. Practice in rural areas and within particular faith communities and cultures makes it difficult to consistently maintain clear, firm, and impermeable boundaries. Thus, from a deontological perspective, the choices that exclude only the CPS clients seem unrealistic and undesirable.

What rules might be implicit in a decision to invite the CPS clients to the party? We would probably agree with the statement "Children should not be ostracized or excluded from activities with friends due to their status as involuntary clients." And while we may not wish it to be a universal law, we would probably favor a policy stating that "Children should be allowed to invite whomever they wish to their parties." To the extent that these two directives are embedded in option 1, our acceptance of them suggests an intention to invite all the children to the party. We should be clear that approving option 1 does not mean encouraging workers to breach boundaries and pursue external relationships with their clients and former clients. Option 1 does not permit or encourage that. Rather, it acknowledges Juli's relationships and allows them to exist without Katie's interference. Stated as a rule, it might read, "If social workers' children befriend clients, workers should not discourage those relationships." As parents, we might not be comfortable with this in all situations all the time, but it is probably preferable to (and more realistic than) the alternative.

Autonomy and justice are the most relevant ethical principles for Katie's dilemma. As always in individual-vs.-other scenarios, we must ask, "Whose autonomy?" and "Justice for whom?" These questions lead us to different choices. For example, to the extent that seven-year-olds are allowed to exercise autonomy, Juli's is advanced by the decision to permit her to choose from all her friends or classmates in making the invitation list. The classmates who received or currently receive services from Katie have the greatest autonomy if they are invited. In response, they or their parents can accept or decline, whereas if they are summarily excluded from invitation, the decision is made for them. On the other hand, Katie's autonomy to be free and authentic in her role as Juli's stepmother is best served if she can avoid inviting clients to the party. Preferencing the autonomy of different actors leads to different conclusions.

The principle of justice leads to less divergent outcomes. It seems unjust to exclude clients and former clients from the party simply because of their relationship with Katie. Especially in light of the circumstances under which they came to her attention, it seems cruel to exclude them from the party solely on the basis of their clienthood. Yet there are situations in which we must distinguish among and between clients and non-clients for legitimate nondiscriminatory reasons, such as safety, client capacity, and role clarity. Is justice served if there are within-group distinctions (e.g. if clients whose interactions with Katie were traumatic or hostile are excluded, but those with whom she had a positive experience are invited)? Is this a more rational, acceptable, and just way to fashion the guest list?

Laws and policies. The fact that the law has little interest in matters such as this makes them no less vexing. The agency may have policies relating to this problem, but they may not be operationalized with enough specificity to be of help. For example, the agency likely has policies regarding dual relationships. However, it is not clear whether this case would fit in standard definitions of that concept. If a client's relationship is with Katie's stepchild, not with Katie herself, is it her relationship? Would attending a single party be considered a relationship? Would it apply if Katie makes the rule that clients can't come to her home and her child can't go to theirs but that clients and former clients may be included in a group event? Consultation is vital to the interpretation of agency policies for situations such as Katie's and others that commonly arise in small towns.

Katie's employer likely has policies about accepting gifts from clients. This adds an additional wrinkle to her problem. Does the agency's no-gifts policy apply if clients or former clients are invited and bring Juli gifts? Do the gifts Juli receives create the possibility of a conflict of interest as Katie makes decisions in the children's cases? Does the expectation that guests will bring gifts to the party create undue financial and social hardship for any of the children, particularly those Katie knows as clients? Again, consultation will help ensure that Katie complies with the spirit and the letter of the policy.

Agency policies would also dictate that interactions with clients should be noted in the case record. Though a child's attendance at the birthday party would not be a professional interaction per se, Katie should still document the interaction. While this might make for an odd case note, it provides a measure of protection for Katie if questions are raised by clients, colleagues, or anyone else at a later date.

Values. Given her struggle with the decision of whom to invite, Katie appears to value taking an active role to make her stepdaughter's birthday a happy one. She also seems to value keeping a firm demarcation between her work relationships and her personal contacts. These values are understandable, particularly given her role as a new stepmother and the nature of her work. Without such boundaries, it might be impossible to fairly carry out difficult responsibilities, make life-and-death decisions, and avoid burnout while preserving her own well-being and comfort as a member of the community in which she works.

The social work profession's values have relevance for Katie's choices as well. In particular, she should consider social justice, the dignity and worth of the person, and the importance of human relationships. The value of social justice emphasizes attending to issues such as discrimination and other forms of injustice. It calls for workers to promote sensitivity to and knowledge about oppression and ensure that all people have equal opportunities and the chance to participate meaningfully in decision making. Social workers enhance the dignity and worth of others by treating them in a caring and respectful manner, encouraging their self-determination, and respecting their capacity for change. The value placed on human relationships emphasizes that these connections are the vehicles that enable change to occur. Specifically, "social workers seek to strengthen relationships among people in a purposeful effort to promote, restore, maintain, and enhance the well-being of individuals, families, social groups, organizations, and communities" (NASW, 1999, p. 6). This provision can be interpreted as encouraging workers to promote healthy connections between clients and their social systems. In this case, the relationships for some of the CPS clients include their friendships with Katie's stepdaughter Juli.

Taken together, these values seek to decrease the distance between professional and client, between the person who is helping and the one who is receiving help. They don't suggest that boundaries are irrelevant or erasable, but they do encourage sensitivity to the child clients and constructive inclusion in Juli's party.

Information. Information about the norms in Katie's community, workplace, and family would help us sort out the options for action. For example, some schools and classes have policies that students who wish to invite some of their classmates to a party must invite them all. Is this the case at Juli's school? Clearly, if it is, it would be harsher and more difficult to hold a party with only some of her classmates. What are the norms regarding parties in this area and for this age group? How much do parents tend to discuss among themselves such things as planning, transportation, and gifts? Is it common for parents of guests to attend if they wish?

If one possible area of tension or concern is the expectation that guests bring gifts, is it possible to have a party without gifts? Alternatively, can gifts be for something else (food for an animal shelter, for example)? A creative solution that is acceptable to Juli will allow Katie to avoid putting any of the children in a position of financial hardship or social pressure due to the expectation that they must buy gifts for Katie's stepdaughter.

It would be helpful to know more about the nature of the relationship between Katie and Juli. If theirs is a tenuous or fractious relationship, Katie may feel particular pressure to be part of Juli's celebration and to support Juli's wishes to the greatest extent possible. If their relationship is trusting and solid, Katie may be more comfortable standing back from the party planning or asserting her own needs and wishes to plan a more selective or family-oriented event.

Similarly, it would help to know specifically about Katie's relationships with the families and children who may attend the party. The more contentious or fragile the relationships, the more difficult it may be to negotiate their inclusion, especially if Katie plays a substantial role in chaperoning the party. For example, a child whose removal from the home was traumatic may associate Katie with that negative event. In light of this, would an invitation to the party be beneficial to the child, or would it lead to recollections of a sad and troubling time? Will a child who is no longer able to celebrate birthdays with her own family be distressed at the sight of Juli's interactions with Katie? A family that blames Katie and CPS for intruding in their private affairs may have such animosity that their involvement would jeopardize the event for Juli and the other participants. Conversely, a family reported for neglect or a child Katie protected from harm may have no qualms or difficulties interacting with Katie and seeing her with her family at the party.

This issue raises questions about the norms of the rural community in which Katie resides and the norms of her practice setting. Workers in rural settings must quickly come to terms with the heightened visibility and the permeable boundaries that characterize practice in small communities (Manning & Van Pelt, 2005). It would help to know how much experience and comfort Katie has juggling her roles as a member of the community and a CPS worker. Surely there have been other instances of interactions with clients, at school events, in the grocery store, at local functions, or on the streets. Her ability to negotiate these encounters will be telling in terms of her capacity to manage more personal interactions at Juli's party. Does Katie chafe at her visibility or take it in stride? Can she carry out her daily activities without excessive worry about how she is seen, or does she alter her behavior to avoid any possible unplanned contact with clients? The answers to these questions may indicate that a far more fundamental issue is embedded in Katie's dilemma. That is, how can Katie learn to reconcile her individuality and autonomy as a resident of the community with her job? If this is indeed a problem, it warrants attention in supervision or counseling, as it will arise repeatedly over the course of her career, no matter how she decides to resolve the dilemma at hand.

Standards. The NASW Code of Ethics cautions against an array of conflicts of interest that have the potential to compromise the worker's professional judgment and place clients at risk of exploitation. For example, "Social workers should be alert to and avoid conflicts of interest that interfere with the exercise of professional discretion and impartial judgment. Social workers should inform clients when a real or potential conflict of interest arises and take reasonable steps to resolve the issue in a manner that makes the clients' interests primary and protects clients' interests to the greatest extent possible. In some cases, protecting clients' interests may require termination of the professional relationship with proper referral of the client" (NASW, 1999, 1.06a). More specifically, the Code offers broad interpretation of multiple relationships, as a particular form of such conflicts: "Social workers should not engage in dual or multiple relationships with clients or former clients in which there is a risk of exploitation or potential harm to the client. In instances when dual or multiple relationships are unavoidable, social workers should take steps to protect clients and are responsible for setting clear, appropriate, and culturally sensitive boundaries. (Dual or multiple relationships occur when social workers relate to clients in more than one relationship, whether professional, social, or business. Dual or multiple relationships can occur simultaneously or consecutively)" (NASW, 1999, 1.06c).

Our discussion has identified the various difficulties that might arise for Katie and her clients if she assumes multiple roles with them (social worker and stepmother of a friend). When social workers are faced with unavoidable and problematic dual relationships, one alternative is to end the helping relationship. Doing so is not a perfect solution, but it does remove potential future complications that may arise once the worker has related to the client in multiple capacities. This seems an unlikely and unsatisfactory option in Katie's case, as the nature of her community is such that overlapping relationships are a way of life. Further, her involvement with the cases has already been intense and powerful. Termination might end her personal involvement, but it will not erase what she knows of the children and their families or what they know of her. It does not seem that transferring the cases will make the conflicts of interest go away, though this is certainly an option Katie and her supervisor can explore.

What would setting "clear, appropriate, and culturally sensitive boundaries" mean in Katie's case, should she decide to relate to the CPS clients in her capacity as Juli's stepmom? Practice standards and concepts on boundaries in helping relationships are relevant in light of the risks and benefits already discussed. They would require Katie to be forthright about her two roles and the ways that she keeps them distinct. This might mean offering assurances of confidentiality as part of initial informed consent discussions and clarification about how she will behave when interacting with the children in different circumstances outside the helping relationship. These conversations must allow clients to opt out of such an arrangement if they are uncomfortable with the terms of the overlapping contacts. While peremptory discussions such as these are helpful in managing community contacts, such conversations may be inappropriate or unfeasible in light of the crises and conflicts that frequently characterize Katie's cases.

What constitutes an "appropriate" boundary depends greatly on the type of contact Katie has in the worker role and the intensity of her involvement in her role as Juli's stepparent (Gottlieb, 1993; Reamer, 2001). The notion of thick and thin boundaries is relevant here. The concept of thick boundaries refers to situations and clients with whom very firm and impermeable boundaries must be enforced, as opposed to those where more flexible (or thinner) boundaries suffice. For example, some of the children may be able to understand and tolerate the two types of involvements with Katie due to their maturity, their positive bond with her, or the low level of rancor between CPS and their family of origin. In these instances, co-occurring relationships are unlikely to be harmful and may carry benefits. Conversely, in cases where there is the threat of harm, confusion, or retribution; the risk of manipulation of Juli or the private relationship; or other hazards, any efforts to relax boundaries will be more harmful than helpful. And, in reality, it may be easier to make these distinctions than to act on them. If Katie determines that most of her clients or former clients could tolerate the dual relationship, but that two cannot, can she realistically differentiate between them in issuing birthday invitations? The distinction may work in some situations (such as decisions regarding whose home Juli could visit), but it won't help with the birthday party.

The expectation that social workers will be culturally sensitive in setting boundaries in dual relationships applies in Katie's case. Because rural areas present their own challenges and conventions, Katie and her coworkers must consider the local norms in deciding how to manage the junction between their personal and professional lives (Boisen

& Bosch, 2005; Burkemper, 2005; Schank & Skovholt, 1997; Strom-Gottfried, 2005). Similarly, the degree to which her clients are accustomed to overlapping relationships with the children of teachers, doctors, and other adults in their lives may indicate how easily they will understand and adapt to interacting with her as Juli's stepmother.

Be Mindful of Process

What will Katie say to Juli as she tries to exclude certain children from the guest list? Is there any way to do so without revealing her connection to these children? Might she simply say, "I know some of your classmates' families through my work and that means I have to avoid seeing them during our family time"?

It may also be awkward to excuse herself from the party. Juli may wonder why Katie is not taking part and Katie may feel diminished in her role as stepmother. However awkward and undesirable these consequences may be, they are less troublesome than those that might occur should she take an active role in hosting a party to which clients are invited. Perhaps Katie could explain to Juli, "I know some of the children who will be attending, and they may be more comfortable if I am not at the party." This statement may satisfy Juli or it may pique her curiosity, but if it works, it explains Katie's reticence about attending the party without identifying any particular children as clients and makes it clear to Juli that Katie would come if she could. Katie's assessment of Juli's capacity to understand and honor this information will be crucial as she decides whether this (or any other) explanation is sufficient and acceptable.

A similarly sensitive conversation will need to take place if Katie concludes that a family-only party is the safest option. Juli will likely be disappointed at the change of plans and wonder why a party with her peers is forbidden. She may hold Katie responsible for it, and thus her father and Katie will have to think creatively to brainstrom an appealing alternative event in which Katie can take part.

If the family decides to invite all the children, how transparent should Katie be about the fact that her family is hosting the party? She and her husband may be tempted to put only Juli's name on the invitations, obscuring their role and the risk that some of the parents will react negatively to it. However, having Katie's name on the invitation is the more transparent alternative, and it allows the parents of her clients to choose not to permit the children to attend if they are uncomfortable with it. If her name is not there and the families later find out about her connection to Juli, they may feel deceived or suspicious of her motives.

Consult

Consultation will be important for Katie as she struggles to effectively reconcile her professional and personal roles. She can talk with her husband about the dilemma, without identifying specific children, in order to understand Juli's needs and interests and discuss possible compromises and complications. His actions and attitude may diminish the risk of negative effects for Katie and Juli's relationship if it appears that the party being planned is not in keeping with Juli's expectations and desires. It may also lead to a tradition of two parties, one with Juli's friends and hosted by her father, and one with the family, hosted by Katie. This hybrid solution allows Katie to avoid engaging in a dual role with her clients and to participate, in some fashion, in Juli's special day.

Clearly, Katie should consult with her supervisor and colleagues for interpretations of agency policies, creative strategies other workers have used in similar situations, and assistance in anticipating the risks and benefits of her choices. Individuals who understand ethics, her workplace, and her community can help Katie anticipate repercussions now and in the future. Regardless of how the birthday party question is solved, there will be future variations as other events and friendships arise, as Juli is invited to other children's homes, and as she begins to have more say in these matters. For assistance in evaluating these possibilities and further help in navigating dual relationships, Katie might refer to more formal resources, such as her professional association or licensure board or written works on the topic of boundaries in rural practice.

One last process and consultation issue involves talking directly with the parents involved. In other child-serving settings, social workers who are trying to manage situations like Katie's might discuss the issue directly with the child's parent. Such a conversation would allow Katie to determine their views on the issue and their comfort with the merging of roles and involve them as allies in identifying difficulties, setting boundaries, and explaining the role distinctions to the child client. In Katie's case, however, these may be difficult or impossible conversations to initiate. Even if the relationships are not adversarial, Katie is in a power position relative to the families, and this may make them uncomfortable working with her and making their true feelings and wishes known. The direct contact unrelated to her professional role may be perceived as inappropriate, coercive, or distracting from the work at hand. However, Katie's supervisory and collegial consultations are the perfect venues for examining the feasibility of such conversations, strategies for effectively initiating them, and the possible advantages of respectful and direct links to the classmates' parents.

Document

To properly document her quandary and decision-making process and the results, Katie should address the situation in the clients' case files. She should also include information about it in her notes from supervisory sessions, to verify that she raised her concerns with her supervisor, and indicate the nature of their discussions before, during, and after the decision is reached. She might also keep personal notes about other consultations and ideas on handling such predicaments. These notes offer a record of her actions in this instance, but they may also provide wisdom and guidance for future dilemmas of this sort, which are sure to arise, given her positions in the community.

Evaluate

Since the birthday party is likely only the first of many challenges in reconciling her personal and professional roles, Katie should pay careful attention to the effects of her choices and the way she carries them out. This will mean determining whether Juli understands the nature of her work and the times and ways it might affect Katie's availability and actions (for example, talking with apparent strangers, requiring privacy for emergency phone calls, or excusing herself from certain activities with other families). Evaluation will involve observation, conversation, and consultation to determine the reactions that clients and former clients have to whatever resolution she reaches on the party invitations and other events and adjusting practices as appropriate. It will also involve Katie monitoring her own reactions. Can supervision and practice teach her to reconcile her two roles, distinguishing more easily those cases where they can successfully coexist from those where firm boundaries are required?

Case Conclusion

There is no refuge from self-vs.-other dilemmas. Living in a different community from one's workplace or avoiding civic and social activities all have unfortunate implications for the worker's personhood and his or her efficacy as a social worker with the population he or she is trying to avoid. As in Katie's case, the easiest, safest, and most conservative path may only be a temporary solution in light of all the challenges involved in integrating one's personal and professional lives.

Social workers in all settings must reconcile their professional roles and responsibilities with their personal lives, family relationships, and human frailties. The worker who shouts at his teenager at the mall within earshot of a family he is treating for parenting deficits must come to terms with the visibility of such behaviors and the discomfort they create. Maturity and confidence help professionals acknowledge that they can be effective helpers without being perfect themselves. In fact, the appreciation of common human struggles can build empathy, compassion, and authenticity, thereby enhancing the helping relationship.

Yet even if these experiences are common, it doesn't diminish their impact and the dilemmas they create. Social workers facing self-vs.-other choices must seek a delicate balance between inappropriately putting their needs and interests before those of their clients and asserting proper rights and boundaries for their personal well-being and integrity. An understanding of concepts such as thick and thin boundaries may help in differentiating those situations in which personal and professional spheres of life can safely overlap from those in which they must be separate. Effective decision making in self-vs.-other scenarios also requires appreciation for the long-term and short-term implications of action, particularly when boundary crossings are involved. The handling of distinct and seemingly innocuous situations like a birthday party can open the door to more significant clinical and ethical repercussions. Consultation helps workers such as Katie to anticipate and accommodate these possibilities.

SUMMARY

By their very nature, individual-vs.-other dilemmas require us to favor one person's rights, risks, or opportunities over those of another individual or group. This choice is often painful and gives rise to apprehensions about liability, feelings of sympathy, and fears of injustice in privileging one person or group over another. The difficulty is compounded when these dilemmas involve minors. Given their limited legal rights and developmental capacities, choices involving children bring up responsibilities and protective impulses that are unlikely to emerge with adult clients. Dilemmas are further complicated by limitations in the child's ability to voice preferences, to understand risks and benefits, and to act autonomously. Thus, the weight the decision maker must bear is increased.

Thorough decision making helps workers establish the proper basis for deciding in favor of one party or another. It ensures that the choice is well grounded even if it is not wholly satisfactory. Consultation and creative problem solving in the process can allow win-win scenarios to emerge from what appear to be win-lose dilemmas.

Chapter 9

Hard Truths

In 2006, the parents and doctors of Ashley X, a six-year-old with profound brain damage, sought permission to use surgical and medical procedures to permanently stunt her growth. Once the consent of medical specialists and the hospital ethics committee was obtained, physicians performed a hysterectomy, surgically removed Ashley's breast buds, and administered high doses of estrogen to attenuate her development (Gunther & Diekema, 2006).

Ashley is assessed to have the mental capacity of a three-month-old. She cannot sit upright, talk, eat, or walk. She is responsive to her environment, though, and smiles and vocalizes in her interactions with others. When she began showing signs of early puberty, her parents considered the ways that her growth would affect her comfort and their ability to care for her. They argued that the hysterectomy was necessary to alleviate discomfort and confusion arising from her menstrual cycle and that the reduction in breast size would make Ashley more comfortable when strapped in a wheelchair (as an additional consideration, the parents have stated that breast cancer is common on both sides of the family). The family contends that "Ashley's biggest challenge is discomfort and boredom and the 'Ashley Treatment' goes straight to the heart of this challenge" (Ashley Treatment, 2007). Attenuating her growth is expected to maximize her involvement with her parents and siblings by allowing her to be moved from room to room, be present at meal times, and participate in car trips and other outings. The anticipated benefits of limiting her size are psychological (it is easier to include her in family activities), physical (reduced risk of bedsores and discomfort of menses), and practical (her parents can continue to act as caregivers, thus avoiding institutionalization for Ashley and its negative psychosocial effects).

The cost-benefit analysis of Ashley's case must take into account the risks of the procedures and the concerns that they raise. Some would suggest that it is really the parents who are benefiting from the treatment, not Ashley, and that they are in fact putting their fears and needs before her fundamental human rights (Brosco & Feudtner, 2006; United Cerebral Palsy, 2007). Further, the extreme and irreversible procedures performed on Ashley bring to mind the sad history of the eugenics movement, which forced people who were presumed to be defective to undergo sterilization procedures to ensure that their "defects" were not passed on to a subsequent generation. According to the disability rights perspective, this intervention sends the message that people with disabling conditions are unacceptable as they are and can be manipulated and deprived of natural life processes for the convenience of others (Somerville, 2007). The treatment raises particular ire among those who have suffered from discrimination, marginalization, and medical experimentation because their lives are considered to be of little value. "Stop it. We are not mice or rats or kitty cats. The final affront is to suggest that this matter is worthy of ethical attention" (Ellis, 2007, p. 419).

Ashley's family emphasizes how much they love and value her as a member of their family. The growth-limiting interventions are intended to enhance her participation in family activities, not to marginalize her and render her invisible. They refer to her as their "Pillow Angel," a reference to her sweet disposition and the fact that she stays where she is placed, usually on a pillow (Ashley Treatment, 2007). The term also appears to be coming into wider use as other families use it to refer to their youngsters in the same condition, and journalists use it in their accounts of these children (Gibbs, 2007). While the families clearly consider it a term of affection, it creates disturbing images of the objectification of Ashley and other children like her. One has to worry that such labels inadvertently permit intrusions into the personhood of these children that would be more disturbing if they were happening to Ashley, a six-year-old girl, rather than to a "Pillow Angel."

Those who support growth attenuation in Ashley's case acknowledge concerns that such processes may be misused or taken to even more troubling extremes. They advise careful screening and evaluation processes before the use of such measures. As to whose needs are being met by the procedure, advocates maintain that because Ashley is fully dependent on her parents, "the line between improving Ashley's life and making it easier for her parents to handle her scarcely exists, because anything that makes it possible for Ashley's parents to involve her in family life is in her interest" (Singer, 2007). The rationale for the treatment is akin to the rationale for other interventions that parents permit in order to alter natural processes in their children for long-term benefits, for example, immunizations or orthodontic braces. It is also similar to other interventions intended to arrest unnatural processes, for example surgery or chemotherapy for cancer and insulin shots for diabetes. In these cases as well, long-term benefits are believed to outweigh short-term suffering.

Whichever position one takes, Ashley's case, like many of those in this book, demonstrates several hard facts for which ethical decision making offers little comfort: even sound decisions may be troubling or unpalatable, child-serving systems are flawed, resources are finite, and parents are imperfect. Let's examine these barriers in light of Ashley's case and consider the strategies by which we can advance ethical decision making despite their effects.

SOLUTIONS ARE IMPERFECT

Even those decisions made with the soundest of methods may still yield results with which people are individually or collectively unhappy. By all reports, the processes used to weigh the pros and cons in Ashley's case were thorough and fully informed. We can't determine Ashley's satisfaction with the result, but clearly her parents and the treatment team feel they made a rational decision that ultimately enhances Ashley's quality of life. Still, the interventions to attenuate her growth are controversial and discomfiting.

Sometimes decisions are "good" because they are arrived at through thoughtful, deliberative processes, not because they are unanimous, risk-free, or satisfying. Sometimes good decisions are the least bad among many choices. Professionals in any field as complex as social work must come to terms with those cases in which there are no easy answers. The fear of risks, errors, and condemnation must be offset by confidence in the process, particularly in thoughtful, shared decision making and skillful execution of the decision. Evaluation can help to mitigate the ill effects of the decision or to improve future decisions. In Ashley's case, the decision required diverse sources of expertise to weigh the long- and short-term risks and consequences in light of her profoundly and permanently disabling condition. Those involved in the decision clearly documented and have openly shared the bases for their decisions. They feel it was appropriate, as do ethicists viewing the case from a distance (Ross, 2007a, 2007b; Singer, 2007). The fact that the decision is not wholly popular does not mean it should have been avoided or deferred. Evaluation, however, may improve future decision-making processes in similar cases. For example, it appears that no advocate with "explicit expertise in disability rights and autonomy" was invited or appointed to act on Ashley's behalf (American Association on Intellectual and Developmental Disabilities, 2007, ¶ 10). The inclusion of such a person in the decision-making process would have ensured that those perspectives were taken into account in the deliberations. Similarly, it later became evident that the hospital violated state law in performing the hysterectomy in the absence of a court order, required in all cases involving the sterilization of minors (Associated Press, 2007). Evaluation helps decision makers flag necessary steps and considerations that were not taken but will be necessary in future cases.

SYSTEMS ARE IMPERFECT

The evaluation of Ashley's case revealed a weakness in the decision-making process that can be rectified in future cases, though not in hers. Other cases in this book raised concerns about the limitations or frailties of the organizations and processes put in place to help children. Chapter 4 discussed some of the historical, political, and financial variables that limit systems' effectiveness. When service delivery falls short of aspirations, the professionals, consumers, and citizens involved must provide the critical feedback and advocacy necessary to encourage change. This is not a short or easy process, but failing to do so signals capitulation to the status quo and to a lifetime spent facing the same dilemmas the flawed system is now creating. Thus, unless fundamental changes are made to health care, education, welfare, and wage systems in the United States, social workers and their clients will continue to confront the same intractable dilemmas with the same unsatisfying results. The vital interface between micro- and macro-change efforts becomes abundantly clear in situations such as these.

As the J. Daniel Scruggs case revealed, some systems' problems are more about the humans working in the systems than the systems themselves. When employees' egos, attitudes, jealousies, apathy, or ignorance are the cause of system failures, new strategies must be employed. Different problems call for different measures, but communication, evaluation, and education can all be used to increase workers' quality and accountability. Ethical action may involve strategies for improving systems and the people who work in them (Netting, Kettner, & McMurtry, 2004).

RESOURCES ARE IMPERFECT

Many ethical dilemmas are, at their core, problems regarding the distribution of scarce resources. While it doesn't appear that money was an overt consideration in Ashley's case, the possibility of her family continuing to provide her care rather than placing her in an institutional setting is clearly a resource issue. Some who object to Ashley's treatment have suggested that the dilemma involves more than one family's choices and responsibilities. Rather, it reveals the insufficiency of funding and supports for the many families who must care for loved ones with chronic life-limiting conditions (Grossberg, 2007). As Brosco and Feudtner (2006) state, "If we as a society want to fundamentally revise the nature of the harrowing predicament that these parents face, then, in the end, more funds for home-based services, not more medication, is what is called for" (p. 1078). Whether or not home-based services are the answer, the fundamental point is that "easy," short-term, or case-specific solutions may derail efforts to look for long-term medical, structural, and service solutions that allow families to avoid the permanent and irreversible strategies undertaken with Ashley. More broadly speaking, at what point should social workers and other helping professionals stop trying to make do with untenable resource constrictions and turn their attention to the causes of the scarcity of those resources?

Even if we accept that funds are finite and societal needs are not, questions must still be raised about the processes by which decisions are made on how to utilize fixed resources. For example, within the U.S. health care system alone, could priorities be reallocated to create greater benefits for more citizens, in the form of prevention or early intervention? Could expenditures for advertising, shareholders, executive salaries, and stadium skyboxes be better used for patient care? Why is it that states can afford to spend millions of dollars on incentives to lure corporations to their regions but feel the need to nickel and dime their social and health services? Ethical practice requires critical awareness and action regarding resource allocation issues. Social workers and other professionals must transform frustration and outrage about individual clients' dilemmas into action on the core causes of those dilemmas. This action may take many forms, including personal education, public speaking, civic participation, testimony to legislative and regulatory bodies, lobbying, and activism in movements to address societal inequities. This goes beyond the social work standard that "Social work administrators should advocate within and outside their agencies for adequate resources to meet clients' needs" (NASW, 1999, 3.07a). Rather, it speaks to the fact that a "historic and defining feature of social work is the profession's focus on individual well-being in a social context and the well-being of society" (NASW, 1999, p. 1). Ethical action thus requires attention to the environmental forces that create enduring resource dilemmas.

PARENTS ARE IMPERFECT

The media's reports in Ashley's case frequently emphasized her parents' virtues. They were described as loving, well-educated professionals concerned with their daughter's interests. Advocates for interventions such as Ashley's insist that any such case must be carefully and individually assessed. Presumably, medical personnel and ethicists would not condone such interventions for children whose parents have ulterior motives, limited care-giving capacity, deficient communication skills, or the inability to appreciate the risks and benefits involved. One wonders if parents without the same socioeconomic means, educational attainment, and other forms of privilege would have even been offered the option of such treatment, much less allowed to pursue it. Had other parents sought the procedures, would authorities such as child protective services been contacted to pass judgment on their suitability to represent the child's interests?

Several cases in this text featured parents who are, perhaps, unlikable, unlucky, unscrupulous, or uninformed. Like the social workers in the vignettes, some readers may have chafed at the parents' decisions, and perhaps even at their right to make those decisions. As described in chapter 3, contemporary U.S. policies have attempted to balance the rights of children with the rights of their parents and guardians. Alternatives to those checks and balances come with unacceptable costs and risks. For example, who should decide what charitable gifts a child should receive, if not his parents? Where does the slippery slope end if parents are not allowed to make decisions about their child's care, privacy, or safety? As in most balancing acts, the price we pay for rights and protections is the conferral of those rights and protections in cases we may deem unworthy of those privileges.

It is sometimes easy to write off people with whom we disagree. However, effective ethical practice demands more of the professionals involved, if only for the sake of the child clients. A fundamental part of social work education involves the development of self-awareness and self-regulation and the capacity to bridge differences with client systems. In this process students learn to look beyond labels and stereotypes to understand the person behind the tough facade, laissez-faire attitude, or offensive actions. They learn to comprehend the principle of countertransference and the ways their experiences and relationships may play out in their work with clients. They are taught to understand value differences and to employ their professional values to give precedence to clients' needs. These lessons are not easy ones, and even when achieved, their impact can erode over time, as social workers contend with families who routinely and reprehensibly mistreat their most vulnerable members.

It is easy to understand how workers can lose patience and hope in light of the failure of parents to act wisely and honorably in regard to their children. Yet giving up on or demonizing parents creates significant problems for helping minor clients. Aside from exceptional circumstances, parents hold all the cards. Writing them off means alienating the very avenue by which the worker can interact meaningfully with the child. Despite their imperfections, incorporating the parents as partners in service delivery is the means to the end of helping the child. Further, children are incredibly loyal, even to families who have repeatedly failed them. The social worker who repudiates the family may put the minor client in an untenable position of choosing sides. Not only is this unfair to the child, but such triangulation often leaves the social worker as the alienated party. Forced to choose, the child will select the familiar, even over a well-meaning stranger.

There is a final rationale for looking beyond parents' deficiencies. Many parents are victims of the same abuses and injustices that we are trying to avert for their children. Who will help them if social workers view them only as impediments and problems? Who will stand up for the families disadvantaged by unjust systems and institutional racism if we as helpers write them off? Will alienating the parents help the kids? Will it fulfill the fundamental mission of social work?

To be sure, some parents do not deserve the right to speak for their children. In those cases, social workers must act to advance the interests and safety of the minors involved, even at the expense of the parents' wishes and well-being. But many more cases are less clear. In these, the professional aim is to find ways to help kids to be heard and to be healthy, even in unhealthy circumstances.

EFFECTIVE AND ETHICAL PRACTICE IN A WORLD OF IMPERFECTION

Despite the hard realities, strategies for avoiding and addressing ethical dilemmas exist. These include focusing on long-term as well as short-term goals; speaking truth to power; refusing to surrender to stereotypes, labels, powerlessness, or hopelessness; and maintaining clarity about the core objectives. Even when we do these things, many things are out of our control, yet our development as ethical decision makers is not. The strategies to ensure a lifetime of effective, ethical practice involve awareness, alliances, attention, and action.

Awareness in this context refers to self-knowledge. For ethical decision making, it means knowing our preferences and tendencies, prejudices, values, and weaknesses. For example, do we tend to prefer rules-based decisions? Do we typically champion the underdog? Do we worry so much about our liabilities that we avoid any decision that leaves us unsettled and sleepless? Do we habitually capitulate to authority, or do we bristle at it? Awareness asks us to be attuned to these tendencies and mindful of the ways they can subvert thorough and balanced decision making.

Awareness also requires us to think about the ways that our roles and experiences influence the stance we take when faced with ethical dilemmas. This is especially relevant to decisions involving minors. The concept of countertransference suggests that professionals unconsciously bring experiences from other realms of their lives to their helping relationships. The psychologist who was an adopted child, the physician who overcame learning disabilities and an inhospitable educational system, the social worker who investigated the death of a shaken baby, or the teacher continually berated by parents of underperforming students—each one brings those and other experiences to his or her ethical decision-making process. Awareness makes such perspectives tangible, allowing the professionals involved to use those experiences constructively and transparently, and preventing the contaminating effects they may have if they remain unexamined.

The recommendation for alliances means forging ongoing, trusting, honest relationships as a means for ethical action. This involves creating the kinds of supervisory or collegial relationships in which we can bring out our fears and frustrations and get effective advice. The suggestion that alliances should be ongoing and honest is grounded in the belief that we are most able to grow in ethical sophistication if we are comfortable examining our choices and actions and learning from them. Solid allies support us, but they also push us to know ourselves and to improve ourselves. Long-term relationships are the best mechanisms for both. Allies are also needed when ethical decisions are unpopular or when acting on a decision demands moral courage. Sometimes doing the right thing isn't the same as doing the easy thing. People who make hard, highly visible, or unpleasant decisions deserve the support of caring others.

Different but similarly important alliances are recommended for the ethical actions needed in long-term change strategies. In these cases workers can join groups, create coalitions, and contribute to causes that address the issues that are embedded in some of the hard truths discussed above.

Attention, the third strategy for ethical effectiveness, refers to a host of efforts to keep ethics on one's personal radar. It means being alert to dilemmas, taking lessons from the ethical actions of others, seizing opportunities to learn more, and applying those lessons in new contexts. Paying attention means we look for the ethical dimensions in our daily lives, in our environments, and in the events that surround us. Consider, for example, the following situations:

- Your daughter tells you her best friend is cheating on her boyfriend. How does the ensuing conversation with her proceed when we are attentive to ethics?
- Music videos and lyrics are often condemned for slurring and demeaning others. How do we introduce ethics into a discussion of respect, civility, free speech, and artistic freedom on this topic?
- Kids in a Head Start program rampage when Santa brings hand-me-down toys to the Christmas party. How do we understand their behavior? How do we respond as their Head Start workers, as donors, and as citizens?
- Therapists portrayed on TV and in film routinely violate professional standards on confidentiality and patient boundaries. Are we alert to the effects of those examples?
- A massive school shooting mesmerizes the nation. Are we capable of discerning the ethics involved as victims and perpetrators are portrayed by the media, the events are dissected, and remedies are offered?

Perhaps this makes it sound as if ethics is a full-time occupation. This is, admittedly, not a very appealing prospect. Yet, as we contend in chapter 2, the practiced struggle with ethical dilemmas improves our decisions and our conclusions. Critical thinking is enhanced when we pay attention to opportunities to learn more and exercise the skills of practiced ethics.

The last strategy for building our ethical capacity is action. Acting on our convictions and decisions is not easy. In doing so, we may encounter hatred, retribution, marginalization, and strife. But acting to uphold principles despite our fears is the very essence of moral courage. As Miller (2000) suggests, moral courage is also "the capacity to overcome the fear of shame and humiliation in order to admit one's mistakes, to confess a wrong, to reject evil conformity, to renounce injustice, and also to defy immoral or imprudent orders" (p. 254).

Some of us may look at the examples of whistle-blowers or other morally courageous individuals closer to home and conclude that there is simply too high a price to be paid for ethical action. Yet where are we without action? What sense is there in valuing professional or civic principles if no one is willing to stand up for them? While we may focus on the price to be paid for ethical action, we may lose sight of the cost of our failure to act. Obviously, there are ramifications for a community, a profession, or any other group when people are unwilling to speak up in support of accountability and shared values. There are implications for individuals as well that are evident when we calculate the erosion of self-respect that results from moral cowardice.

SUMMARY

Whatever the settings or populations involved, ethics is a complex exercise. There is no perfect, complete, and final recipe for ethical effectiveness. It is a process. The steps we take to have a better understanding of dilemmas and improve our decisions will surely help advance that process. Perhaps it will also help us seed strength in others. If, individually and collectively, we can avoid becoming paralyzed by cynicism, hopelessness, fear, or anger, we can encourage ethical action as well as ethical thinking. Each of us has abilities to contribute to the effort, which will, in the short run and the long run, honor the voices and choices of young people.

References

Adam, E. K. (2004). Parental and residential stability and children's adjustment. *Current Directions in Psychological Science, 13*, 210–213.

Adoption and Safe Families Act. (1997). P.L. 105-89, 111 Stat. 2115.

Ahrons, C. R., & Tanner, J. L. (2003). Adult children and their fathers: Relationship changes 20 years after parental divorce. *Family Relations, 52*, 340–351.

American Academy of Child & Adolescent Psychiatry. (2002). *Facts for families: The adopted child.* Retrieved April 16, 2007, from http://aacap.org/page.ww?name=The+Adopted+Child§ion=Facts+for+Families

American Association on Intellectual and Developmental Disabilities. (2007, January 11). *Board position statement: Growth attenuation issue.* Retrieved April 21, 2007, from http://www.aamr.org/Policies/board_positions/growth.shtml

Annie E. Casey Foundation. (2002). *Family to family: Tools for rebuilding foster care*. Baltimore, MD: Author.

Ashley Treatment. (2007). *Welcome to Ashley's blog.* Retrieved April 30, 2007, from http://ashleytreatment.spaces.live.com/blog

Associated Press. (2007, May 10). Hospital admits sterilization of disabled girl broke law. *News & Observer.* Retrieved May 10, 2007, from http://www.newsobserver.com/news/health_science/story/572451.html

Bandman, E., & Bandman, B. (2002). *Nursing ethics through the life span* (4th ed.). New York: Prentice Hall.

Bazemore, G., & Umbreit, M. (1995). Rethinking the sanctioning function in juvenile court: Retributive or restorative responses to youth crime. *Crime & Delinquency, 41*(3), 296–316.

Beauchamp, T. L., & Childress, J. F. (1994). *Principles of biomedical ethics* (4th ed.). New York: Oxford University Press.

Beauchamp, T. L., & Pinkard, T. P. (1983). *Ethics and public policy: An introduction to ethics.* Englewood Cliffs, NJ: Prentice-Hall.

Behrman, R. E., Kliegman, R. M., & Jenson, H. B. (2004). *Nelson textbook of pediatrics* (17th ed.). Philadelphia: Saunders.

Bernard, T. J. (1992). *The cycle of juvenile justice*. New York: Oxford University Press.

Boisen, L. S., & Bosch, L. A. (2005). Dual relationships and rural social work: Is there a rural code? In L. H. Ginsberg (Ed.), *Social work in rural communities* (4th ed., pp. 189–204). Alexandria, VA: Council on Social Work Education.

Boyle, P. J., & Callahan, D. (1995). Managed care in mental health: The ethical issues. *Health Affairs, 14*(3), 7–22.

Brager, G., & Holloway, S. (1983). A process model for changing organizations from within. In R. M. Kramer & H. Specht (Eds.), *Readings in community organization practice* (pp. 198–208). Englewood Cliffs, NJ: Prentice-Hall.

Braver, S. L., Ellman, I. M., & Fabricius, W. V. (2003). Relocation of children after divorce and children's best interests: New evidence and legal considerations. *Journal of Family Psychology, 17*(2), 206–219.

Brosco, J., & Feudtner, C. (2006). Growth attenuation: A diminutive solution to a daunting problem. *Archives of Pediatric and Adolescent Medicine, 160*, 1077–1078.

Burkemper, E. M. (2005). Ethical mental health social work practice in the small community. In L. H. Ginsberg (Ed.), *Social work in rural communities* (4th ed., pp. 175–188). Alexandria, VA: Council on Social Work Education.

California Department of Social Services. (2003). *The California child abuse and neglect reporting law: Issues and answers for mandated reporters.* Sacramento: State of California, Department of Social Services, Office of Child Abuse Prevention.

Centers for Disease Control and Prevention. (2006). *2002, United States suicide injury deaths and rates per 100,000, National Center for Injury Prevention and Control.* Retrieved September 4, 2006, from http://webappa.cdc.gov/sasweb/ncipc/mortrate10.html

Christ, G. H., Siegel, K., & Christ, A. E. (2002). Adolescent grief: "It never really hit me . . . until it actually happened." *Journal of the American Medical Association, 288*(10), 1269–1279.

Cleveland, C. (2005). A desperate means to dignity: Work refusal amongst Philadelphia welfare recipients. *Ethnography, 6*, 35–60.

Congress, E. (1999). *Social work values and ethics: Identifying and resolving professional dilemmas*. Chicago: Nelson-Hall.

Corey, G., Corey, M. S., & Callahan, P. (2003). *Issues and ethics in the helping professions* (6th ed.). Belmont, CA: Brooks/Cole.

D'Aprix, A. S. (2005). Ethical decision-making models: A two phase study. *Dissertation Abstracts International, 66* (05), 1957A. (UMI No. AAT 3177652)

Darr, K. (1997). *Ethics in health services management* (3rd ed.). Baltimore, MD: Health Professions Press.

Davis, J. K., & Shah, K. (1997). Bioethical aspects of HIV infection in children. *Clinical Pediatrics, 36*, 573–579.

De Jong, P., & Berg, I. K. (2001). Co-constructing cooperation with mandated clients. *Social Work, 46*, 361–374.

Dickson, D. T. (1998). *Confidentiality and privacy in social work: A guide to the law for practitioners and students.* New York: Free Press.

Dilut, E. (1972). Adolescent thinking a la Piaget: The formal state. *Journal of Youth and Adolescence, 4*, 281–301.

Divorce Magazine. (n.d.). *U.S. divorce statistics.* Retrieved May 3, 2007, from http://www.divorcemag.com/statistics/statsUS.shtml

Dougy Center. (n.d.). *Bill of rights of grieving teens.* Retrieved March 18, 2007, from http://www.dougy.org/default.asp?pid=8497582

Drake, R. E., Goldman, H. H., Leff, H. S., Lehman, A. F., Dixon, L., Mueser, K. T., et al. (2001). Implementing evidence-based practices in routine mental health service settings. *Psychiatric Services, 52*, 179-182.

Ebert, B. W. (1997). Dual-relationship prohibitions: A concept whose time never should have come. *Applied and Preventative Psychology, 6*, 137-156.

Ellis, E. B. (2007). Disabling children with disabilities. *Archives of Pediatrics & Adolescent Medicine, 161*(4), 419.

Emery, R. E. (2003). Symposium: Hearing children's voices: Children's voices: Listening and deciding is an adult responsibility. *Arizona Law Review, 45*, 621-627.

Emery, R. E., Otto, R. K., & O'Donohue, W. T. (2005). A critical assessment of child custody evaluations: Limited science and a flawed system. *Psychological Science in the Public Interest, 6*, 1-29.

Erikson, E. H. (1963). *Childhood and society*. New York: Norton.

Freud, S. (1973). *A general introduction to psychoanalysis*. New York: Pocket Books. (Original work published in 1924)

Freundlich, M. D. (1998). The case against preadoption genetic testing. *Child Welfare League of America, 77*(6), 663-679.

Frey, G. (1990). Framework for promoting organizational change. *Families in Society, 7*(3), 142-147.

Gambrill, E. (1997). *Social work practice: A critical thinker's guide.* New York: Oxford University Press.

Gibbs, N. (2007, January 7). Pillow angel ethics. *Time* [Electronic version]. Retrieved April 9, 2007, from http://www.time.com/time/nation/article/0,8599,1574851,00.html

Gladwell, M. (2005). *Blink: The power of thinking without thinking*. New York: Little Brown.

Goldstein, J., Freud, A., & Solnit, A. (1973). *Beyond the best interests of the child.* New York: Free Press.

Goldstein, J., Freud, A., & Solnit, A. (1979). *Before the best interests of the child.* New York: Free Press.

Goldstein, J., Solnit, A., Goldstein, S., & Freud, A. (1996). *The best interests of the child: The least detrimental alternative.* New York: Free Press.

Gottlieb, M. C. (1993). Avoiding exploitive dual relationships: A decision-making model. *Psychotherapy, 30*(1), 41-48.

Green, J. P., Duncan, R. E., Barnes, G. L., & Oberklaid, F. (2003). Putting the informed into consent: A matter of plain language. *Journal of Pediatric Child Health, 39*, 700-703.

Grossberg, R. I. (2007). Closing facilities for children: An unrealistic position. *Archives of Pediatrics & Adolescent Medicine, 161*(4), 418-419.

Gunther, D. F., & Diekema, D. S. (2006). Attenuating growth in children with profound developmental disability: A new approach to an old dilemma. *Archives of Pediatrics and Adolescent Medicine, 160*(10), 1013-1017.

Gutman, A., & Thompson, D. (1984). *Ethics and politics: Cases and comments.* Chicago: Nelson-Hall.

Health Insurance Portability and Accountability Act. (1996). 45 C.F.R. § 164.

Heyman, J. D. (2003, October 20). Did bullying—or a mother's neglect—drive a 12-year-old boy to commit suicide? *People*, 117-118.

Houk, C. P., Hughes, I. A., Ahmed, S. F., & Lee, P. A. (2006). Summary of consensus statement on intersex disorders and their management (special article). *Pediatrics, 118*(2), 753-757.

Houston-Vega, M. K., Nuehring, E. M., & Daguio, E. R. (1997). *Prudent practice: A guide for managing malpractice risk.* Washington, DC: NASW Press.

Huesman, L. R., Eron, L. D., Leftkowitz, M. M., & Walder, L. O. (1984). Stability of aggression over time and generations. *Developmental Psychology, 20*, 1120-1134.

Hussey, D., & Guo, S. (2005). Characteristics and trajectories of treatment foster care youth. *Child Welfare, 84*(4), 485-506.

Illinois Coalition Against Sexual Assault. (2004). *Service standards.* Retrieved May 3, 2007, from http://www.resourcesharingproject.org/ResourceFiles/RapeCrisisProgramStandards/ICASAServiceStandardsApproved604.pdf

Indyk, D., Belville, R., Lachapelle, S. S., Gordon, G., & Dewart, T. (1993). A community-based approach to HIV case management: Systematizing the unmanageable. *Social Work, 38*(4), 380-387.

In re Gault. 387 U.S. 1 (1967). Retrieved December 24, 2006, from http://web.utk.edu/~scheb/gault.html

Jarlais, D. C., Sloboda, Z., Friedman, S. R., Tempalski, B., McKnight, C., & Braine, N. (2006). Diffusion of the D.A.R.E. and syringe exchange programs. *American Journal of Public Health, 96*(8), 1354-1358.

Kaltenborn, K. F. (2001). Children's and young people's experiences in various residential arrangements: A longitudinal study to evaluate criteria for custody and residence decision making. *British Journal of Social Work, 31*, 81-117.

Kelly, A. E., & Yip, J. Y. (2006). Is keeping a secret or being a secretive person linked to psychological symptoms? *Journal of Personality, 74*, 1349-1370.

Kelly, J. B., & Lamb, M. E. (2003). Developmental issues in relocation cases involving young children: When, where and how? *Journal of Family Psychology, 17*(2), 193-205.

Kidder, R. M. (1995). *How good people make tough choices: Resolving the dilemmas of ethical living.* New York: Simon and Schuster.

Kidder, R. M. (2005). *Moral courage: Taking action when your values are put to the test.* New York: HarperCollins.

Kirst-Ashman, K. K. (2008). *Human behaviors, communities, organizations, and groups in the macro social environment: An empowerment approach* (2nd ed.). Belmont, CA: Thomson, Brooks/Cole.

Kirst-Ashman, K. K., & Hull, G. H. (1997). *Generalist practice with organizations and communities.* Chicago: Nelson-Hall.

Koocher, G. P., & DeMaso, D. R. (1990). Children's competence to consent to medical procedures. *Pediatrician, 17*, 68–73.

Koocher, G. P., & Keith-Spiegel, P. C. (1990). *Children, ethics, and the law: Professional issues and cases*. Lincoln: University of Nebraska Press.

Kuther, T. L. (2003). Medical decision-making and minors: Issues of consent and assent. *Adolescence, 38*(150), 343–358.

Lazarus, A. (1994). The illusion of the therapist's power and the patient's fragility: My rejoinder. *Ethics and Behavior, 4*(3), 299–306.

Lidz, C. W., Meisel, A., Zerubavel, E., Carter, M., Sestak, R. M., & Roth, L. H. (1984). *Informed consent: A study of decision making in psychiatry.* New York: Guilford Press.

Lochman, J. E., & Dodge, K. A. (1994). Social-cognitive processes of severely violent, moderately aggressive, and nonaggressive boys. *Journal of Consulting and Clinical Psychology, 62*(2), 366–374.

Loewenberg, F., Golgoff, R., & Harrington, D. (2000). *Ethical decisions for social work practice* (6th ed.). Itasca, IL: F. W. Peacock.

Lopes, G. (2007, April 25). HPV vaccine concerns give legislatures pause. *Washington Times* [Electronic version]. Retrieved on May 1, 2007, from http://www.washtimes.com/business/20070424-114157-2717r.htm

Madden, R. G. (1998). *Legal issues in social work, counseling, and mental health: Guidelines for clinical practice in psychotherapy*. Thousand Oaks, CA: Sage.

Makwana, R. R. (2003a, January 23). Child Advocate's report finds everyone at fault in suicide of 12-year-old. *Record-Journal*, 1.

Makwana, R. R. (2003b, January 24). Child Advocate's report sets stage for sweeping changes in policies. *Record-Journal*, 1.

Manning, S. S., & Van Pelt, M. E. (2005). The challenges of dual relationships and the continuum of care in rural mental health. In L. Ginsberg (ed.), *Social work in rural communities* (4 ed., pp. 259–282). Alexandria, VA: Council on Social Work Education.

McCain, J., & Salter, M. (2004). *Why courage matters: The way to a braver life.* New York: Random House.

McCarthy, J., Marshall, A., Irvine, M., & Jay, B. (2004). *An analysis of mental health issues in states' child and family service reviews and program improvement plans*. Retrieved March 27, 2007, from http://gucchd.georgetown.edu/object_view.html?objectID=3802.

Meaux J. B., & Bell, P. L. (2001). Balancing recruitment and protection: Children as research subjects. *Issues in Comprehensive Pediatric Nursing, 14*, 241–51.

Mellins, C. A., Brackis-Cott, E., Dolezai, C., Richards, A. Nicholas, S. W., & Abrams, E. J. (2002). Patterns of HIV status disclosure to perinatally HIV-infected children and subsequent mental health outcomes. *Clinical Child Psyhcology and Psychiatry, 7*, 101–114.

Merlo, A. V., & Benekos, P. J. (2003). Defining juvenile justice in the 21st century. *Youth Violence and Juvenile Justice, 1*(3), 276–288.

Migeon, C. J., Wisniewski, A. B., Gearhart, J. P., Heino, F. L., Meyer-Bahlburg, H. F. L., Rock, J. A., et al. (2002). Ambiguous genitalia with perineoscrotal hypospadias in 46 XY individuals: Long-term medical, surgical, and psychosexual outcome. *Pediatrics, 110*(3), 611.

Miller, W. I. (2000). *The mystery of courage.* Cambridge, MA: Harvard University Press.

NASW. (1999). *Code of ethics of the National Association of Social Workers.* Washington, DC: NASW.

Netting, F. E., Kettner, P. M., & McMurtry, S. (2004). *Social work macro practice* (3rd ed.). New York: Longman.

O'Donohue, W. T., & Ferguson, K. E. (2003). *Handbook of professional ethics for psychologists: Issues, questions, and controversies.* Thousand Oaks, CA: Sage.

Office of the Child Advocate and the Child Fatality Review Panel. (2003, January). *Investigation of the death of Joseph Daniel S.* Retrieved September 4, 2007, from http://www.ct.gov/oca/lib/oca/josephdaniel.doc

Office on the Higher Commissioner on Human Rights. (1990). *Convention on the rights of the child.* Retrieved December 3, 2006, from http://www.unhchr.ch/html/menu3/b/k2crc.htm

Parents of Kids with Infectious Diseases. (2006). *Advocacy: Legal protections for children with viral hepatitis.* Retrieved on May 1, 2007, from http://www.pkids.org/pdf/phr/11-01civilrights.pdf

Parsons, R. D. (2001). *The ethics of professional practice.* Needham Heights, MA: Allyn and Bacon.

Piaget, J. (1970). Piaget's theory. In P. H. Mussen (Ed.), *Carmichael's manual of child psychology* (3rd ed., pp. 103–128). New York: Wiley.

Practice basics: Avoid legal trouble with custody evals and boundary issues. (2005, March). *Psychotherapy Finances, 31*(3), 4–5.

Rachels, J. (2003). *The elements of moral philosophy* (4th ed.). Boston: McGraw-Hill.

Reamer, F. G. (2001). *Tangled relationships: Managing boundary issues in the human services.* New York: Columbia University Press.

Reamer, F. G. (2005). Documentation in social work: Evolving ethical and risk-management standards. *Social Work, 50*(4), 325–334.

Reamer, F. G. (2006). *Social work values and ethics* (3rd ed.). New York: Columbia University Press.

Ross, L. F. (2007a). Growth attenuation by commission and omission may be ethically justifiable in children with profound disabilities. *Archives of Pediatrics & Adolescent Medicine, 161*(4), 418.

Ross, L. F. (2007b). Is it ever appropriate to attenuate growth in profoundly developmentally disable children to facilitate their care? *AAP Grand Rounds, 17*, 2–3.

Rutter, M. (1990). Psychosocial resilience and protective mechanisms. In J. Rolf, A. Masten, D. Cicchetti, K. Neuchterlein, & S. Weintraub (Eds.), *Risk and protective factors in the development of psychopathology* (pp. 181-214). New York: Cambridge University Press.

Saltzman, A., & Furman, D. M. (1999). Locating and using the law. In A. Saltzman & D. M. Furman (Eds.), *Law in social work practice* (pp. 77-116). Chicago: Nelson-Hall.

Schank, J. A., & Skovholt, T. M. (1997). Dual relationship dilemmas of rural and small-community psychologists. *Professional Psychology: Research and Practice, 28*(1), 44-49.

Schulman, D. (2007, May/June). Don't whistle while you work. *Mother Jones,* pp. 52-57, 92.

Singer, P. (2007, January 26). A convenient truth. *New York Times* [Electronic version]. Retrieved February 4, 2007, from http://www.nytimes.com/2007/01/26/opinion/26singer.html?ex=1170738000&en=ea7946829736b4c2&ei=5070

Smith v. Seibly, 72 2n.2d 16. (Wash. 1967). Retrieved December 24, 2006, from http://www.mrsc.org/mc/court/supreme/072wn2d/072wn2d0016.htm

Smith, B. D., & Donovan, S. E. F. (2003). Child welfare practice in organizational and institutional context. *Social Services Review,* 77, 541-562.

Somerville, M. (2007, February 7). The story of Ashley: Hard case, bad ethics: How we treat our weakest citizens still matters. *Globe and Mail,* p. A19.

Sommer, D. B., Bravender, T., & Hogan, V. (2004). Residential relocation and risk of attempted suicide in adolescents. *Journal of Adolescent Health, 34*(2), 115.

Sowell, E. R., Thompson, P. M., Holmes, C. J., Jernigan, T. L., & Toga, A. W. (1999). In vivo evidence for post-adolescent brain maturation in frontal and striatal regions. *Nature Neuroscience, 2*(10), 859-861.

Sowell, E. R., Thompson, P. M., Tessner, K. D., & Toga, A. W. (2001) Mapping continued brain growth and gray matter density reduction in dorsal frontal cortex: Inverse relationships during postadolescent brain maturation. *Journal of Neuroscience, 21*(22), 8819-8829.

Strauch, B. (2003). *The primal teen: What new discoveries about the teenage brain tell us about our kids.* New York: Anchor Books.

Strom-Gottfried, K. J. (1999). Professional boundaries: An analysis of violations by social workers. *Families in Society, 80*(5), 439-449.

Strom-Gottfried, K. J. (2005). Ethical practice in rural environments. For L. Ginsberg (Ed.), *Social work in rural communities* (4th ed., pp. 141-155). Alexandria, VA: Council on Social Work Education.

United Cerebral Palsy. (2007). *UCP and the ARC issue joint statement on "Ashley's treatment."* Retrieved April 30, 2007, from http://www.ucp.org/ucp_generaldoc.cfm/1/9/10020/10020-10020/7108

U.S. Department of Health and Human Services. (1999). *Mental health: A report of the surgeon general.* Rockville, MD: U.S. Department of Health and Human Services, Substance Abuse and Mental health Services Administration, Center for Mental Health Services, National Institutes of Health, National Institute of Mental Health.

U.S. Department of Health and Human Services. (2007, March 26). *Personal representatives and minors FAQs*. Retrieved April 8, 2007, from http://www.hhs.gov/hipaafaq/personal/

U.S. General Accounting Office. (2003). *Youth illicit drug prevention: D.A.R.E. long-term evaluations and federal efforts to identify effective programs.* Washington, DC: General Accounting Office. [Report No. GAO-03-172R]

Urban, L. S., St. Cyr, J. L., & Decker, S. H. (2003). Goal conflict in the juvenile court. *Journal of Contemporary Criminal Justice, 19*(4), 454–479.

Walden, T., Wolock, I., & Demone, H. W. (1990). Ethical decision making in human services: A comparative study. *Families in Society, 72*(2), 67–75.

Weir, D. (2003). A child's journey. *MADDvocate.* Retrieved March 18, 2007, from http://www.madd.org/victims/6231

Wiener, L., Mellins, C. A., Marhefka, S., & Battles, H. B. (2007). Disclosure of an HIV diagnosis to children: History, current research, and future directions. *Journal of Developmental and Behavioral Pediatrics, 28*, 155–166.

Zahn-Waxler, C., Kochanska, G., Krupnick, J., & McKnew, D. (1990). Patterns of guilt in children of depressed and well mothers. *Developmental Psychology, 26*, 51–59.

Index